The MINISTRY OF WOMEN in the EARLY CHURCH

The MINISTRY OF WOMEN in the EARLY CHURCH

by
Roger Gryson

Translated by
Jean Laporte and Mary Louise Hall

THE LITURGICAL PRESS
Collegeville, Minnesota

Second printing, 1980

The Ministry of Women in the Early Church is the authorized English translation of *Le ministére des femmes dans l'Église ancienne* (Recherches et synthèses, Section d'histoire,[4]) by Roger Gryson, published by Éditions J. Duculot, S.A., Gembloux, Belgium.

Printed by The North Central Publishing Company, St. Paul, Minnesota, U.S.A.

ISBN 0–8146–0899–X

ABBREVIATIONS

ANF	*Ante-Nicene Fathers*
Apost. Const.	*Apostolic Constitutions*
Apost. Trad.	*Apostolic Tradition*
AV 1	*Die apostolischen Väter*
CCL	*Corpus christianorum. Series latina*
CH	*Canons of Hippolytus*
CIL	*Corpus inscriptionum latinarum*
CJ	*Code of Justinian*
CSEL	*Corpus scriptorum ecclesiasticorum latinorum*
CT	*Code of Theodosius*
DACL	*Dictionnaire d'archéologie chrétienne et de liturgie*
DDC	*Dictionnaire de droit canonique*
Didasc.	*Didascalia Apostolorum*
DTC	*Dictionnaire de théologie catholique*
ECA	*Ecclesiastical Canons of the Apostles*
GCS	*Griechischen christlichen Schriftsteller*
JTS	*Journal of Theological Studies*
LNPF	*Nicene and Post-Nicene Fathers*
MGHAA	*Monumenta Germaniae historica, Auctores antiquissimi*
MGHL	*Monumenta Germaniae historica, Leges*
NJ	*Novellae of Justinian*
PG	*Patrologia graeca*
PGL	*Patristic Greek Lexicon*
PL	*Patrologia latina*
PLS	*Patrologiae latinae supplementum*
PO	*Patrologia orientalis*
SC	*Sources chrétiennes*
SEA	*Statuta Ecclesiae antiqua*
TDNT	*Theological Dictionary of the New Testament*
Test.	*Testament of Our Lord Jesus Christ*
TU	*Texte und Untersuchungen zur Geschichte der altchristlichen Literatur*

CONTENTS

Chapter 4

THE ALEXANDRIAN FATHERS OF THE THIRD CENTURY

Chapter 5

DIDASCALIA APOSTOLORUM

Chapter 6

GREEK CANONICAL SOURCES FROM THE FOURTH TO THE SIXTH CENTURY

Chapter 7

THEOLOGICAL WRITINGS AND OTHER GREEK DOCUMENTS FROM THE FOURTH TO THE SIXTH CENTURY

INTRODUCTION

The question of the ministry of women in the Church arises today with ever-increasing insistence. The adherents of the status quo readily claim a tradition which goes back, so they say, to earliest antiquity; the partisans of evolution reject this argument as insufficient. Generally, however, neither one side nor the other has a precise knowledge of the early tradition of the Church in this matter. While this study does not take the position of either side, it recognizes that a lack of historical understanding is the reason why, without being adequately informed in this area, one side invokes this ancient tradition and the other challenges it. This study, therefore, sets out to examine exactly what this ancient tradition involves.

One thing is undeniable: there were in the early Church women who occupied an official position, who were invested with a ministry, and who, at least at certain times and places, appeared as part of the clergy. These women were called "deaconesses" and at times "widows." For a long time the historians of the Church have been interested in them. They have questioned, in particular, whether they constituted two different ministries and, if the answer to this query is affirmative, what was the relationship of the one group to the other.

Up until about a hundred years ago, the almost unanimous opinion was that the early Church had known only one type of feminine ministration. It was entrusted first to old widows, and for this reason, in the beginning, these ministers were simply called "widows." Later, virgins also assumed the same ministry, and this could be the reason why, from the third century on, the title "deaconess" was used concurrently with that of "widow."[1] However, in the long run this theory failed to account for all the implications contained in the sources. Also, Thomas Zahn, in his important work on St. Ignatius of Antioch published in 1873, suggested the existence in the early Christian communities of a group of aged widows supported by the Church who were charged with certain pastoral tasks on behalf of women and who occupied a place of honor in the community, and, along with these, a group of deaconesses, who were much younger. Later on, after a period of eclipse during which feminine ministries were generally the privilege of a few widows only, the feminine diaconate flourished again in the East and even tended to include widows.[2]

L. Zscharnack, in one of the most detailed monographs on this question, while presenting somewhat differently the particular aspects of their history,[3] emphasized the distinction between the functions of widows and deaconesses. Nevertheless, since the new theory retained only the evidence for their distinction, and the old, for their assimilation, the theory of Zahn and of Zscharnack appeared as powerless as the theory of identity, generally admitted before, to interpret as a whole the texts referring to widows and deaconesses. In spite of Zahn and Zscharnack, the theory of identity found new supporters.[4] Scholars, however, generally have adopted a middle position. They accept either (1) the existence of two ministries, which never occurred simultaneously in the same place but which appeared successively;[5] or (2) the coexistence of two distinct groups, deaconesses and widows, sharing the same ministry, since to be a widow does not mean to exercise a specific ministry.[6]

Among the works which defend the position just traced, A. Kalsbach's "Die altkirchliche Einrichtung der Diakonissen bis zu ihrem Erlöschen"[7] deserves special notice. Although this work is written in a confused manner and in muddled language, making the reading twice laborious, it offers the most complete documentation regarding widows and deaconesses. Kalsbach had read most of the earlier literature on this subject. What escaped his attention — or what he judged useless to mention — may generally be considered unimportant, consisting especially of dictionary articles or pages of handbooks, in which the authors do not propose to be original.[8] Kalsbach, though, should have pointed out the articles regarding "Diaconesse(s)" in the *Dictionnaire de théologie catholique* and in the *Dictionnaire d'archéologie chrétienne et de liturgie*.[9] The first work is certainly marked by many errors, and the second is extremely brief. However, since they are widely known and commonly used as references, their positions will be analyzed when the occasion arises.

Neither does Kalsbach mention the voluminous study by A. Rosambert regarding the position of widows in canon law up to the fourteenth century;[10] but in spite of its size, this work may be neglected purely and simply because of its methodological errors.[11] It is also unfortunate that Kalsbach omitted in his bibliography an interesting "bulletin," published anonymously in the *Church Quarterly Review* of 1899 and titled "On the Early History and Modern Revival of Deaconesses," which contains many pertinent remarks.[12]

In order not to increase the discussions and notes, since Kalsbach has given a sufficient account of their opinions and has separated the chaff from the grain, except for the literature already mentioned in the Introduction, this study will refrain from citing and criticizing authors before Kalsbach.

The next important publication after Kalsbach's is a collection of ancient texts (in the original or in the Latin version for those in Oriental languages) concerning widows, deaconesses, and virgins. This large collection, which includes 182 texts, is substantial and certainly useful, but it is still quite incomplete.[13] We could also mention a large number of dictionary articles and sections of manuals which are introductory, but they would not offer any original views.[14]

Very few studies are now devoted exclusively to the question of widows and deaconesses. C. H. Turner, who is always an engaging author, wrote some pages on this topic; his conclusions compare well with Kalsbach's.[15] L. Bopp's work regarding widows is hardly better than Rosambert's.[16] To determine if a restoration of the feminine diaconate is conceivable in the Oriental Church today, E. D. Theodoros has written a thorough study of the tradition; but it is regrettable that, although well documented, it is difficult for the Western reader because of the language in which it is written.[17] In the third part of his book on the function of the diaconate in the early Church, J. Colson deals with deaconesses; this section is only twenty pages long, and the author simply quotes a few ancient texts, interspersing them with poor comments which are not even all his own.[18] In an article by J. B. Davies concerning deacons, deaconesses, and minor orders in the patristic period, five pages deal with deaconesses.[19] On the basis of a small selection of documents, Davies concludes that the order of deaconesses appeared in the first part of the third century, evolved from the masculine diaconate, with which it shared certain functions, and recruited its first members from the order of widows, who in the beginning exercised an active ministry among women in the community. Deaconesses were essentially a creation of the East; they were not seen in the West before the fifth century and were not accepted by Rome before the end of the eighth century.

For the rest, studies on the ministry of women in the early Church, or simply on woman in the early Church or in the Church in general, provide new reflections on the problem of widows and deaconesses. This restoration of a particular question to the wider context, where it rightly belongs, is a good thing. The abundant literature published earlier about widows and deaconesses exclusively seemed to forget that this question is only one aspect, although a privileged one, of a much broader problem, i.e., the ministry of women in the Church. Actually, women did not exercise any other ministry properly so called in the early Church except that of deaconesses and occasionally of widows.

But it is essential to inquire why access to other ministries was refused, whether any attempts to gain access were made, and, in particular, what kind of tradition grew out of the famous text of 1 Corinthians 14:34, "the women should keep silence in the churches." Already in 1905, precisely this topic was studied in an article by P. de Labriolle, who chose Paul's famous words for its title. The subtitle of this article, "Un aspect de la lutte anti-montaniste," reflects the importance of the Montanist crisis for the ministry of women.[20] An entire issue of the magazine *Eine heilige Kirche*, in 1939, was devoted to the ministry of women in religions and Churches; it included an extremely superficial article on the ministry of women in the Church and another more penetrating one on the history of the ordination of deaconesses.[21]

At Vanves, in 1959, during a session of a conference sponsored by the Centre de Pastorale Liturgique, whose theme was "Liturgical Functions in Tradition," J. Daniélou spoke on the ministry of women in the early Church. His lecture, published in full in the review of the Centre, emphasized the outstanding role played by women in the Church of the first centuries, but at the same time stressed the fact that they have always been denied admission to the priesthood. The scriptural and traditional argument supporting this prohibition appeared impressively solid to Daniélou.[22] In the first chapter of his thesis regarding admittance to orders in ancient canon law, P. H. Lafontaine examined the same question from the viewpoint of a canonist. Unfortunately this chapter is by far the weakest in a work which includes many excellent sections. Satisfied with giving a series of juxtaposed notes, the author never reached a true synthesis.[23]

After these studies centering on the problem of the ministry of women in the early Church, others appeared which investigated the image of woman in the early Church, or quite simply the priesthood of woman in the early Church, or more generally woman in the Church. But the generality of these inquiries precluded the close study — with primary research, in-depth treatment, and sufficient development — which the precise question with which we are dealing here required. Since the authors did not focus enough on the exact point, it was difficult for them to say anything but banalities or approximations.

This is the case, for example, in the works of H. Borsinger, Fr. Heiler, G. Huls, J. Leipoldt, and H. van der Meer,[24] as well as in two recent dissertations of C. Vaessen and J. A. Wahl. The dissertation of Vaessen[25] consists of three parts: (1) equality of man and woman according to Scripture; (2) equality and inequality of man and woman according to canon law and the Church; and (3) equality of man and woman according to the declarations of recent popes. In the second part, the only one which is published, the thirty pages dealing with widows and deaconesses[26] is a work of compilation. For each text which he quotes he mentions the opinions found in previously published literature, without criticizing them or taking a position himself. The dissertation of J. A. Wahl[27] also consists of three chapters: (1) the social role of women; (2) the participation of women in Christian ministry; and (3) the Catholic doctrine excluding women from holy orders. In the printed extract, only the third chapter appears in its entirety; the first two chapters are only briefly summarized. The third chapter, which proposes to interpret the Pauline texts, is merely a juxtaposition of comments from some "ancient" exegetes (the Fathers) and the "moderns" (Estius, Cornelius a Lapide, etc.) relevant to these texts.

This study will confine itself to presenting information relative to the ministry of women in the early Church from the first to the sixth century. We will strive to be as complete and objective as possible. To avoid imposing on the material a preconceived plan, the texts will be arranged in a strictly chronological order. The work, however, does not pretend to be definitive; all is not finally said. After the facts concerning the history of women ministers in the early Church, the details of legislation on this matter, and the motives advanced by ancient writers to justify these facts and legislation, the question still remains whether the motives explicitly alleged were the only ones operative, and, in particular, whether the refusal of the early Church to admit women to the priesthood was not influenced by a conception of woman, the components of which had not been completely and clearly analyzed, since some of them may have been foreign to the gospel and derived from the Greco-Roman milieu in which the Church was born.

This question is not only historically inescapable, but it is also theologically crucial. It is, however, a question that cannot be answered immediately. Because of the complexity of this question and the research needed to gain a true knowledge of its many aspects, no one today can explain with sufficient accuracy and certainly what concept of women the ancient Church had.

The early Church extended from the first to the sixth century, from Clement of Rome to Gregory the Great, from Ireland to Egypt, and from North Africa to the shores of the Black Sea. We can suspect that the concept of woman varied from one period to another and from one place to another. To say bluntly that the early Church had such and such a concept of woman and that it was due to this concept that women were refused access to the priesthood is, at least, premature.[28] This same remark applies also to the image and the legal status of women in the Greco-Roman world, which some scholars denounce too easily as an influence contrary to the principles of the gospel.

In any case, there is an enormous difference in this regard between the East and the West, and, of course, many subtle differences due to the diversity of time and place. There is a whole world, on the one hand, between codified Roman law in the legislative collections of the fifth and sixth centuries, and, on the other hand, the customary laws of small cities of Egypt or of Asia Minor at the time of Ignatius of Antioch. To justify the right of the Church to make a change in regard to the accession of women to sacred orders without disobeying the gospel,[29] much research still has to be done before one is able to determine, in a rigorous manner, whether the customs and the canons of the Church in this matter have or have not been conditioned by the cultural milieu in which it developed.

For all these reasons, this study has very strict and narrow limitations. It represents only a step, and its conclusions should be considered within the framework of greater reflection. But it was necessary both to achieve this first step, because it directs the research of the future, and to stop here temporarily while awaiting the information needed for further reflection. Before such information is available, the conscientious historian, accustomed to affirm nothing except through strict investigation, must protest the naive self-confidence of those for whom all these matters are simple and evident at first sight.

The MINISTRY OF WOMEN in the EARLY CHURCH

1 THE NEW TESTAMENT

The earliest sources of knowledge about the ministry of women in the early Church are the texts of the New Testament. Since entire books have been written on one or two verses, such as the famous sentence of First Corinthians which imposes silence on women in the assemblies (14:34), the reader will understand that this study deals with the essentials and, for the rest, refers to the commentaries and specialized works which are available.

1. Preliminary Note: The Ministry of Women in the Old Testament [1]

The condition of woman in ancient Israel, while more advanced than it was in most contemporary civilizations of the Near East, did not permit her to play an active role in the political and religious life of the chosen people. Since she was subject to multiple legal impurities, it was inconceivable that she would have access to the priesthood or that she would be part of the personnel attached to the sanctuary.[2] Furthermore, the sacred prostitution of old Canaanite cults was still too vivid a memory for the intervention of a woman in the celebration of sacred rites not to appear immediately ambiguous and suspect. And the charism of prophecy, even though it escapes the narrow frames of political and religious institutions, was not frequently bestowed on women. The Old Testament mentions by name only four "prophetesses": Miriam, the sister of Aaron;[3] Deborah, in the time of Judges;[4] Huldah, during the reign of Josias;[5] and Noadiah, in the time of Nehemiah.[6] If she is considered as still belonging to the old economy of salvation, Anna, the daughter of Phanuel, according to the Infancy Gospel of Luke.[7] may be added to this list of prophetesses. The prophet Joel announced, however, that at the end of time, after the pouring out of the Spirit, women as well as men would prophesy.[8]

2. The Women Accompanying Jesus

The preaching of Jesus, addressed indiscriminately to men and women, seems to have been particularly well received by the latter. According to some early variants of the Third Gospel, the Jews accused Jesus before Pilate not only of fomenting riots and dissuading people from paying taxes to Caesar but also of entrapping the minds of women and children and of causing the former to neglect the customary Jewish purifications.[9] Luke mentions a certain number of women following Jesus, along with the Twelve:

> Soon afterward he went on through cities and villages, preaching and bringing the good news of the kingdom of God. And the twelve were with him, and also some women who had been healed of evil spirits and infirmities: Mary, called Magdalene, from whom seven demons had gone out, and Joanna, the wife of Chuza, Herod's steward, and Susanna, and many others, who provided for them out of their means.[10]

Though unparalleled in the other two Synoptics, this text is not a mere figment of Luke's imagination. According to Mark, at the moment of Jesus' death

> there were women looking on from afar, among whom were Mary Magdalene, and Mary the mother of James the younger and of Joses, and Salome, who, when he was in Galilee, followed him, and ministered to him.[11]

Therefore Mark, like Luke, attests that some women ministered to Jesus when he was preaching in Galilee.

The fact that these two texts, and many other sections in the Evangelists, mention specific names[12] indicates the consideration those people enjoyed in the early community, and, at the same time, confirms the historicity of these references and makes it unlikely that one writer had merely projected into the life of Jesus a ministry of the early community.[13] Then, when all the disciples except one had abandoned the Master, these women accompanied him to the place of his execution and were present at his burial. The same women also, according to the unanimous testimony of the four Gospels, found the empty tomb on Easter morning, met the resurrected Christ or his angel, and announced the news to his unbelieving disciples.[14] None of them, though, is included among the number of the Apostles, and it must be noted that the women who placed themselves at the service of Jesus during his wanderings in Galilee, according to Luke, did not do so because they had been the object of an explicit call by the Master, like the Twelve, but because they were moved by the sight of his miracles.

3. Women in the First Christian Communities

Probably these are the same women who reappeared in the small community which, according to Luke, awaited in prayer the coming of the Holy Spirit after the ascension of the Lord.[15] They are the first-fruits of many women converts who, according to the Acts of the Apostles, joined the new faith.[16] Just as during the life of Jesus, many women served the Master in his Church, in his Apostles, and in the poorest members of the community. At Joppa a woman named Tabitha, who "was full of good works and acts of charity," made tunics and other garments, which she gave away.[17] Mary, the mother of John-Mark, opened her house for gatherings of the Christian community of Jerusalem.[18] Lydia, a seller of purple goods in the city of Thyatira, compelled Paul and his companions to stay at her house.[19]

The long list of greetings at the end of the Epistle to the Romans [20] suggests how much the Apostle of the Nations benefited from the kindness of numerous women in his missionary journeys. The first woman named is Phoebe, a minister (*diakonos*) of the church of Cenchreae:

> I commend to you our sister Phoebe, a *diakonos* [minister] of the church at Cenchreae, that you may receive her in the Lord as befits the saints, and help her in whatever she may require from you, for she has been a helper of many and of myself as well.[21]

Many scholars boldly connect this text with those of the third century where the institution of deaconesses appeared clearly defined for the first time and translate *diakonos* as "deaconess" instead of the more general term "minister," which we prefer; they consider Phoebe the first deaconess. If this assumption is true, then this order goes back to apostolic times.[22]

It is necessary, however, to apply certain distinctions to this affirmation. Scholars have noted that toward the end of the decade 50–60, *diakonos* (servant, minister) did not designate a specific function.[23] Even Paul introduces himself, as well as his co-workers, as *diakonos* (servant, minister) of Christ, of the gospel, of the New Covenant, etc., and speaks of his apostolic works as a *diakonia* (service, ministry).[24] First Corinthians speaks of Stephanas and his household, "the first converts in Achaia," who "have devoted themselves to the service of the saints" (*eis diakonian tois hagiois etaxan heautous*).[25] The *diakonia* appears among the charisms mentioned by Paul in Romans between the gift of prophecy and the gift of teaching.[26] It must be noted, however, that in the case of Phoebe, *diakonos* refers to a specific service, not to the general service of God, which includes the whole of Christian life.

This title is used as intelligible in itself, and the works of Phoebe are not described until later. The meaning of this term is determined by a genitive ("minister *of* the church at Cenchreae"), not by a dative indicating the beneficiary of the service, as was the case with Stephanas and his household, who "devoted themselves to the service of the saints" (*eis diakonian tois hagiois*).[27] The service of Phoebe is briefly characterized as follows: "she has been a helper of many and of myself as well." The term "helper" (*prostatis*) evokes a custom known by the ancients as "patronage," by which material assistance and moral support were given by more fortunate and influential persons to the communities or to some individuals, who made up their "clientele."[28]

With this background, it is easy to imagine the role played by Phoebe in Cenchreae. In this city, which was a harbor depending on Corinth, there were many travelers and strangers; consequently, there were daily opportunities to practice the virtue of hospitality. As everywhere, there were misery and distress to be relieved. Phoebe also apparently opened her home for religious meetings.[29] All these activities, no doubt, made up the substance of her ministry, a ministry, according to all evidence, freely accepted under the influence of the Holy Spirit, "who apportions to each one individually as he wills."[30]

Phoebe's ministry was, therefore, like that of Stephanas and his household; they all worked hard to help the saints. However, such a ministry is recognized as a function of the Body of Christ, which is the Church, and brings to those who assume it honor and consideration. Without a doubt, A. Oepke is closest to the truth when he writes: "The description of Phoebe as the *diakonos* of the church at Cenchreae indicates the point where the original charisma is becoming an office."[31]

In Romans, after Phoebe appears the couple Prisca and Aquila, whom Paul calls his "fellow workers" in Christ Jesus (*tous synergous mou en Christō Iēsou*), a title which he habitually gives to his direct associates in the work of the gospel: Timothy,[33] Titus,[34] Epaphroditus,[35] Clement,[36] and others.[37] Paul mentions that these two Christians risked death to save his life,[38] an event which may have taken place at Ephesus during the riot of the goldsmiths,[39] or later perhaps at the time of Paul's captivity in this city. Paul made the acquaintance of Aquila, a Jew from Pontus, and his wife Priscilla (or Prisca, a diminutive form of the same name) in Corinth, where they arrived from Italy, driven out by an edict of the Emperor Claudius ordering all Jews out of the city. Like Paul, they were tentmakers and he lived with them.[40] When Paul left for Syria, they accompanied him, but they remained at Ephesus while Paul continued his journey alone.[41] They perfected the Christian instruction of Apollos, an Alexandrian Jew, eloquent and versed in the Scriptures, who was to become a leading figure in the life of the church of Corinth.[42] It is significant that in two places in Acts, as in Romans, Priscilla, a woman, is mentioned before her husband.[43] She must have been the dominant personality in this marriage, and John Chrysostom may be close to the truth when he attributes to her the whole merit of having instructed Apollos correctly in Christian doctrine.[44] It is not surprising to read that the home of the couple was a meeting place for a group of the faithful.[45]

After Prisca and her husband Aquila, Paul greets still other women: a certain Mary,[46] then Tryphaena, Tryphosa, and Persis,[47] all of whom "worked hard" in the Lord. Here again Paul uses the term *kopian* to refer to the work of evangelization; he typically employs this word in reference to evangelization, whether accomplished by himself or others. Later, Paul greets the mother of Rufus, who, he says, is his mother, too.[48] He also greets Nereus and his sister.[49] In Philippians, he mentions Euodia and Syntyche, who "have labored side by side with me in the gospel together with Clement and the rest of my felllow workers."[50] In short, there is no doubt that Paul often benefited from the cooperation of women in his apostolic labors and that the women did not prove themselves less fervent than the men in spreading the Good News.

4. The Prophetesses of the New Testament

The Holy Spirit, "who apportions to each one individually as he wills," did not deny women the gift of prophecy, which he gave abundantly to Christians in the early Church. The evangelist Philip, "one of the seven," with whom Paul stayed at Caesarea on his last journey to Jerusalem, had four unmarried daughters who prophesied.[51] In the community of Corinth, under the inspiration of the Holy Spirit, women as well as men prophesied and prayed aloud.

Paul had no objection to this practice, but he held firmly to the custom that women had to have their heads covered when they prophesied, just as they did when they were in public, whereas men, on the contrary, had to be bareheaded.[52] The reason for his insistence on this point is that at Corinth a dualist Gnosticism tended to deny any distinction between a man and a woman, on the ground that sex belongs to flesh and matter, and is, therefore, indifferent to the spirit. For Paul it is true that "there is neither male nor female; for you are all one in Christ Jesus,"[53] in the sense that neither of the sexes should pretend to a closer proximity to the Deity; both sexes are equal before God. But in spite of their equality "in the Lord," men and women are not the same. "In the Lord," man remains man, and woman, woman; each has a specific role to play; the relation which unites them is not reversible.

Contrary to the Gnostic contention, God the Creator is not different from God the Savior. God the Savior did not destroy his first work by redeeming it but raised it to a new perfection. Therefore the chief characteristics of the first work remain in the new creation as long as the "glory of the sons of God" has not been fully revealed; and, in particular, the difference between man and woman evident in the order of creation is not abolished in the order of redemption. Because the Gnostics saw a sign of this difference in the custom, which imposed one attitude toward men and another toward women when they were prophesying or praying, they wanted to be free of this practice; but Paul insisted that it be maintained.

The fact that a woman has her head covered when she prophesies or prays is not a sign of woman's "subjection" to man [54]; in fact, saying that "the head of a woman is her husband" [55] is not affirming that woman is inferior to man, any more than saying that "the head of Christ is God" [56] means that Christ is inferior to God. Consequently, the veil worn by women in the early Church was a sign that by not trying to deny, in the name of the redemption, the distinction of the sexes inscribed in their creation,[57] they agreed to submit to the order established by God.

5. Women Are To Remain Quiet at Meetings!

Since apparently, according to 1 Corinthians 11, Paul does not object to a woman's prophesying or praying aloud in the Christian assembly, provided she have her head covered, the reader is understandably surprised to find a few pages later a passage which categorically orders women to keep silent in the assemblies:

> As in all the churches of the saints, the women should keep silence in the churches. For they are not permitted to speak, but should be subordinate, as even the law says. If there is anything they desire to know, let them ask their husbands at home. For it is shameful for a woman to speak in church.[58]

Some authors try to settle the contradiction by declaring that in chapter 11 Paul mentions merely the fact that women prophesy and pray in Corinth, without judging its lawfulness, since he is dealing only with the rule that women should cover their heads. They further claim that in chapter 14, when the opportunity arises to pass judgment on the fact that women speak in the Christian assembly, he formally condemns this abuse.[59]

This explanation does not stand criticism. If Paul really considered it an abuse for a woman to speak in the Christian assembly, he had, without a doubt, the chance to make this point in chapter 11. Instead of arguing for the custom which required that women cover their heads in public, he would have taken advantage of such a strong argument against the supporters of a mistaken understanding of the equality of men and women.

Really the contradiction has a simpler solution. Although eliminating a text to eliminate a difficulty is always bad, in the present instance both the external and the internal evidence suggest that the verses cited above (1 Cor. 14:34-35) are an interpolation which has nothing to do with the genuine text of chapter 14 or Paul's true thought. In some important manuscripts these verses are given at the end of chapter 14 after verse 40. Since verse 36 logically follows after verse 33, the verses in question break the continuity of the reasoning process. Several lexicographic and syntactic details are unusual in Paul's vocabulary and style, such as the formula "as even the law says" (*katōs ho nomos legei*).

Finally, some of the ideas of this text disagree with what Paul says elsewhere about women. This short passage actually means that in the assemblies women must not speak, in the most general and the most natural sense of the word. If they do not understand something, all they have to do is to ask their husband at home. They should not indulge in whispering or interrupting the speaker or disturbing the order of the meeting in any way. This type of behavior would be unbecoming and contrary to the subordinate condition in which the law intends they should remain.

If the text in question, forbidding women "to speak" (*lalein*) and requiring them "to keep silence" (*sigan*) had been inserted precisely at the end of chapter 14 of First Corinthians, it undoubtedly would have been due to the fact that this section deals extensively with "speaking" and "keeping silent." The origin of this interpolation can probably be ascribed to the Jewish-Christian milieu.[60] The reference made to "the law," without further distinction, and the anti-feminist tendency manifested in the formulation of this rule point to late Judaism rather than to Hellenistic society. The addition is certainly very ancient, not only because it is found in all manuscripts, although not always in the same place, but also because First Timothy plagiarizes it, warning women to "learn in silence" and forbidding them not only to speak but also to teach:

> Let a woman learn in silence with all submissiveness. I permit no woman to teach or to have authority over men; she is to keep silent. For Adam was formed first, then Eve; and Adam was not deceived, but the woman was deceived and became a trangressor.[61]

This "recasting" is manifestly far from the idea of 1 Corinthians 14:34-35. It has had, nevertheless, a resounding effect; the theologians of later centuries have nearly always interpreted 1 Corinthians 14:34-35 in light of 1 Timothy 2:11-12. They have also retained the two reasons which motivated the interdiction against women in this second text: that woman was created after man and that she was primarily responsible for original sin.

6. The Women of 1 Timothy 3:11

Since women were not permitted "to teach or to have authority over men," [62] they were naturally excluded in Pastoral Epistles from the functions of *episkopos* and presbyter, whose purpose was the management and instruction of the community.[63] Were there other functions in which their zeal found an outlet? A direction in this matter is actually found in chapter 3 of First

Timothy, which deals with the qualities required for an *episkopos* and deacon. The middle of this section regarding deacons contains the following sentence:

> The women likewise must be serious, no slanderers, but temperate, faithful in all things (*gynaikas ōsautōs semnas, mē diabolous, nēphalious, pistas en pasin.*).[64]

This sentence interrupts the development relative to deacons, and C. Spicq, who tends to be rather conservative in his exegesis, in his commentary on the Pastoral Epistles, does not discard the possibility that a marginal note was inserted in the text here.[65] Actually, the whole problem of the composition of the Pastoral Epistles should be raised at this point. More than once Spicq notes that First Timothy is "poorly composed,"[66] or that such a verse "breaks the logical development";[67] and it is true that the continuity of ideas in many parts of this letter is logically less than satisfying. Spicq, though, does not in every instance consider the litigate verses strangers to the original text; after all, if they had to be deleted from it, almost nothing of the Epistle would survive. Why then make an exception in the case of 1 Timothy 3:11?

According to J. G. Davies, this sentence refers to women in general,[68] an opinion which cannot be seriously supported, since, whether it be from the pen of the principal writer of the Epistle or whether it was inserted there by some interpolator, the place itself of the sentence suggests that in the mind of the author these women have a certain relation with deacons. Many interpreters think that this sentence refers to the wives of deacons.[69] Nothing, though, is said earlier about the wife of the *episkopos*; and if that were the meaning, another formulation would be expected, such as: *hai de gynaikas autōn estōsan semnai*, for example, instead of *gynaikas ōsautōs* without any determination.

The parallelism between the formulation of verses 8 and 11, on the one hand,[70] and between the qualities required of deacons and of the women in question, on the other hand,[71] shows that the author refers, after the *episkopos* and the deacons, to a new category of ministers, who are feminine this time. Although they are not given a specific title and are simply referred to as "the women," the context is sufficient to indicate that these women carried out a function in the community. The nature of this function cannot be known precisely, but the fact that these women are mentioned along with deacons strongly suggests that their service was analogous to that of deacons.[72]

7. Widows

In 1 Timothy 5, an extended text deals with widows.[73] The interpretation given in old commentaries and in the literature on the ministries of women is often influenced by the idea one has of the later evolution of the status of widows in the Church. According to some scholars, widows appear already in this text as an order invested with properly clerical functions.[74] Others vehemently reject the idea that the widows referred to in this passage are anything else but women assisted by the Church.[75] For the former scholars, who are inclined to compare the ministry of widows to that of deaconesses, the widows appear as the subject of the *diakonia* of the Church, but for the latter they are only the object of this *diakonia*, as in chapter 6 of Acts, where the Hellenists complain that their widows are neglected in the daily *diakonia*.[76] It is necessary, therefore, without taking into consideration the later evolution of these institutions and holding strictly to the letter of the text, to determine exactly the status of widows in these texts.

Paul exhorts Timothy to honor women who are truly widows.[77] As the general usage of the word and the sequence of the text clearly indicate, "to honor" must be understood as giving material assistance as well as respect.[78] The Old Testament, which frequently associates widows with the orphan, the stranger, the poor, and the oppressed, constantly refers to the duty of assisting them.[79] The Epistle of James echoes this tradition when it declares that "religion that is pure and undefiled before God and the Father is this: to visit orphans and widows in their affliction, and to keep oneself unstained from the world." [80] First Timothy repeats three times that widows who have relatives must be assisted by them so that the Church will not be obligated to take care of them and may use her resources to support the "real widows." [81]

The "true widow" had to be completely alone, have set her hope in God and persevered day and night in prayer.[82] Her conduct had to be irreproachable.[83] To be registered as a widow, i.e., to be inscribed on the list of widows recognized as such by the Church, a woman had to be at least sixty years old. She also had to have been the wife of only one husband, brought up children well, and multiplied good deeds; in brief, all through her life she must have been an exemplary wife, mother, and Christian.[84] Young widows, who might be too easily tempted to remarry and thus fail in their pledge, were excluded. Further, they would be more apt to waste their time and to gossip, and, finally, "to stray after Satan" into debauchery. For these reasons they were advised to remarry as soon as possible, to have children to raise and a house to govern, and so to keep from laziness, the mother of all vices.[85]

We find in this text essentially the portrait of the "real widow" or the outline of a feminine ideal whose realization begins in marriage and continues in widowhood under the form of a consecration to God lived in prayer. This way of life implied a profession of continence and was granted official recognition by the community, which took charge of these older women deprived of all natural help. Of a ministry exercised by these widows, nothing is expressly said. Of course, if formerly they had "shown hospitality," if they had "relieved the afflicted," if they had "devoted [themselves] to doing good in every way," [86] there is no reason why they should stop doing so. On the other hand, as indicated in the Epistle to Titus, their age and experience made them the most natural counselors of young women.[87] They do not, however, seem to have been invested with a specific function; but they seem, instead, to display only the effects of a living faith and spontaneous charity. These remarks do not imply that widows did not play a significant role in the life of the community and that their influence was not a tremendous blessing.[88]

2 TEXTS OF THE SECOND CENTURY

The texts of the second century confirm the essential impression of widows and women "ministers" conveyed by the New Testament. On the other hand, these writings reveal that women assumed an important role in the heterodox sects which multiplied at this time.

1. The Writings of the Apostolic Fathers and of the Apologists

In the writings of the Apostolic Fathers, following the biblical tradition, widows seem to have been assisted persons, in the same sense orphans, the needy, strangers, the sick, and prisoners were. One of the chief signs distinguishing the just man has always been his concern for the oppressed, the orphan, and the widow. Reference is made to the injunctions of Isaias: "Learn to do good, seek justice, correct oppression; defend the fatherless, plead for the widow." [1] Those who listen to the voice of evil have no regard for the widow and the orphan.[2] Heretics in particular care for neither the widow, nor the orphan, nor the oppressed, nor the prisoner and the man who has just been freed, nor those who are hungry or thirsty.[3]

Ignatius of Antioch made it clear that in the Christian community widows should not be neglected, and he warned Polycarp to take care of them: "After the Lord, you must be their protector." [4] Echoing Ignatius' exhortation, Polycarp insisted:

> Also the presbyters must be compassionate, merciful to all, turning back those who have gone astray, looking after the sick, not neglecting widows or orphans of one that is poor.[5]

Justin remarked that after the Sunday Eucharist, those who were well-to-do gave what they wished, and with these donations the president of the assembly "assisted orphans, widows, those who were in need because of sickness or any other reason, prisoners, and sojourning strangers — in a word, all those who were in want." [6] Among the works which one has to do to be saved, Hermas also listed "helping widows, looking after orphans and the needy." [7] When a person fasts, Hermas said, he must add up the price of the food which he would have eaten that day and give that amount to a widow or an orphan or some person in want.[8] Just as in Acts 6, widows appear in *The Shepherd of Hermas*, not as the subject, but as the object of the *diakonia* of the Church:

> Therefore, instead of lands, purchase afflicted souls, as each is able, "and look after the widows and orphans," and do not despise them, and spend your wealth and all your establishments for such fields and houses as you have received from God. For, for this reason did the Master make you rich, that you should fulfil these ministries for him (*hina tautas tas diakonias telesēte autō*).[9]
>
> And from the ninth mountain, which was desert and had in it creeping things and wild beasts which devour men, are such believers as these: Those with spots are ministers who ministered amiss (*diakonoi kakōs diakonēsantes*), and devoured the living of widows and orphans, and made gain for themselves from the ministry which they had to administer (*heautois peripoiēsamenoi ek tēs diakonias hēs elabon diakonēsai*). If they remain in the same covetousness, they are dead and they have no hope of life. But if they turn and fulfil their ministry in holiness (*hagnōs teleiōsōsi tēn diakonian autōn*), they shall be able to live.[10]
>
> And from the tenth mountain, where were trees sheltering some sheep, are such believers as these: Bishops and hospitable men who at all times received the servants of God into their houses gladly and without hypocrisy; and the bishops ever ceaselessly sheltered the destitute and the widows by their ministration (*tē diakonia heautōn*), and ever behaved with holiness.[11]

Just as widows in each of the Apostolic Fathers appear essentially as assisted women, do they not here also sublimate their widowhood in concretizing a Christian ideal, as in 1 Timothy 5:3-16? Polycarp's letter to the Philippians seems to echo this Pauline text:

> And the widows should be discreet in their faith pledged to the Lord, praying unceasingly on behalf of all, refraining from all slander, gossip, false witness, love of money — in fact, from evil of any kind — knowing that they are God's altar, that everything is examined for blemishes, and nothing escapes him whether of thoughts or sentiments, or any of the secrets of the heart.[12]

The "faith" (*pistin*) which widows owe to the Lord parallels the "pledge" (*pistin*) in 1 Timothy 5:12. "Praying unceasingly on behalf of all" recalls 1 Timothy 5:5, she "continues in supplications and prayers night and day." Also, "refraining from all slander, gossip, false witness" echoes Titus 2:3, "not to be slanderers," and 1 Timothy 5:13, "gossips and busybodies, saying what they should not." The idea that widows are the "altar of God" and, as such, are closely scrutinized by the eye of God,[13] may be understood in two different ways: (1) that widows, who live by the generosity of the faithful, are like altars upon which these gifts are offered to God;[14] or (2) that widows owe uninterrupted prayer to God.[15] Both meanings may have been simultaneously present in the mind of the author.[16] Regardless of the exact nature of this connection between the text of Polycarp and 1 Timothy, there is no doubt that the word *chēra* at this time was used as a technical term meaning an ideal life-style, and not merely the fact of being a widow.

In his Letter to the Smyrneans, after greeting the bishop, priests, and deacons, Ignatius of Antioch wrote:

> Greeting to the families of my brothers, along with their wives and children, and to the virgins called widows.[17] (*Aspazomai tous oikous tōn adelphōn mou syn gynaixi kai teknois, kai tas parthenous tas legomenas chēras*).

The community of Smyrna, therefore, included virgins who were called "widows." But why were they given this title? Some scholars think that this title indicates that they exercised the same function as widows.[18] Since in the writings of the Apostolic Fathers, just as in the New Testament, there was never a question of a function fulfilled by widows, this explanation does not seem valid. Besides, the holders of ecclesiastical offices (bishops, presbyters, deacons) had already been greeted in Ignatius' Letter to the Smyrneans.[19]

The point is that in First Timothy the widows recognized and "registered" as such professed continence; in fact, since young widows might want to remarry later on and thus break their "first pledge," (*prōtēn pistin*), they were refused registration.[20] Consequently, Christian virgins who resolved to remain chaste "for the honor of the Lord's flesh"[21] were called "widows"; since both groups of women had a profession of continence as their chief characteristic, their ideals and life-styles seemed similar. In the case of these virgins, continence most probably went hand in hand with asceticism, prayer, and acts of charity; when no close relatives were available, they also, like widows, were assisted by the community.

The only text of the Apostolic Fathers in which a woman seems to have assumed a more or less official mission in the community is found in *The Shepherd of Hermas*. In a vision an old woman, who represented the Church, gave Hermas a book of revelations, which he copied. In a later vision the same woman asked whether he had already given the book to the presbyters. When Hermas answered no, she said:

> You have done well, for I have words to add. When, therefore, I have finished all the words, they shall be made known by you to all the elect. You shall therefore write two little books and send one to Clement and

> one to Grapte. Clement then shall send it to the cities abroad, for that is his duty; and Grapte shall exhort the widows and orphans; but in this city you shall read it yourself with the elders who are in charge of the church.[22]

This is the only passage that mentions Grapte; there is absolutely nothing else known about her. She is charged with the task of communicating to widows and orphans the warnings contained in the little book which presents Christians with a last opportunity to do penance before the end of the world. Nothing is said of her being a widow nor of the reason for her appointment to this mission. The literary genre of vision and fiction which introduces the author, who was a brother of Pius, the bishop of Rome (*ca.* 140–150) according to the Canon of Muratori, as a contemporary of Clement (end of the first century), makes it difficult to derive data of historical value from this text. Demonstrating a particular solicitude for widows and orphans, Grapte may have been, like Clement, a well-known figure in the Roman tradition, and for this reason the author may have used her name as a device to give credibility to the fictitious antedating of his book.

2. The *De Morte Peregrini* of Lucian of Samosata

Like the Apostolic Fathers, Lucian of Samosata, in his *De Morte Pere grini*, does not provide any information about a function exercised by widows. He recounts that at a certain moment of his life, the pagan philosopher Peregrinus had converted to Christianity. He was then arrested as a Christian and thrown into jail. His fellow-Christians, who held him in high esteem, spared no effort to obtain his freedom. Since they could not free him, they surrounded him with all kinds of attention. From early in the morning, old widows and orphans stood before the jail; then in the evening, the most prominent Christians bribed the guards for permission to spend the night with Peregrinus.[23]

This story does not suggest that the widows were in charge of caring for prisoners; and the mention of orphans alongside of widows suggests rather a type of silent support of the prisoner. In addition, the narrative of Lucian is the work of a pagan who despised Christianity and, as an outsider, knew its doctrines and institutions only superficially. His work, consequently, is full of improbabilities and gives little valuable information about the history of the early Church.

3. The Epistle of Pliny the Younger to Trajan

It is possible that a trace of the women spoken of in 1 Timothy 3:11 may be found in the famous letter of Pliny the Younger to Trajan concerning Christians. To know the truth about the Christian sect, Pliny declared, it was necessary to torture two servants, who were called *ministrae*: "*Necessarium credidi ex duabus ancillis, quae ministrae dicebantur, quid esset veri et per tormenta quaerere.*" [24] In this sentence, *ancilla* is a term designating the social condition of these women, and *ministra* a title given to them by the Christians. It is probable, although not absolutely certain, that the Greek word *diakonos* corresponds to the Latin *ministra.*[25]

This text, however, does not give any precise information about the status and functions of these women in the Christian community. On the basis of the title given them, they may be compared to the women associated with deacons in 1 Timothy 3:11, but even this association is itself loose and uncertain. The beginnings of a feminine diaconate are indeed hidden in shadow and darkness, and difficult to perceive with any exactness.

4. Women in the Heterodox Sects of the Second Century

In the heterodox sects of the second century, the role of women was important. For evidence of this role, one can consider the place occupied by women of the Gospel in Gnostic literature: Mary, the mother of Jesus, Mary Magdalene, Martha, Salome, etc.[26] The Nicolaitans read a work attributed to Noria, whom they considered Noah's wife.[27] The Naassenes pretended that they had received their doctrines from a certain Marianne, who, they said, received them from James, the brother of the Lord.[28] The *Acts of Philip* introduce Marianne as the sister of this Apostle and associate her with his apostolate,[29] just as the *Acts of Paul* associate Thecla with the ministry of the Apostle of the Gentiles.[30] The *Acts of Paul* introduce numerous other prophetesses: Theonoe, Stratonica, Eubulla, Artemilla, Nympha, and Phila.

The Gnostics certainly tended to listen to prophetesses, such as Jezabel, probably symbolically named, who, according to the Apocalypse, was doing her evil work in the church of Thyatira trying to win the faithful to the Nicolaitan doctrines.[31] Some of the great Gnostic teachers had a prophetess at their side. The literature concerning Simon Magus associated with him a woman named Helena, whom he presented as "the first thought of his mind"; [32] in the same way that Simon himself was worshipped by members of the sect as Jupiter, she was adored as Minerva.[33] According to St. Jerome, Marcion, before going to Rome to try his chance, had sent ahead a woman envoy to prepare the people to receive his errors.[34] Apelles, a former disciple of Marcion, although then on bad terms with him, strongly supported the influence of a prophetess named Philcumene and wrote her revelations.[35] In his *Adversus haereses*, St. Irenaeus speaks at length of a Gnostic of the Valentinian school, called Marcus, who seduced many women in the region of Lyons. Marcus associated these women in complicated and spectacular manipulations which he accomplished with chalices of wine mixed with water, and he pretended to infuse them with the spirit of prophecy.[36] The sect in which women seem to have played the most prominent role is the Montanists, where the zeal and prestige of the famous prophetesses Maximilla and Priscilla were not inferior to Montanus himself, the founder of the group.[37] Proud of these illustrious predecessors, women always held a significant place in the life of the Phrygian prophetic sect.[38]

3 WESTERN WRITERS OF THE THIRD CENTURY

With Tertullian and Hippolytus, the picture of the institution of widows in Carthage and Rome at the beginning of the third century appears more clearly. However, there is no question of feminine "ministers" in their writings, and Tertullian strongly opposed the idea of women exercising ecclesiastical functions.

1. Tertullian

In his Catholic period, Tertullian could not find words vehement enough to stigmatize the abusive pretensions of women in the heretical sects he opposed. Noting the absence of all discipline in these communities, he wrote:

> And the women of these heretics, how wanton they are! For they are bold enough to teach, to dispute, to enact exorcisms, to undertake cures — maybe even to baptize.[1]

Tertullian did not tolerate women pretending to teach or to discuss. He denied them, too, the right to exorcise. He did not see this action as an infringement upon priestly functions. Whether the exorcism be performed by touching, breathing, or calling upon the name of Christ, Tertullian did not consider this amazing power of the Christian over demoniacs, a power he regarded as strong evidence of the truth of Christianity, reserved solely to ministries duly appointed for this purpose. Not until the middle of the third century did the exorcist appear as a member of the clergy in the West.[2] In Tertullian's eyes, every Christian in possession of divine grace was entitled to cast out devils;[3] however, he understood this power as exercised by men only, not by women. He applied the same principle to another specifically charismatic activity close to exorcism, the power of healing. Finally, for all the more reason women should leave to men an act as holy as giving baptism. The restriction which Tertullian introduced at this point — "*maybe* even to baptize" — seems to indicate that this abuse was not widespread and that the author looked upon it as a hypothesis rather than as an established fact.

The same position appears in his treatise *On Baptism*, which he wrote about the same time as *On Prescription against Heretics*. The occasion of treatise was the propaganda conducted in Carthage by a woman of the Cainite sect, which rejected baptism.[4] Regardless of the contents of the propaganda in question, in his introduction Tertullian noted the unprecedented nature of the fact itself, i.e., that a woman was teaching.[5] Further on he spoke in the same manner about the minister of baptism. The right to confer baptism, he said, belongs first to the bishop, if he is present, then to presbyters and deacons, with the agreement of the bishop. In case of necessity, lay people also have this right. He reasoned that what all receive in the same degree, all may give in the same degree; he viewed baptism, therefore, as he did the word of God, which no one has the right to keep for himself alone. Since baptism comes from God, all may confer it.[6] But here again he referred only to men, not to women:

> But the impudence of that woman who assumed the right to teach is evidently not going to arrogate to her the right to baptize as well — unless perhaps some new serpent appears, like that original one, so that as that woman abolished baptism, some other should of her own authority confer it. But if certain Acts of Paul, which are falsely so named, claim the example of Thecla for allowing women to teach and to baptize, let men know that in Asia the presbyter who compiled that document, thinking to add of his own to Paul's reputation, was found out, and though he professed he had done it for love of Paul, was deposed from his position. How could we believe that Paul should give a female power to teach and to baptize, when he did not allow a woman even to learn by her own right? "Let them keep silence, he says, and ask their husbands at home." [7]

Since the woman whom Tertullian attacked as a "monstrous viper" rejected baptism, she is not thought to have claimed for herself the right to baptize after usurping the right to teach. But apparently Tertullian did not discard the hypothesis that other women, relying for support on the *Acts of Paul*, actually claimed this right. In one section of this book, which, before scholars discovered that it belonged to a larger corpus, was called the *Acts of Paul and Thecla*, a young girl from Iconium, Thecla, who had been converted by Paul, breaks her engagement and joins the Apostle to assist him in his missionary work. After many pathetic episodes, Paul, who trusted her intelligence and devotion, sends her back to Iconium to teach the word of God.[8] On different occasions, for instance, at Antioch, in the home of Tryphaena, a rich widow who granted her hospitality,[9] and later on at Seleucia,[10] Thecla appears catechizing and converting. Although she never is seen baptizing, when she is condemned to death at Antioch without yet being baptized, she baptizes herself in the amphitheater by throwing herself into a ditch full of water.[11]

Since it was an apocryphal book, the work of a presbyter of Asia, who was deposed for writing this false story, Tertullian said that women would be poorly inspired to use this piece of writing to claim the right to teach and to baptize. In addition, it would be quite wrong, Tertullian insisted, to assume that St. Paul, since he did not even permit women to open their mouth in public and instead ordered them to ask their husbands for instruction at home, acknowledged the right of women to teach and to baptize.

One might imagine that when Tertullian joined Montanism, because of the role played in the beginning of the sect by the prophetesses Maximilla and Priscilla, whose oracles he quoted on two different occasions,[12] he would have compromised his earlier restrictions. One might think, particularly, that he would have refrained from citing the Pauline texts imposing on women silence in church. Such is not the case. In his treatise *On the Veiling of Virgins*, he categorically declared:

> It is not permitted to a woman to speak in church.[13] Neither may she teach, baptize, offer, nor claim for herself any function proper to a man, least of all the sacerdotal office.[14]

This rule was for all women, including virgins; the only kind of priesthood that they might exercise was the "priesthood of chastity." [15] Tertullian, however, because of his Montanist allegiance, made an exception in the case of prophecy. By doing so, he did not think that he was contradicting himself or the Apostle, since the latter, while forbidding women to speak in church, implicitly recognized their right to prophesy, bidding them only to keep their heads covered. A remark in *Against Marcion* reveals his new concern:

> Once more, when he enjoins upon women silence in the church,[16] that they are not to speak, at all events with the idea of learning — though he has already shown that even they have the right to prophesying [17] — it was from the law that he received authority for putting the woman in subjection,[18] that law which, let me say it once at all, (you suppose) he had no right to take note of except for its destruction.[19]

Far from being a difficulty, the matter of Montanist prophetesses became an argument against Marcion, whom Tertullian challenged to name among his disciples any genuine prophetesses.[20] It cannot be concluded, however, that Tertullian believed that all women who said that they were inspired by the Holy Spirit could be allowed to speak freely in church. A text from the treatise *On the Soul* reveals the precautions which he judged necessary to take with prophetesses:

> There is among us a sister who is favored with sundry gifts of revelation, which she experiences in the Spirit by ecstatic vision during the sacred rites of the Lord's day in the church: she converses with angels, and sometimes even with the Lord; she both sees and hears mysterious communications; she understands some men's hearts, and to them who are in need she distributes remedies. Whether it be in the reading of Scriptures, or in the chanting of psalms, or in the preaching of sermons, or in the offering up of prayers — all these religious services offer matter and opportunity to her for seeing visions. One day, while this sister of ours was rapt in the Spirit, we discoursed in some ineffable way about the soul. After the people are dismissed at the conclusion of the sacred services, she regularly reports to us whatever things she may have seen in visions (for all her communications are examined with the utmost scrupulous care, in order that their truth may be probed). "Among other things," she said, "there has been shown to me a soul in bodily shape, and a spirit has been in the habit of appearing to me; not, however, a void and empty illusion, but such as could even be grasped by the hand. It is soft, and transparent, and of an ethereal color, and in form resembling a human being in every respect." [21]

It is significant that the prophetess did not disclose immediately the visions she had received during the Sunday assembly. It was after the ceremony, when the people had gone home, that she explained them to the heads of the sect, who were entitled to pass judgment on their authenticity. Surely Tertullian would not have admitted that the reading of Scripture, the singing of psalms, the preaching of the homily, and the saying of the common prayer would be interrupted by a woman, even one speaking under the influence of the Holy Spirit.

From one end to the other of his religious evolution, Tertullian remained adamant in his refusal to acknowledge the right of women to teach in church or to perform a sacramental act. He testified, however, that there were women in the *ordo* (or in the *ordines*), i.e., within the clergy. The term *ordo*, borrowed from ancient Roman institutions, was applied analogously by Tertullian to those who occupied an official position in the Church.[22] That there were women as well as men in these positions is evident from the following text:

> How many men and how many women in ecclesiastical "orders" owe their position to the practice of continence! They have preferred to be wedded to God; they have restored their flesh in its first dignity and have already dedicated themselves as sons of the other world by slaying in themselves desire, the fruit of lust, in everything which could not be admitted within Paradise.[23]

These women, who in the "orders" of the Church gave the example of continence, were the widows. Just like the male members of the hierarchy (bishops, presbyters, deacons), the widows who were admitted to the *ordo* could have been married only once and they could not enter into a second marriage later on:

> How detrimental to faith, how obstructive to holiness second marriages are, the discipline of the church and the prescription of the Apostle declare when he does not allow men twice married to preside (over a church),[24] when he would not grant a widow admittance into the *ordo* unless she had been "the wife of only one man"; [25] for it behooves God's altar to be set forth pure.[26]

Although there is no question of an explicit profession of widowhood,[27] these widows were certainly under the obligation of continence. They were not forbidden, though, to contract a "spiritual marriage" with a widower who saw to their needs while they looked after his house.[28]

The text quoted above points to the official character of the position in the Church of the women admitted to the "order" of widows. But this position appears even more clearly in the following text, where widows are mentioned in an enumeration just after the male members of the hierarchy; they belonged to the representatives of the community to whom a Christian had to submit his project of marriage, and Tertullian derived from their way of life an argument against second marriages:

> With what face do you request (the solemnizing of) a matrimony which is unlawful to those of whom you request it: of a monogamist bishop, or presbyters and deacons bound by the solemn engagement, of widows whose way of life you have in your own person refused? [29]

All the scholars who comment on this text affirm without any reservation that Tertullian ranked the widows among the clergy.[30] As found in other texts, this official position appears concretely in the fact that widows occupied a place apart in the assemblies of the community. For instance, sinners seeking reconciliation prostrated themselves in the center of the assembly before the widows and before the presbyters (*in medium ante viduas, ante presbyteros*).[31] An important text of *De virginibus velandis*, in which Tertullian gives his most detailed information on widows, also mentions seats reserved for them. In this work Tertullian insists upon the idea that Christian virgins should not neglect the custom which requires women to have their heads covered in assemblies. In this context he relates the following event:

> I know plainly that in a certain place a virgin less than twenty years old has been placed in the order of widows (*in viduatu*)! Whereas if the bishop had been bound to accord her any relief, he might, of course, have done it in some other way without detriment to the respect due to discipline, that such a miracle, not to say monster, should not be pointed at in the church, a virgin-widow! The more portentous, indeed, that not even as a widow did she veil her head, denying herself either way: both as virgin, in that she is counted a widow, and as widow, in that she is

> styled a virgin. But the authority which licenses her sitting in that seat (*illic sedet*) uncovered is the same which allows her to sit there as a virgin: a seat (*ad quam sedem*) to which (besides the sixty years) not merely "single-husbanded" (women) — that is, married women — are at length elected, but mothers to boot, yes, and educators of children; [32] in order that their experimental training in all the affections may, on the one hand, have rendered them capable of readily aiding all others with counsel and comfort, and that, on the other, they nonetheless have traveled down the whole course of probation whereby a female can be tested. So true it is that, on the ground of her position, nothing in the way of public honor is permitted to a virgin.[33]

From this text it is obvious that there existed in the community a group of widows referred to here by the term *viduatus*. Admission into this group depended on the authority of the bishop. The conditions for admission, generally, were those mentioned in First Timothy: they had to be at least sixty years of age, have been married only once, and have raised their children properly. Nevertheless, there were bishops who neglected this rule and admitted among the widows younger women who were unmarried.

Ignatius of Antioch already spoke of "virgins called widows." [34] Tertullian considered this practice a monstrous abuse. Since Tertullian put forth the hypothesis that the bishop perhaps saw himself obliged to provide for the needs of this young virgin, and that he could have done differently and not violated the rule, admission into the group of widows probably implied material help from the Church. This text deals solely with the role of widows in counseling and encouraging other women. It does not support their comparison to deaconesses in the manner that they appear, for instance, in the *Didascalia*; there is no evidence of widows exercising any liturgical ministry nor of their being especially appointed to care for the sick. Those scholars, therefore, who interpret *vidua* in Tertullian as a synonym for *diaconissa*, and *viduatus* as a synonym for *diaconatus*, do so arbitrarily.[35] Tertullian, like all the West up to the end of the fourth century, ignored completely the institution of deaconesses.

2. Hippolytus of Rome

In Hippolytus' *Apostolic Tradition*, just as in the texts of the second century, widows appear among the privileged beneficiaries of Christian charity. When Hippolytus examined candidates for admission to baptism, he asked, among other questions, if they have "honored widows":

> And when they are chosen who are set apart to receive baptism, let their life be examined, whether they lived piously while catechumens, whether "they honored the widows," whether they visited the sick, whether they have fulfilled every good work.[36]

Since these are signs of the dispositions that prepare people to fulfill the great commandment of Christian charity, so to honor widows was one of the good works highly appreciated in candidates for baptism. Here, as in First Timothy, "to honor" does not mean only to show respect but also to give material assistance. A difficult passage of the *Apostolic Tradition*, whose text is now preserved only in the Ethiopian version but whose authenticity is guaranteed by parallels in the *Canons of Hippolytus* and in the *Testament of Our Lord*,[37] blames those who do not give immediately the gifts committed to their care to the beneficiaries for whom they are intended:

> If there is any one who takes it (the gifts) away, let him bear it to the widows and the sick. And let him who is occupied with the church take it away. And if he did not take it away, on the morrow having added of that which was with him, he shall take it away; for it remained with him as bread of the poor.[38]

In this text also, widows are mentioned along with the sick. There is the further question of "him who is occupied with the Church," a puzzling formula; one cannot affirm, in terms of the three successive versions (Greek-Coptic, Coptic-Arabic, Arabic-Ethiopic), exactly who this person was. Since the gifts destined for widows were called "the bread of the poor," these widows, as in the *Shepherd of Hermas*, were the object of the *diakonia* of the Church.

One of the ways of assisting widows was to invite them to a meal:

> If at any time any one wishes to invite those widows who are advanced in years, let him feed them and send them away before sunset. But if he cannot (entertain them in his house) because of his clerical office, let him give them food and wine and send them away, and they shall partake of it at home as they please.[39]

The beginning of the text is easily understood. The author wanted to be sure that meals arranged for widows — a kind of *agape* — did not become occasions for abuse. He directed that only elderly women should be invited and that they should leave before nightfall. The following is less clear. It envisions the case of someone who cannot receive widows because of the function allotted to him. The Coptic version indicates that in the Greek the words used here were *klēros* and *klēroun*, which in the *Apostolic Tradition* always designate an ecclesiastical office.

But it is difficult to understand the reason for preventing a Church official from receiving widows at his table. The difficulty increases when, instead of "the office he has received" in the Latin version, the Coptic and Arabic texts read "the office they [the widows] have received."[40] However, this last reading apparently should not be retained, for one does not see in the *Apostolic Tradition* that widows received a *klēros* nor that they figured among the clergy; the contrary situation seems apparent in Chapter XI, which will be studied shortly. However this text is interpreted, the fact remains that widows were designated with a special title to Christian charity because of the precariousness of their means of subsistence.[41]

Among widows, some were "appointed"; Chapter XI of the *Apostolic Tradition* treats this subject in detail:

> When a widow is appointed, she is not ordained but she shall be chosen by name. But if she lost her husband a long time previously, let her be appointed. But if she lately lost her husband, let her not be trusted. And even if she is aged, let her be tested for a time, for often the passions grow old with him who gives place for them in himself. Let the widow be instituted by word only and (then) let her be reckoned among the (enrolled) widows. But she shall not be ordained, because she does not offer the oblation nor has she a (liturgical) ministry. But the widow is appointed for prayer, and this is (a function) of all (Christians).[42]

The author stresses first that when a widow was appointed (*kathistasthai*), she was not ordained (*cheirotonein*), as were the bishop, the presbyter, and the deacon. Ordination for these involved each time an imposition of hands accompanied by a prayer.[43] In the case of a widow, there was nothing similar; she was simply "named," just as a subdeacon was.[44] A declaration was made, according to a formula which is now unknown and which was not uniform, that so-and-so was admitted among the enrolled widows. The reason for this difference is that ordination (*cheirotonia*) is conferred on members of the clergy (*klēros*) because of their role in liturgical services (*leitourgia*).

But widows did not have a special liturgical function; they were instituted for prayer, a duty common to all Christians. This duty, though, like fasting, which is frequently associated with prayer in traditional Christian spirituality, was imposed on them in a special way. Widows could be compared to virgins in this regard, since the latter were not "ordained" nor even "appointed," but they were exhorted to combine with the "profession" (*proairesis*) [45] of continence the practice of asceticism and prayer: "Widows and virgins shall fast often and pray on behalf of the Church." [46]

There is, therefore, a common ground for comparing virgins and widows. In effect, like the virgins who took a vow of virginity, the appointed widows obligated themselves to a life of continence. This obligation is apparent from the rule which forbade the appointment of a widow whose husband had died only recently; and even if she was aged, the text says, she had to be placed on probation (*dokimazein*) for a certain period, since often the passions endure with those who compromise with them. This remark makes sense here, of course, only if the remarriage of a widow who had been appointed is considered wrong, a matter which consequently appears as forbidden.

4 THE ALEXANDRIAN FATHERS OF THE THIRD CENTURY

While Tertullian and Hippolytus were flourishing in the West, the Alexandrian School with Clement and Origen was thriving in the East. The manner in which these authors spoke of widows does not have the same connotation of actuality as that of their Western contemporaries had. For them, women deacons seem to have been an institution of the past. When he denounced the pretension of women to exercise a ministry of teaching, Origen, however, was no less strong than Tertullian.

1. Widows and "Senior Women" in the Exegesis of the Alexandrians

More than once the Alexandrians cited widows in the same listing with bishops, presbyters, and deacons. For instance, Clement of Alexandria declared:

> Innumerable commands such as these are written in the holy Bible and directed to chosen persons, some to presbyters, some to bishops, some to deacons, others to widows.[1]

The same type of enumeration appeared in Origen, when he commented on the fifth petition of the Lord's Prayer: "Forgive us our trespasses, as we forgive those who trespass against us."

> Apart from these more general obligations, there is the debt of the widow, who is provided for by the Church; the debt of the deacon; that

> of the priest; and the heaviest of all, that of the bishop exacted from him under penalty of punishment by the Savior of the whole Church.[2]

Another example exists in the seventeenth homily on Luke:

> Not only fornication but also second marriages shut off access to ecclesiastical dignities: neither the bishop, nor the presbyter, nor the deacon, nor the widow may be married twice.[3]

Also, in his *Commentary on Matthew*, Origen writes:

> For Paul wishes no one of those in the Church who has attained to any eminence, as is attained in the administration of the sacraments, to make trial of a second marriage. For laying down the law in regard to bishops in the First Epistle to Timothy, he says, "If a man seeks the office of a bishop, he desires a good work. The bishop, therefore, must be without reproach, the husband of one wife, temperate, sober-minded," [4] etc. In regard to deacons, "Let the deacons," he says, "be the husbands of one wife, ruling their children and their own houses well," [5] etc. And also when appointing widows, he says, "Let there be no one as a widow under threescore years old, having been the wife of one man"; [6] He adds to this the things of second or third importance. In the Epistle to Titus, "For this cause," he says, "I left you in Crete to set in order the things that were wanting, and to appoint elders in every city as I gave you charge. If anyone is blameless, the husband of one wife, having children, that believe" [7] — of course — and so on.[8]

It is clear that in these four texts, the widow is closely associated with the bishop, the presbyter, and the deacon. It is necessary, however, to guard against drawing conclusions too quickly, and therefore it is fitting to pursue the investigation further.

On two occasions Origen revealed incidently how to understand one of the conditions asked at the registration of a widow in First Timothy — whether she has "washed the saints' feet." Explaining, in his *Commentary on John*, the account of the washing of the feet, the teacher of Alexandria seeks the spiritual interpretation of this gesture which the Lord asked his disciples to repeat in their turn toward their brethren. At this point Origen refers to the same demand prescribed for widows in 1 Timothy 5:10 and concludes that it should not be understood literally:

> In my opinion, it would be ridiculous to stick to the letter of the text and — if I may take the liberty to say — to insist that a woman who shows all the marks of a holy widow except this one not be admitted to this ecclesiastical dignity, even if often, through the intermediary of servants and domestics, she proved her generosity, and, when she was well-to-do, she cared for strangers and those who, for whatsoever reason, needed to receive a witness to their humanity. Do not hesitate to interpret symbolically the expression, "washed the saints' feet," [9] since senior women, just as senior men, are ordered to be the "teachers of good things." [10]

If one interprets "washed the saints' feet" in a literal sense, he arrives at the absurd conclusion that a widow who has never personally poured water on the feet of a stranger but who has frequently been helpful to all those in need, using her servants for this good work, would nevertheless be excluded from the dignity of widow. This example shows well that "washing the feet" must be understood in a figurative sense. Origen derived this interpretation from a part of the Epistle to Titus; this letter, in fact, requires senior women, among other things, to "teach what is good" (*kalodidaskalous einai*), as earlier it requires senior men [11] — or more exactly the bishops,[12] but Origen does not seem to make a distinction — who are able "to give instruction in sound doctrine" (*parakalein en tē didaskalia tē hygiainousē*).[13] To wash the feet of someone means, therefore, to purify the blemishes of his soul with fitting words.

The same interpretation is suggested in the text of the sixth homily on Isaiah:

> If you wish to understand more clearly how the widow "washes the feet of the saints," [14] listen to Paul, who, in another place, commands widows "to teach what is good, and in such a way that young women may remain chaste," [15] thus washing the stain off the feet of the young women. And these widows are worthy to be honored in the Church who wash the feet of the saints through spiritual instruction — by saints I mean not men, but women. For: "I permit no woman to teach or to have authority over men." [16] He wants women "to teach what is good" in the sense that they have to inculcate chastity in "young women," not young men, for it is not becoming for a woman to be a teacher of men; but they must train young women in chastity and love of their husbands and of their children.[17]

Here again Origen interpreted the expression "washed the saints' feet" as signifying teaching, and he referred to the same text of the Epistle to Titus to support this reading. Besides, this time he emphasized that this teaching, coming from women, should be addressed only to women. In effect, he said the Apostle does not permit women to teach nor to govern men. Since it was not becoming for a woman to dare to teach a man, the senior women were invited to train "young women," not young men. In this statement Origen was faithful to 1 Timothy 2:12.[18]

In his *Commentary on the Epistle to the Romans*, the Alexandrian teacher also referred to the exhortation addressed to senior women to train the young women and to the additional duty "to wash the saints' feet":

> "Greet Mary, who has worked hard in the Lord." [19] Here also he teaches [20] that women, too, ought to labor diligently for the churches of God. They toil assiduously, indeed, when they teach young women to be sober, to love their husbands, to raise their children, to be modest, chaste, to be good housekeepers, to be submissive to their husbands,[21]

> to be kind, to practice hospitality, to wash the feet of the saints,[22] and to fulfill in all chastity all the other duties which are ascribed to women in Scripture.[23]

For a woman, "to work hard in the Lord" meant to inculcate in young women the qualities which make them good wives, good mothers, good housekeepers, gracious and charitable Christians. At this point Origen was not preoccupied with stressing that women teach women only, and he apparently did not intend that the duty of "washing the feet of the saints" be read "figuratively."

In a comment on 1 Corinthians 14:34-35 preserved in a *catena*, Origen expanded at length on the interdiction of teaching which is given to women, referring again to the verses of Titus about senior women and commenting in the same sense as in the sixth homily on Isaiah. In this text Origen attacked the Montanist prophetesses:

> Although all speak and are allowed to speak when they are granted a revelation, "the women," he says, "should keep silence in the churches." [24] They in no way fulfill this command, those disciples of women, who chose as their master Priscilla and Maximilla, not Christ, the Spouse of the Bride.[25] But, let us be good-natured players, and cope with the arguments which they judge convincing. The Evangelist Philip, they say, had four daughters, and all prophesied.[26] If they prophesied, what is strange, they ask, if our own prophetesses — as they are called — also prophesy? Let us then resolve this difficulty. First, since you say: "Our women prophesied," show in them the signs of prophesy. Second, if the daughters of Philip prophesied, at least they did not speak in the assemblies; for we do not find this fact in the Acts of the Apostles. Much less in the Old Testament. It is said that Deborah was a prophetess.[27] Mary, the sister of Aaron, tambourine in hand, led the choir of women.[28] There is no evidence that Deborah delivered speeches to the people, as did Jeremias and Isaias. Hulda, who was a prophetess, did not speak to the people, but only to a man, who consulted her at home.[29] The Gospel itself mentions a prophetess, Anna, the daughter of Phanuel, of the tribe of Aser; [30] but she did not speak publicly. Even if it is granted to a woman to prophesy and show the sign of prophecy, she is nevertheless not permitted to speak in an assembly. When Mary, the prophetess, spoke, she was leading a choir of women. For: "It is improper for a woman to raise her voice at meetings," [31] and: "I am not giving permission for a woman to teach" and even less "to tell a man what to do." [32] Although those given above say more categorically that a woman does not have the right by her word to guide a man, I shall further prove this position from another text. "Bid the old women to behave themselves as befits holy women, teaching what is good, in order to form young women in wisdom," and not simply "Let them teach." [33] Certainly, women should also "teach what is good," but men should not sit and listen to a woman, as if there were no men capable of communicating the word of God. "If they have any question to ask, they should ask their husbands at home: it does not seem right for a woman to raise her voice at meetings." [34] It seems to me that the expression "their hus-

> bands" does not refer only to husbands; for if that were the case, either virgins would speak in the assembly, or they would have nobody to teach them, and the same is true for widows. But could "their husbands" not also mean a brother, a relative, or a son? In short, let a woman learn from the man who is her own, taking "man" in its generic sense, as the counterpart of "woman." "For it is improper for a woman to speak in an assembly," no matter what she says, even if she says admirable things, or even saintly things, that is of little consequence, since they come from the mouth of a woman. "A woman in an assembly": clearly this abuse is denounced as improper — an abuse for which the entire assembly is responsible.[35]

Although the behavior of the Montanist prophetesses who spoke in public, such as Maximilla and Priscilla, is obviously condemned by Paul's categorical command: "Women are to remain quiet at meetings," Origen consented to discuss the argument of those whom he scornfully called "the disciples of women." If the daughters of Philip prophesied, they say, why is it so astonishing that we have these prophetesses? Sketching at first a parade without pushing too far, Origen invited his adversaries to show in their prophetesses the "signs of prophecy." This expression recalls that of Paul when he mentioned to the Corinthians the "signs of the apostle" (*ta sēmeia tou apostolou*), which they were able to observe on the occasion of his apostolic activities.[36]

The "signs of prophecy" seem to be the criteria that the first Christian generations established to distinguish between those who exploited popular credulity and sought to gain advantage, on the one hand, and those who authentically interpreted the Spirit, on the other hand. Chief among these criteria were a strict orthodoxy, an irreproachable morality, and a perfect disinterestedness.[37] But Origen did not insist on this argument. He preferred to emphasize that in the Acts of the Apostles there is no evidence that the daughters of Philip prophesied in mixed assemblies, and moreover that the same held true for the few prophetesses mentioned in the Old Testament. In addition, the duty of teaching, or more exactly, of "formation," entrusted to senior women in the Epistle to Titus concerns only young women. It is not a question of men sitting down and listening to women, as if there were no men capable of transmitting the word of God. The rule expressed by Paul is clear: under no pretext may a woman open her mouth in an assembly where there are men, for she is not permitted to make herself the guide of men by the word.

As we have seen, the Alexandrians were not interested in widows or in "senior women" for themselves. They did not speak of them as an institution existing in their time; they dealt, instead, with the biblical texts relevant to widows and senior women. Before developing this conclusion, it is necessary to examine women deacons, about whom a similar observation can be made.

2. Women Deacons According to the Alexandrians

Besides widows and "senior women," Clement of Alexandria and Origen likewise wrote about "women deacons." Clement spoke about the women who accompanied the Apostles according to 1 Corinthians 9:5, "Have we not the right to take a woman around with us as a sister, like all the other apostles?"

> But the latter, in accordance with their particular ministry, devoted themselves to preaching without any distraction, and took their wives with them, not as women with whom they had marriage relations, but as sisters, that they might be their fellow-ministers (*syndiakonous*) in dealing with housewives. It was through them that the Lord's teaching penetrated also the women's quarters without any scandal being aroused. We also know the directions (*hosa*) about women deacons (*diakonōn gynaikōn*) which are given by the noble Paul in his second letter to Timothy.[38]

The text to which Clement alluded in the last line can be only 1 Timothy 3:11. Kalsbach, in defiance of the evidence, it seems to me, approves Stählin, the editor of the Berlin Corpus, who refers to 1 Timothy 5:9.[39] Kalsbach's arguments, however, are not convincing. The relative pronoun used by Clement in the last sentence (*hosa*) does not necessarily imply that an extended passage must result, for in late Greek it can be almost the equivalent of the simple relative (*hos*). In addition, this text does not necessarily contain a prescription regarding the sexual behavior of women deacons, which would be the case in 1 Timothy 5:9 but not in 1 Timothy 3:11.

The point of this reference to the wives of the Apostles is not that they must renounce conjugal relations to be associated with the ministry of their husbands; moreover, it would be difficult to find a confirmation of this rule in 1 Timothy 5:9 or in the context, which simply prescribes that a widow, to be registered as such, must have been the wife of only one man. The point of this reference to the wives of the Apostles is that the Apostles were married and that, consequently, the character of marriage is licit and good, contrary to the pretention of Gnostics of the Encratic tendency.[40] However, the Apostles, according to 1 Corinthians 9:5,[41] treated their wives not as spouses but as sisters, for they intended to devote themselves wholly to preaching. Clement deduced from this text that their wives accompanied them on their missionary journeys to be their collaborators in ministering to women.

Without relying directly on 1 Corinthians 9:5, this last affirmation explains the reference to First Timothy. Having shown the wives of the Apostles as collaborators of their ministry, as their *syndiakonoi*, Clement remembered that in the passage of First Timothy on deacons, there are "women" who, because of the place where they are mentioned, seem to have exercised a ministry similar to that of deacons and even collaborated with their masculine colleagues. This was the truth that Clement wanted to bring out when he referred to the prescriptions contained in one of the letters to Timothy regarding deacons.

Here is Origen's comment explaining the text of Romans concerning Phoebe: [42]

> This text teaches with the authority of the Apostle that even women are instituted deacons in the Church.[43] This is the function which was exercised in the church of Cenchreae by Phoebe, who was the object of high praise and recommendation by Paul. He enumerated her outstanding works; she assisted everyone, he said — i.e., she helped them in their needs — she also helped me in my needs and my apostolic work with a perfect devotion. I readily compare her action with the hospitality of Lot, who never failed to welcome guests who presented themselves, and thereby deserved one day to grant his hospitality to angels.[44] In the same manner, likewise, Abraham, who always came forward to greet his guests, deserved to have the Lord with his angels visit him and stay under his tent.[45] Also this pious Phoebe, while giving assistance and rendering service to all, deserved to assist and to serve the Apostle himself. And thus this text teaches at the same time two things: that there are, as we have already said, women deacons in the Church, and that women, who have given assistance to so many people and who by their good works deserve to be praised by the Apostle, ought to be accepted in the diaconate. He also exhorted that those who are active in good works in the Church receive likewise in return from their brethren consideration and be treated with honor, in whatever matter is necessary, even in material services.[46]

Here again Kalsbach is wrong when, at any cost, he finds in this text the influence of 1 Timothy 5:9-10.[47] The only detail that tends to warrant this assertion is the reference to the hospitality of Lot and Abraham, which Kalsbach compares to the hospitality required for the admission of a widow in 1 Timothy 5:10, "shown hospitality" to strangers. But the practice of hospitality is not a widow's distinctive virtue; according to other texts of the New Testament,[48] all Christians must show hospitality. In addition, the point of the comparison between Phoebe with Lot, on the one hand, and Abraham, on the other, is not that Phoebe practiced hospitality as Lot and Abraham did; it is much more the following idea: in the same manner that Lot and Abraham deserved to receive the Lord and his angels one day because they always welcomed travelers liberally, so too Phoebe, because she assisted all those in need of help, deserved the honor of assisting and serving an apostle of the Lord.

If Kalsbach is preoccupied at this point with discovering references to 1 Timothy 5:9-10 in the Alexandrian texts about women deacons to prove that their authors assimilated the ministry of "deaconesses" with that of widows, it is because, for him, the widows of the first two centuries represent a union of an ideal of ascetic life and one of service to the community, and because the institution of widows in the course of the third century split into its two essential components; and as service to the community developed more and more, it became the lot of deaconesses distinct from widows. Since deaconesses originated in Syria, where the Didascalia [49] testified for the first time to their existence, the Alexandrians, writing in Egypt during the first half of the third century, could not know a feminine diaconate distinct from the institution of widows, and they could not, therefore, conceive of a ministry for women other than one modeled on widows. This is the reason why, when the Alexandrians spoke of women deacons, Kalsbach absolutely wants their functions described on the basis of 1 Timothy 5:9-10.

In reality, without renouncing his thesis, Kalsbach could have avoided these complications if he had noticed that whenever the Alexandrians mentioned women deacons or widows, they referred to the past, not to the present. Some other scholars have made this same observation concerning deaconesses. Both Clement and Origen occasionally recognized that women were placed in the service of the Church in the time of St. Paul, but they did not indicate that this office survived later, and even less that it existed in Egypt in their own period. When they spoke of the ministries of their era,[50] deaconesses were never mentioned among the ministers of the Church. Significantly, when he tried to explain what could have been the collaboration of the wives of the apostles with their husbands, Clement did not refer to an institution or to a practice of the Church of his time but to a *text* of St. Paul. Furthermore, Phoebe did not seem to remind Origen of a minister of the contemporary Church, whereas the exegetes of the Antiochian School of the fourth century, for whom deaconesses were a living reality, spontaneously made the comparison.[51]

Origen even gave the impression that the idea of a woman exercising a ministry in the Church was astonishing and needed to be confirmed by the authority of the Apostle: "This text," he said about Romans 16:1, "teaches *with the authority of the Apostle that even women* are made deacons in the Church." [52] If by his time women deacons were frequently found in the churches of Egypt, this remark would have been pointless, for there would have been no need of a text to teach with the authority of the Apostle that women were instituted deacons in the Church.

Similar observations can be made regarding widows. According to Clement, they were among the number of chosen people (*prosōpa eklekta*): according to Origen, they received from the Church a pre-eminence (*hyperochēn tina*) and, just as bishops, presbyters, and deacons, they were granted an ecclesiastical dignity (*ekklēsiastikē timē, ecclesiastica dignitas, ecclesiasticus honor*). Here too, however, one feels that he is dealing with theoretical considerations, not with references to a concrete situation and a living practice. The four texts quoted above indicate that what led the Alexandrians to compare the widow to the bishop, the presbyter, and the deacon was the parallelism between the conditions prescribed in Pastoral Epistles for the enrolling of a widow and for the choosing of a bishop, presbyter, or deacon — especially the fact that remarried persons are excluded — and not the situation or juridical condition which would have been theirs in the Church at that time.

About this point of view, it is interesting to note the contrast with Tertullian, who mentioned the presence of widows in the midst of the Christian assembly, who referred to the testimony of their life, and who gave multiple concrete details about them, and with Hippolytus, who defined their status with precision in his *Apostolic Tradition.* When, in his *Commentary on Matthew*, after citing the passages of the Pastoral Epistles which exclude remarried people from ecclesiastical dignities (bishops, deacons, widows, presbyters), Origen tried to explain the reason for this rule and, forgetting this text for awhile, considered the life of the Church of his time, he was concerned with the bishop, the presbyter, and the deacon — the hierarchical order spontaneously substituting for the order found in biblical citations — and widows were no longer mentioned:

> Now, when we saw that some who have been married twice may be much better than those who have been married once, we were perplexed why Paul does not at all permit those who have been twice married to be appointed to ecclesiastical dignities; for also it seemed to me that such a thing was worthy of examination, and it was possible that a man who had been unfortunate in two marriages and had lost his second wife while he was yet young, might have lived for the rest of his years up to old age in the greatest self-control and chastity. Who, then, would not naturally be perplexed why at all, when a ruler of the Church is being sought, we do not appoint such a man, though he has been twice married, because of the expressions about marriage, but lay hold of the man who has been once married as our ruler, even if he chance to have lived to old age with his wife, and sometimes may not have been disciplined in chastity and temperance? But, from what is said in the law about the bill of divorcement, I reflect whether, seeing that the bishop and the presbyter and the deacon are a symbol of things that truly exist in accordance with these names, he wished to appoint those who were figuratively once married, in order that he who is able to give attention to the matter may find out from the spiritual law the one who was unworthy of ecclesiastical rule, whose soul did not find favor in the eyes of her husband because there had been found in her a unseemly thing, and she had become worthy of the bill of divorcement; for such a soul, having dwelt along with a second husband and having been hated by such a one, can no longer, after the second bill of divorcement, return to her former husband.[53]

When Origen explained that having "washed the saints' feet" should be understood in a spiritual sense, he was not thinking of the widows of his own time. He sought, as an exegete, to illumine the meaning of the word of the Lord: "You must wash one another's feet." It was always as an exegete, and only as an exegete, that he referred on several occasions to the text of the Epistle to Titus about the duty of senior women to teach the younger ones. These senior women seem to have been persons of the past, like Miriam, the sister of Aaron, Deborah, Hulda, Anna, and the daughters of Philip. No connection appeared between them and a present function. Origen, who was ever ready to draw typological parallels and extend them over centuries, who, for instance, recognized immediately in all those who exercised some form of leadership in ancient Israel a prefiguration of leaders in Christianity, when he mentioned the women who accompanied Jesus and ministered to him,[54] did not make any comparison with an actual ministry of his own time, whereas the *Didascalia Apostolorum* found in them a prefiguration of the ministry of deaconesses.

An inquiry into the Alexandrians about a ministry of women in their era, or, more generally, about the status of widows in Egyptian communities, is fruitless. There is absolutely no reason to rank, as J. Daniélou has,[55] the Alexandrians, together with Tertullian, among those who maintain that in the third century widows had become an order in the Church and were incorporated in the ecclesiastical hierarchy.

5 DIDASCALIA APOSTOLORUM

The Eastern documents presented up to this time provide only occasional references to widows or to women who exercised a ministry in the Church. But the *Didascalia Apostolorum*, an ecclesiastical constitution, offers an extended treatment of the status and function of these women.[1]

1. Widows

We shall note in the *Didascalia* data relevant to widows in the order in which they occur. In the chapters of the *Didascalia* dealing with the rights and duties of bishops, widows are mentioned more than once. Among the people entitled to special solicitude on the part of the bishops, widows appear along with orphans, the poor, and strangers.[2] The author immediately adds that this solicitude must not be exercised indiscriminately. If a bishop finds a widow who has enough to live on or who is capable of providing for her own needs, and a woman, not a widow, who is in a difficult material situation because she is in poor health or has children to raise, he must give preference to the second.[3] The bishop ought not use the gifts of the faithful to live luxuriously. He is allowed to take from these gifts only what he needs to feed and clothe himself decently, and he has to distribute the rest to orphans, widows, the destitute, and strangers — in short, to all those in need.[4]

As in the Old Testament, the faithful must offer to God, in the person of those designated by God for this end, their tithes and first-fruits. High priests of the Old Testament correspond to bishops of the Church, and the Levites of earlier times are now the deacons, the presbyters, the widows, and the orphans.[5] The context and the mention of orphans alongside of widows clearly shows that if widows are paralleled with Levites, it is not because they are invested with any kind of ministry, as the deacons and presbyters are, but because they are entitled to receive a part of the donations of the faithful. For the same reason, the author, choosing an image already used by Polycarp,[6] declares that widows and orphans have a right to be considered a symbol of the altar.[7]

Widows, who are generally aged women, belong to a naturally larger group of elderly women. In liturgical assemblies, where the faithful were grouped according to their age, sex, and family situation, senior women and widows, mentioned together, had their own place.[8] At a time when old age pensions did not exist, old women without personal possessions or family help must necessarily have suffered. For this reason, according to the *Didascalia*,[9] generous Christians organized in their behalf[10] brotherly meals[11] and gift distributions.[12] The *Didascalia* recommended that the bishop send to these meals, by preference, those whom he knew to be in want.

Among the widows, there were some who were "appointed"[13] as such and formed the "order of widows."[14] They had to be not less than fifty years old so that their age might provide in a certain measure a guarantee against remarriage.[15] If a young woman who had been admitted into the order of widows should remarry because her state was burdensome to her, she would dishonor the order and she would have to render an account to God: first, because she had belonged to two men, and, second, because she had promised God to remain a widow, and as such she has received gifts, but she has not persevered in this state.[16] But if a young widow, whose age prevented her from entering the order of widows, persevered in widowhood, she would not be less rewarded by God or honored by men.[17] To avoid making them wish for a second marriage because of their poverty, young widows had to be assisted in the same way as "appointed" widows. The bishop had to attend carefully to this duty.[18]

A widow had to be distinguished by her mildness and evenness of temper; she should be without malice and anger, not talkative or quarrelsome, and if she saw or heard anything unseemly, she had to act as if she had neither seen nor heard anything.[19] She had to occupy herself with nothing other than praying for those who gave alms and for the whole Church.[20] If she was questioned by someone, she should refrain from answering unless the question was about the rudiments of faith and morals. She could answer, for instance, that idols are nothing and that there is only one God, but she was not herself to try to explain to pagans the mysteries of the Incarnation and the Passion of Christ or those of the last things. She was to send those who wished to be instructed in these matters to the leaders of the community. Because of her incompetence and, above all, because the unbelievers would have ridiculed what was said by a woman, in doing otherwise she would have created a greater obstacle rather than helping the spread of the gospel.[21]

> It is neither right nor necessary therefore that women should be teachers, and especially concerning the name of Christ and the redemption of His passion. For you have not been appointed to this, O women, and especially widows, that you should teach, but that you should pray and entreat the Lord God. For He, the Lord God, Jesus Christ our Teacher, sent us the Twelve to instruct the people and the Gentiles; and there were with us women disciples, Mary Magdalene and Mary the daughter of James [22] and the other Mary [23]; but He did not send them to instruct the people with us. For if it were required that women should teach, our Master Himself would have commanded these to give instruction with us.[24]

The argument advanced to prove that widows should not concern themselves with teaching is that Christ did not give women the mission to instruct the people with the apostles.

Without transition, the author then returns to the image of the widow as the "altar of God" to demonstrate this time the idea that, just as the altar is immovable and solidly fixed in one spot, the widow must stay at home and not waste her time running from one house to another. There were, in fact, widows who totally lacked reserve and discretion and who went everywhere to obtain gifts, to spread gossip, and to stir up quarrels. These are not widows but wallets, says the author, in an untranslatable play on words (*mē chēras, alla pēras — non viduae, sed viduli*). Their God was their wallet; they turned their state of life into a business. Instead of giving to the bishop what they might have had in excess to help him to receive strangers or to support the destitute, they lent money at exorbitant rates and thought of nothing except getting more money.

It is no wonder that the prayer of such a widow was not heard by God. While she was at prayer, she remembered where she had to go to get money, or that she had forgotten to say something to a friend and could think of nothing but that.[25] On the contrary, the widow who wished to please God remained at home to pray without ceasing, and because her heart was not occupied with anything else, she obtained what she asked. She did not listen to the wicked. She was not greedy or selfish. Quite the contrary, she spun her wool that she might help the destitute, the little that she was able, rather than be in charge of someone herself.[26]

Widows had to be obedient to the bishop and deacons, and they could not take any initiative without their permission. They were particularly forbidden, without an order from the bishop or the deacon, to go to someone's home to eat or drink, to fast with the person, to receive gifts, or to impose a hand and pray over someone. How would the widows know, otherwise, from whom they received these gifts, for whom they fasted, or upon whom they laid their hand? There were widows who, knowing that their sister-widows or their brethren were sick, pretended to have no time to go to their homes to fast with them, to pray, or to lay hands on them. But, since sinners and the excommunicated gave them important donations, these widows showed the greatest eagerness to visit them. They believed that they were wiser than men, and even than presbyters and bishops. They forgot that he who enters into relationship with an excommunicated person and prays with him takes his guilt upon himself and must render to God the same account as this sinner must.[27]

Apparently, since the *Didascalia* mentions at this point that it is forbidden for women to baptize, some widows must have dared to baptize, or at least some of them must have claimed this right:

> That a woman should baptize, or that one should be baptized by a woman, we do not counsel, for it is a transgression of the commandment, and a great peril to her who baptizes and to him who is baptized. For if it were lawful to be baptized by a woman, our Lord and Teacher Himself would have been baptized by Mary His mother, whereas He was baptized by John, like others of the people. Do not therefore imperil yourselves, brethren and sisters, by acting beside the law of the Gospel.[28]

The argument is the same type as given concerning women teaching.

Envy and jealousy are sentiments unbecoming to a Christian, and even more to a widow. If a widow sees that a sister-widow has received a gift, she must give thanks to God and pray for the donor and for the bishop who gave the gift to her companion rather than to her. In return, God will not fail to take care that an even better gift will come to her. On the other hand, a widow who has received a donation must be careful not to reveal the name of the donor, either by praying loudly for him or by answering questions about the origin of the gift; otherwise there is the risk that the pagans, who do not need to be informed about what takes place in the Church, might hear of it. And above all, evil widows might show their bitterness to the giver, pretending to have a greater right to benefit from his generosity than the widow who received his donation. On these occasions, forgetting that they were established to bless, some may even go so far as to curse. Neither a bishop nor a presbyter nor a deacon nor a widow should pronounce a curse, lest he or she be cursed in return. The bishop must take measures that none of the laity curses either.[29]

Bishops and deacons must watch carefully that what is offered at the altar of Christ, i.e., to widows and orphans, is the product of honest labor only.[30] The *Didascalia* gives a long list of people whose gifts should not be accepted, such as the rich who are harsh with the humble and the poor, the dissolute, dishonest merchants and usurers, false witnesses and lying judges, idol-makers, etc.[31] Better for a widow to have only bread to eat that is the product of honest work than to have an abundance that is the fruit of injustice. It would be better even to die of hunger than to accept such gifts. If a widow prays for an unjust man from whom she has received a donation, her prayer will not be heard; but, on the contrary, it will recall to God, who knows the hearts of men, the misdeeds of that sinner. Since, in such a circumstance, people could believe that God is not good and does not answer the prayers addressed to him,[32] she also risks doing injury to the gospel.

But, as someone might contend, if we do not accept the gifts of these people, how shall we provide for widows? It is exactly for this purpose that the faithful must give to the bishop tithes, first-fruits, and offerings. If they are not sufficient, the community should be informed of the situation and a collection organized to gather what is needed.[33] However, if once in a while the bishop finds himself obliged to accept money from an impious man, he should use it to buy firewood for himself and for widows, lest a widow who received the money might use it to purchase food. If the bishop acts thus, he will not be guilty of any sin, and the prayers of the widow will be heard.[34]

As one can see, the *Didascalia* reveals in an exceedingly lively way what the widows stood for in a Syrian community in the first half of the third century. From this information we now will try to define the juridical status and the corresponding rights and duties of these widows. As noted before, there were two kinds of widows, those "appointed," who made up the order of widows, and the others.[35] Since the latter were unquestionably members of the laity and nothing more, it is only the former that pose a question. Were the "appointed" widows members of the clergy or of the laity? On the one hand, they were the object of a special call from God,[36] and they occupied a "place" or "rank" apart from lay people.[37] But, on the other hand, there is no evidence that they were in some way positively associated with the bishops, presbyters, and deacons, so that they too were considered members of the clergy.[38] They seem to have been distinguished from the laity in a manner similar to the religious in the threefold division of the members of the Church in Book II of the *Codex Iuris Canonici*.

The "appointed" widows of the *Didascalia* had also at least two things in common with the nuns of the following centuries: the vow of continence and the duty of prayer. Since she had to promise God to remain a widow, and since a younger woman would have been in danger, according to the *Didascalia*, of failing in this commitment,[39] a woman was not admitted into the order of widows before the age of fifty.

The essential task of a widow was prayer; it was also her special function, and the *Didascalia* refers to it frequently.[40] The supplications of a widow at the bedside of the sick were granted a particular power; these petitions were regularly linked to a propitiatory fast and accompanied by an imposition of the hand.[41] When he declared that widows are appointed, not to curse, but to bless, the author was probably referring to this gesture of blessing.[42] He did not concede any other duty to them,[43] and insisted on the fact that they should not occupy themselves with anything except prayer.[44] They were not to substitute for the leaders of the community in catechizing those who wanted instruction in the Christian faith,[45] since women did not receive from Christ the mission to teach,[46] just as the Gospel never shows them baptizing.[47]

These remarks seem to indicate that some widows were at least tempted to assume these rights. Without hesitation the author denounced what he considered at once an abuse and a mistake: widows did not have the necessary competency, any more than lay people, to teach Christian doctrine fittingly; and, if truths as disconcerting to the mind as the Incarnation and the Passion of Christ had been proclaimed by a woman, the pagans would have only laughed and thought it not worthwhile to listen to these doctrines any more.[48] One easily recognizes here a disdain for women, which is not peculiar to the author but reflects instead the mind-set of his milieu. One must not, however, exaggerate the influence which this environmental disdain had upon the theological positions of the author. He denied women the right to teach and baptize primarily because he did not see in the Gospel that Christ entrusted these ministries to women, even though some women were among his followers.

The "appointed" widows were entitled to assistance from the Church.[49] But they did not have a monopoly on this right; they shared it with all elderly women, whose age naturally placed them in a difficult situation,[50] with younger widows, who were thus persuaded against remarriage,[51] and, in a more general way, with all those who were in need, such as orphans, strangers, and those in difficulty for whatever reason.[52] Although all these people had to be considered the "altar of God,"[53] widows and orphans especially deserved this title,[54] and were the first recommended to the charity of Christians.

There were many abuses which the author bluntly denounced. Covetous, greedy, selfish, evil widows ran the streets, their hand perpetually outstretched, making and breaking reputations, jealous of their sister-widows who seemed to them to be favored over themselves, reserving their prayers for the rich, without any consideration of their sinfulness or excommunication. It is useless to add that under these conditions their prayers would be vain and even dangerous for themselves as well as for those for whom they prayed.[55]

In summary, widowhood appears in the *Didascalia* as a privileged opportunity for spiritual progress. Accentuating the ascetic features of the "real widow" in First Timothy, the author neatly draws the outlines of a spiritual ideal composed of two essentials — continence and prayer. For widows over fifty, agreement with this ideal was sanctioned by entering the "order of widows." But younger widows, even though they could not be "established," were also invited to embrace the same ideal. The *Didascalia* no longer encouraged them to remarry, as Paul did in First Timothy. Correlatively, the right to material help was no longer tied to "enrollment" in a group of widows but was accorded to every widow, as well as to all in need.

2. Deaconesses

Along with widows, the *Didascalia* mentions the presence of deaconesses. Repeating the typology elaborated by St. Ignatius of Antioch, according to which the bishop is the image of the Father, and the deacon of Christ, while the presbyters figure the college of the apostles,[56] the *Didascalia* adds that the deaconess must be honored as a figure of the Holy Spirit.[57] This unusual idea is not found anywhere else and is not particularly developed. The fact that the term designating the Spirit is feminine in Syriac, as in Hebrew, perhaps suggested to the author, a Syrian, to make this analogy, which at first sight seems so startling. The functions of the deaconess are described as follows:

> "Wherefore, O bishop, appoint thee workers of righteousness as helpers who may cooperate with thee unto salvation. Those that please thee out of all the people thou shalt choose and appoint as deacons," a man for the performance of most things that are required, but a woman for the ministry of women. For there are houses whither thou canst not send a deacon to the women, on account of the heathen, but mayest send a deaconess. Also, because in many other matters the office of a woman deacon is required. In the first place, when women go down into the water, those who go down into the water ought to be anointed by a deaconess with the oil of anointing; and where there is no woman at hand, and especially no deaconess, he who baptizes must of necessity anoint her who is being baptized. But where there is a woman, and especially a deaconess, it is not fitting that women should be seen by men: but with the imposition of hand do thou anoint the head only. As of old the priests and kings were anointed in Israel, do thou in like manner, with the imposition of hand, anoint the head of those who receive baptism, whether of men or of women; and afterwards — whether thou thyself baptize, or thou command the deacons or presbyters to baptize — let a woman deacon, as we have already said, anoint the women.
>
> But let a man pronounce over them the invocation of the divine Names in the water. And when she who is being baptized has come up from the water, let the deaconess receive her, and teach and instruct her how the seal of baptism ought to be (kept) unbroken in purity and holiness. For this cause we say that the ministry of a woman deacon is especially needful and important. For our Lord and Savior also was ministered unto by women ministers, Mary Magdalene, and [58] Mary

> the daughter of James and mother of Jose, and the mother of the sons of Zebedee, with other women besides.[59] And thou also hast need of the ministry of a deaconess for many things; for a deaconess is required to go into the houses of the heathen where there are believing women, and to visit those who are sick, and to minister to them in that of which they have need, and to bathe those who have begun to recover from sickness.
>
> And let the deacons imitate the bishops in their conversation: nay, let them even be laboring more than he. And let them not love filthy lucre; but let them be diligent in the ministry. And in proportion to the number of the congregation of the people of the Church, so let deacons be, that they may be able to take knowledge (of each) severally and refresh all; so that for the aged women who are infirm, and for the brethren and sisters who are in sickness — for every one they may provide the ministry which is proper for him.
>
> But let a woman rather be devoted to the ministry of women, and a male deacon to the ministry of men. And let him be ready to obey and to submit himself to the command of the bishops. And let him labor and toil in every place whither he is sent to minister or to speak of some matter to any one.[60]

This text presents the position of the deaconess as analogous to that of the deacon: men and women deacons are the collaborators of the bishop, freely chosen by him from among the people and appointed to assist him in his pastoral duties. This analogy appears clearly in the term used for the deaconess: *gynē diakonos, hē diakonos,* "woman deacon," or simply "deacon" employed as a feminine noun.[61]

However, the attributes of a deaconess are not as extended as those of her masculine colleague. A deacon is a "man occupied with a number of the things that are necessary,"[62] and he must be ready to carry out all the orders given him by the bishop.[63] Other texts show even more clearly that he is the right arm of the bishop, "his ear and his mouth," the intermediary between the bishop and the faithful.[64] He assists the bishop in the celebration of the Eucharist and cares for the order of the assembly.[65]

Nothing like this is said about the deaconess. In reading the text quoted above, one at first gets the impression that the duties of a deaconess were also extensive; a deacon was established "for the performance of many things that were required," a deaconess "for the ministry of women." But, in fact, it appears quite quickly that this service was limited to two things. On the one hand, a deaconess ministered to sick women as an assistant of the male deacon in cases where his being sent to Christian women would have offended the pagans. On the other hand, a deaconess could better anoint the women before they descended into the baptismal waters and receive them when they left it, since it is not becoming that the nudity of women be seen by men.

Several of these statements regarding the ministry of deaconesses sound like pleadings. The author insists on the usefulness, even the necessity, of such a ministry. He recalls that during his earthly existence our Lord himself benefited from the service of women. But it is apparent that there were not deaconesses everywhere, since if no deaconess was present, any woman could serve, and if no woman was present, the male minister of baptism anointed the body of women. This was the only task conceded to a deaconess.

Although a deacon could be delegated by the bishop to administer baptism, there is no doubt that a deaconess was included under the prohibition forbidding women to baptize; in fact, it is clearly stated that even when a deaconess was present and anointed a woman, a man always had to pronounce the baptismal formula. In the same way, a deaconess was certainly included under the prohibition forbidding women to teach, except for the advice she was invited to give a neophyte leaving the baptismal water. In short, one has the impression that the feminine diaconate was a ministry existing only in certain places, and that, although the author of the *Didascalia* personally appreciated the relevancy of this ministry, its duties remained extremely limited.

It is evident from reading the *Didascalia* that deaconesses and widows were two different institutions. The typology of the Church presented in this book is sufficient to establish that: the deaconess, mentioned after the deacon, was to be honored as a "type" of the Holy Spirit; and widows and orphans, mentioned directly after the presbyters, were to be regarded as a "type" of the altar.[66] After these observations, it is startling to see authors asserting, without even a shadow of proof, that the "*Didascalia* refers frequently to deaconesses under the name of widows," [67] or that "it is difficult to see in the *Didascalia* the difference one might expect between widows and deaconesses," [68] or applying without comment, texts concerning widows to deaconesses.[69]

The bishops, who freely chose those who would assist them as deacons in their pastoral duties, could probably call a widow to the function of a deaconess. But there is no evidence that they systematically acted this way.[70] The union of these two qualities in one person could have been only accidental and infrequent. The duty of visiting nurse, which constituted the daily ministry of a deaconess, better suited a young and robust person than an aged woman. The task of a widow was of a spiritual nature: it consisted of praying for benefactors and for the Church. Widows visited the sick, not so much to give them needed care, but rather to fast with them, to pray for them, and to lay their hand on them to obtain from God their recovery. The difference between these two roles is distinctly marked.

6 GREEK CANONICAL SOURCES FROM THE FOURTH TO THE SIXTH CENTURY

All through the canonical sources, especially numerous and abundant from the fourth to the sixth century, one can easily trace the evolution of the status of widows and deaconesses in the different regions of the East during this period.

1. The Ecclesiastical Canons of the Apostles

There is general agreement that *The Ecclesiastical Canons of the Apostles*, also called *The Apostolic Church Order*, was written at the beginning of the fourth century in Egypt. The original Greek text has been preserved, along with complete or partial ancient versions in Latin, Syriac, Coptic, Arabic, and Ethiopic. Two parts are evident in this writing, which is reputed to relate the instructions given by the twelve apostles at the order of our Lord himself. The first part (cc. 4–14) consists of moral precepts presented according to an outline of a description of the "Two Ways," that of good and that of evil; it adapts the corresponding section of the *Didache* to the extremely different situation of the Church in the fourth century. In the second part (cc. 15–28), the only one announced in the introduction (cc. 1–3), the apostles regulate "all things that are required for the foundation of the Church," that is, all the functions that ought to be fulfilled in the Church: bishops, presbyters, deacons, lectors, and widows. They excluded women from exercising a ministry in the celebration of the Eucharist.

The introduction to the *Ecclesiastical Canons* characterizes each of these functions with a particular substantive: for the bishop, dignity (*axia*); for the presbyter, the seat (*hedra*); for the deacon, helping (*paredreia*); for the lector, wisdom (*nounechia*); and for the widow, blamelessness (*anegklēsia*).[1] This term recalls the adjective *anegklētos*, which is used for the bishop in Titus 1:7; it is practically synonymous with *anepilēmptos*, utilized to describe the bishop in 1 Timothy 3:2 and widows in 1 Timothy 5:7. The author of the *Canons*, therefore, seemed to expect widows to be particularly blameless.

What role did widows play in the Church? The answer appears in chapter 21, after the four other functions enumerated in the introduction are examined:

> Cephas said: Three widows shall be appointed: two who persevere in prayer, because of all those who are in temptations and to receive revelations and instructions concerning what is required; and one who, abiding with those who are tried by sickness, is of good service, watchful, informing the presbyters of what is necessary: not a lover of filthy lucre, avoiding much wine in order to be able to watch in the night service of those who are sick, and in case anybody required from her other good works; for these things too are the first treasures of the Lord.[2]

This text is undoubtedly concerned, not with widows in general, but with widows "established"[3] as such. Just like the presbyters,[4] and perhaps like the deacons,[5] they were three in number. This number may seem restrictive, but one must not forget that the communities in the *Canons* were small rural ones, generally of little importance.[6] Of the three widows, two had to persevere in prayer[7] for all those in difficulty. It is not a question here, as it was in the *Didascalia*, of "benefactors," as the primary and privileged recipients of the widows' prayers. These two widows had to keep themselves ready to receive or to pray that they be granted — according to whether one relates *apokalypseis* to *prosmenousai* or to *proseuchē* — the revelations which might be needed. If one accepts the first interpretation, these two widows appear as types of prophetesses, like Anna, the daughter of Phanuel, through whose intervention those with difficult problems rely to receive the lights of the Spirit.

The function of the third widow is explicitly defined: she took care of sick women. Since this duty belongs specifically to the deaconess in the *Didascalia*, the third widow seems to be, at least partially, her equivalent. The first quality required of her was that she had to be *eudiakonos*, literally a "good deacon," ready to give service. Two other qualities asked of her are among those required of deacons in First Timothy: disinterestedness and moderation in the use of wine.[8] Since the widow who visited the sick was certainly accountable for bringing material assistance to them, the requirement of disinterestedness is not stressed. The requirement of sobriety was justified by the fact that this widow had to remain awake for night service, that is, to sit up with or nurse a patient during the night.

It is impossible to understand what permits J. Daniélou to add that "care of the sick implies not only material assistance, but religious ministrations as well."[9] The *Canons* make no mention of widows who prayed or laid their hand on the sick, as the *Didascalia* does.

The end of the cited text, from *kai ei tis hetera bouloito ergagathein*, is difficult to translate. The simplest solution is to suppose, with the Syriac translator,[10] that the fourth word must be accented *hétera* (accusative neuter plural), and, on this basis to connect this clause with the passage read before, as this study's translation has done. On the other hand, if one supposes that the word in question must be accented *hetéra* (nominative feminine singular), as the Latin and Coptic translators do, followed by the Arabic and the Ethiopic,[11] and also by Schermann, the last editor of the Greek text,[12] the meaning is: "and if another wished to do good works. . . ." In this case, it seems impossible to connect this clause with what came before it. But one does not see in the Greek text how these words connect with what follows: *kai gar tauta Kyriou thēsaurismata eisin agatha*. The conjunction *kai gar* seems, indeed, to preclude relating the two grammatical elements as a dependent and an independent clause. Likewise in the Latin version: "*Et si alia voluerit bene operari, nam hae primae Domini sunt bonae thesaurationes*," the independent clause may have disappeared, since the Coptic, followed by Arabic and Ethiopic variants, added a few words here: "Since these are the good works which the Lord had determined, *let her act according to the dictates of her heart*." But it is difficult to say whether the Coptic translator found the words in italics in his Greek text or if, misled by an inaccurate accent on the word *hetera*, which would prevent his logically attaching the dependent clause in the conditional to the preceding sentence, he did not add an independent clause of his own invention. Since the Arabic and Ethiopic versions depend on the Coptic and constitute with it a single version, and since the majority of witnesses (Greek, Latin, Syriac traditions) offer more difficult readings, the latter version seems preferable. The third widow, therefore, in addition to her "night services" to sick women, could have also been expected to perform other good works.

Before making his final point, the author felt that he should return to the question of the ministry of women. In more than one respect, the text is curious and interesting:

> Andrew said: (It would be) very good, my brethren, if we established ministries for the women. Peter said: Having given commandment and directions concerning all these things, we have come thus far. Now we

> will give careful teaching concerning the oblation of the Body and Blood. John said: You have forgotten, my brethren, that our Teacher, when He asked for the bread and the cup, and blessed them, saying: "This is My Body and My Blood," did not permit these (the women) to stand with us. Martha said (concerning Mary): I saw her laughing between her teeth exultingly. Mary said: I did not really laugh,[13] only I remembered the words of our Lord and I exulted; for you know that He told us before, when He was teaching: "The weak shall be saved through the strong." Cephas said: We ought to remember several things, for it does not befit women that they should stand up for prayer, but that they should sit down on the ground. James said: How then with regard to the women can we fix any ministry, except that they strengthen and keep vigil for those women who are in want? [14]

According to this text, the question of the ministry of women was introduced by Andrew, who affirmed that it would be useful to establish a ministry for them. What is to be understood here, as is clear from the following text, is a ministry exercised by women, and not a ministry exercised for the benefit of women. When Peter remarked that some steps had already been taken toward this end, he was undoubtedly referring to the institution of widows, which he had previously mentioned. But then he added: "Now we will give careful teaching concerning the oblation of the Body and Blood," i.e., the Eucharist. The question posed, therefore, was to determine whether women could not be admitted to a role in this oblation.

John, however, immediately objected that to consider such a possibility was to forget that the Master, during the Last Supper, did not permit women "to stand" (*systēnai*) alongside the apostles. Standing is the position of those who officiate in the Eucharistic celebration. The evangelical accounts of the Last Supper present Jesus and the apostles "lying down" or "stretched out" at the table, according to the custom of the time, at least for formal meals.[15] Through this little alteration, the author of the *Canons* manifested clearly what he meant: by not allowing women "to stand" with the apostles at the Last Supper, Christ wished to show that they could not officiate in the Eucharistic celebration, of which the Last Supper is the prototype.

Martha intervened then in the discussion and affirmed that such was not the intention of the Master. If he acted thus, it was not because of a principle; it was simply because he saw Mary smile, and this lack of seriousness under such grave circumstances displeased him. But Mary herself rejected this interpretation and recalled the words of the Lord: "The weak shall be saved through the strong,"[16] i.e., women by men. Since the celebration of the Eucharist provides the grace of salvation, it is not suitable that a woman confer it to a man.

Peter enlarged upon the idea of John and referred to a custom ordering women not to stand but to sit on the ground during prayer. This detail is uniquely singular, and nowhere else is anything like it found.[17] On the contrary, the art of Christian antiquity abundantly shows women praying while standing, just as men did. Concluding this discussion, James asserted that it was impossible to attribute to women any ministry except that of bringing comfort to women in need, precisely the function of the third widow already discussed.

What is the *Sitz im Leben* of this strange debate? It is significant, according to G. Huls, that deaconesses had to be established yet had no active role in the Eucharist.[18] According to J. A. Robinson, on the contrary, the text shows that a feminine diaconate was known in certain churches, but that the author of the Canons rejected it.[19] J. Daniélou also believes that in this passage the author "rejects the Order of Deaconesses as an innovation." [20]

Personally, I do not believe there is any question here of deaconesses. The title "deaconess" does not appear in the *Canons*, any more than in any other Egyptian document.[21] Without carrying the specific title, the third widow assumed one of the functions of the deaconess in the *Didascalia*. The author had already dealt with this ministry in a perfectly lucid manner and did not intend to return to it.

At the end of the book, where the apostles are portrayed with Martha and Mary, the point of the discussion is the possibility of women's "standing," i.e., officiating during the oblation of the Body and Blood of Christ. Apparently some women must have tried to claim this right, and the author, after reviewing the various ministries necessary to the life of the Church, judged the case serious enough to devote a special page to this question. He categorically rejected this claim, justifying his refusal with one fact: the Master did not permit women "to stand" with the apostles at the Last Supper. And he interpreted this fact in terms of a word the Master would have said: "The weak shall be saved through the strong," which implies, according to him, that the weaker sex must receive the graces of salvation in the Eucharist through the ministry of the stronger sex, and not the reverse.

2. Canon 19 of Nicaea

The nineteenth canon of the First Council of Nicaea, 324 A.D., prescribed the following:

> Concerning the Paulianists who have flown for refuge to the Catholic Church, it has been decreed that they must by all means be rebaptized; and if any of them who in the past time have been numbered among their clergy should be found blameless and without reproach, let them be rebaptized and ordained by the bishop of the Catholic Church; but if the examination should discover them to be unfit, they ought to be deposed. Likewise in the case of their deaconesses, and generally in the case of those who have been enrolled among their clergy, let the same form be observed. And we mean by deaconesses those who have assumed the habit, but who, since they have no imposition of hands,[22] are to be numbered only among the laity.[23]

This text deals with the reintegration of the Paulianists, or disciples of Paul of Samosata, whose Trinitarian doctrine was heterodox. For this reason, the Nicaean Fathers judged their baptism invalid and ordered rebaptism if they returned to the Catholic Church. Also, the ordination of clerics in this heresy was, of course, invalid. If they were otherwise without reproach, the Council agreed to maintain them in their functions by reordination by the Catholic bishop. In the opposite case, they had to be deposed. The same rule applied to deaconesses, and, generally, to all those mentioned in the canon, i.e., in the list of persons who perform a function within limits determined by ecclesiastical legislation and who, by this title, receive a subsidy from the Church.[24]

This last sentence has frequently been unsatisfactorily interpreted. The rule in question is that if someone is considered worthy to exercise the function which was his in the heresy, he may continue to exercise it. The words "Likewise . . ." (*hōsautōs de kai*) at the beginning of the sentence refer precisely to this rule. Regarding deaconesses and all those mentioned in the canon, the text does not speak of the necessity of reordination. The fact that they are mentioned apart, in a second section, indicates that their case is quite a bit different.

Because of not having seen this difference and having taken it upon themselves to extend the similarity of the rule about the necessity of reordination equally to the case of deaconesses, many scholars have been trapped in an unsolvable difficulty: the text affirms immediately afterwards that deaconesses do not receive the imposition of hands and are, therefore, numbered among the laity. To escape this contradiction, these scholars have put together diverse hypotheses, quite sophisticated, groundless, and unverifiable. There is no need to mention and discuss them here; they are clearly summarized and well criticized in a thorough study made by Kalsbach on Canon 19 of Nicaea.[25]

In reality, the contradiction exists only in the mind of these scholars. The Council in no way affirmed that deaconesses, if they fulfilled their duties blamelessly, had to be reordained, as did the other clergy. To maintain that they had to be reordained contradicts the statement of the Council that they had not received ordination. The meaning, therefore, is that even though they had not received ordination, as the clergy had, they could be maintained in their function, if their conduct had been irreproachable. The reason is that their case is different from that of the clergy; actually they belong to the laity.

3. The Canons of Hippolytus

The *Canons of Hippolytus* are a pseudepigraphical recasting of the *Apostolic Tradition* of Hippolytus compiled in Egypt between the general Councils of Nicaea and of Constantinople, more specifically perhaps between 336 and 340 A.D. Although the work was written in Greek, only an Arabic version, which was itself made from a Coptic one, is extant. Like the *Apostolic Tradition* and the *Ecclesiastical Canons of the Apostles*, this book deals only with widows, never with deaconesses. The first text treating of widows is Canon 9:

> The appointed widows should not be ordained, since we have in their regard the prescriptions of the Apostle. Let them not be given ordination, but prayed over, since ordination is for men. The function [26] of the widows is important, because of all their duties: frequent prayer, care for the sick, and frequent fasting.[27]

Coming after the rules about ordinations, this text undoubtedly corresponds to chapter 11 of the *Apostolic Tradition* (Dix).[28] The rule concerning widows comes last in the *Canons of Hippolytus*, after those relating to virgins and healers.[29] The only prescription, however, that the *Apostolic Tradition* and the *Canons* of *Hippolytus* have in common is that widows must not be "ordained"; they must simply be "appointed." Furthermore, the *Canons* do not treat the question of whether widows who have recently lost their husband must be tested before their appointment. The two documents also give a different reason for refusing ordination to a widow. According to the *Apostolic Tradition*, a widow does not offer the oblation and does not exercise a liturgical ministry; according to the *Canons*, "ordination is" simply "for men." The mode of her appointment is equally different. In the *Apostolic Tradition*, a widow is established "by word alone," in the sense, probably, that she is "designated by this title"; but in the *Canons*, "she is prayed over."

Concerning her duties, in chapter 11 (Dix), the *Apostolic Tradition* says only that a widow is "enrolled for prayer"; but Chapter 25 (Dix) imposes on her an additional obligation — frequent fasting.[30] This last text is reproduced exactly in Canon 32: "Virgins and widows should fast often and pray for the Church." [31] Earlier in the *Canons*, Canon 9 mentioned this duty of fasting. A third obligation, with no parallel in the *Apostolic Tradition*, is added — the care of the sick. This duty recalls the third widow of the *Ecclesiastical Canons of the Apostles*, who was charged especially with the care of ill women.[32]

Finally, it is evident that the *Canons of Hippolytus* refer explicitly to the "prescriptions of the Apostle," i.e., probably to 1 Timothy 5:3-16, where there is no question of ordaining widows. The influence of this passage may also lie in the choice of the term "honor" (probably *timē* in the original Greek, as R. Coquin suggests) in speaking of the "function" (or better the "dignity") of widows.[33]

Besides Canons 9 and 32, widows are mentioned in Canons 5 and 35, but here they are spoken of as assisted persons. Canon 5, which deals with the ordination of deacons, includes the following sentence, which is unparalleled in the *Apostolic Tradition*: "Let them [the deacons] also serve those who receive alms from the bishops, and let them give to widows, to orphans, and to the poor."[34] As noted by R. Coquin,[35] this unwonted plural, "Let them serve," appearing in the text with a whole series of verbs in the singular, reveals a Coptic passive. The original text probably read: "Let also what belongs to the episcopal alms be distributed and imparted to widows, orphans, and the poor." Although this explanation does not clarify much, it at least suggests that widows had a part in the distribution of alms along with orphans and the poor. Canon 35 parallels chapter 27 of the *Apostolic Tradition*:[36]

> When someone wishes to feed widows, let him feed them and send them home before sunset. If they are numerous, lest they get excited and do not depart before night fall, let him give each of them enough to eat and drink, and let them leave before dark sets in.[37]

Like several references in the preceding canons,[38] this passage alludes to a meal of charity, or *agape*. Here again, widows appear as privileged beneficiaries of the faithful's charity.

4. The Canons of Basil

The three so-called "canonical" letters addressed by St. Basil to Amphilochius of Iconium contain some rules which concern this study. Canon 44 declares, first, that the "deaconess who committed fornication with the Greek is to be admitted to repentance (*eis metanoian*); and she shall be admitted to the oblation in the seventh year if she lives in chastity."[39] One cannot say with certainty whether this punishment was heavier or lighter than that imposed on fornicators in general, which, according to Canon 22, was four years,[40] but according to Canon 57, was seven years, and those culpable were not readmitted to communion until the eighth year.[41] In both cases, it is obvious that the sinners had to go through all the stages of public penance.

It is possible that the deaconess may have escaped this last demand, at least if the term *metanoia* in Canon 44 is taken in its technical sense; this term sometimes designates, as in Canon 22, the third of four classes of penitents, and the term *epitimēsis* refers, then, to the whole penitential process.[42] In any case, the fact that a deaconess guilty of fornication was deprived of communion and subjected to penance indicates that she was not a part of the clergy. The clergy, regardless of their rank, who were guilty of a grievous fault,[43] particularly a deacon guilty of fornication,[44] were deposed but not excommunicated, according to the principle "Thou shalt not impose a penalty twice for the same offense."

Apart from the fact that the two cases deal with a "pagan," it is hard to see the logical link connecting the first sentence of Canon 44 with the second: "But the Greek who, after accepting the faith, returns to his vomit, again enters upon sacrilege."[45] The canon then goes back to the deaconess: "But the body of the deaconess, on the ground that it has been consecrated (*hōs kathierōmenon*), we no longer permit to remain in carnal usage."[46] After stating at the beginning of the canon the traditional rule, it seems that Basil gives here, as he does more than once in his canons,[47] his personal opinion or the rule he keeps himself. If this interpretation is correct, Basil imposed on the deaconess a more exacting rule than the one contained in the first sentence of Canon 44, which punished only the illegitimate union of a deaconess with a pagan, but did not deal with the case of a regular marriage with a Christian. For Basil, the deaconess was committed to continence; her body, because of its consecration, could no longer serve a carnal usage.

What "consecrated" the body of a deaconess? Was it the ordination that she received? In spite of the insinuation of Kalsbach,[48] the term used here (*kathierōmenon*) does not denote ordination. Since, in another canon, Basil spoke of a virgin as "a sacred vessel dedicated to the Lord" (*skeuos hieron anatethen tō Despotē*),[49] it is possible that the body of a deaconess is declared "consecrated" because of her vow of continence. According to the *Apostolic Constitutions*, a deaconess had to be a pure virgin or at least a widow vowed to continence.[50] Canon 44 is the only one in which Basil mentions deaconesses. One cannot, therefore, say more about the status and functions of deaconesses in the Cappadocian Church of his time.

Basil declared that in principle widows were free to remarry,[51] but they were required to perform the penance prescribed in this case.[52] However, those who were enrolled as widows (*tēn katalegeisan eis ton arithmon tōn chērōn*), i.e., those who were assisted by the Church (*tēn diakonoumenēn hypo tēs Ekklēsias*), could no longer remarry. The fact that a widow accepted help from the Church by having herself registered among the widows implied, therefore, that she would then practice continence. A woman over sixty who violated this rule had to be excommunicated until she renounced her impure passion. The bishop who took it upon himself to enroll a widow before the age of sixty was personally responsible for an eventual failure.[53]

Finally, the *Short Rules* ascribed to Basil mention "senior women" (*presbytera*), but only in a well-determined milieu, which is that of the monastic communities. Asked whether it was proper for a sister to confess her sins to a "senior man" (*tō presbyterō*),[54] in the presence of a "senior woman" (*kai tēn presbyterian pareinai*),[55] Basil answered that it was more suitable and more prudent.[56] On the other hand, he judged that if the "senior man" gave orders to the community without first consulting the "senior woman,"[57] it was normal for her to become angry. In such a context, it is obvious that the function of these "senior women" was certainly not of a clerical nature. This term simply designated the superior of a religious community of women.[58]

5. Canon 11 of Laodicea

The Greek canonical collections ascribe to a council which is supposed to have met at Laodicea in Phrygia a series of fifty-nine canons, which were inserted between the canons of Antioch or of Sardica, on the one hand, and those of Constantinople, on the other. The stereotyped form and extreme brevity of the canons of Laodicea, and the kinship of the contents of some of these canons with the canons of earlier councils, suggest that they are titles or résumés rather than a complete text of original canonical rulings. In addition, the formulation of the canons reveals the existence of two distinct series, originating from different sources (canons 1–19 and 20–59); the presence of duplicates confirms this conclusion. Finally, most scholars agree that the canons of Laodicea constitute a kind of summary of the canonical rules used in Phrygia, a summary which may have been approved by one or two successive synods held in this province. The discipline reflected in these canons suggests, by comparison, the end of the fourth century.

The concise form of the canons adds to the difficulty of their interpretation. This problem is particularly evident in Canon 11, which reads: " 'Senior women' or 'female presidents' are not to be appointed in the Church"[59] (*Peri tou mē dein tas legomenas presbytidas ētoi prokathēmenas en Ekklēsia kathistasthai*). According to some scholars, *presbytis* in this canon refers simply to deaconesses,[60] and in this supposition the council protested against their being ordained.[61] But in no document where deaconesses appear do they hold a rank or perform functions which would justify the title "senior women" or "female presidents." The term used constantly from the end of the fourth century for the rite marking the beginning of a deaconess' office is *cheirotonein*, which properly means "to ordain," not *kathistasthai*, which means more generally "to appoint" or "to establish."

According to other scholars, this canon refers to older deaconesses or deaconesses of a higher rank.[62] To a certain degree, this hypothesis answers the first objection but not the second; there is no evidence anywhere of a hierarchy within the order of deaconesses.

P. H. Lafontaine believes that these women were not deaconesses but widows, more precisely "established" (*kathistasthai*) widows, in the sense of the *Didascalia Apostolorum* and the *Apostolic Constitutions*; that they constituted in some way a higher rank among the widows, and that the council tried to abolish this institution.[63] This interpretation seems more plausible. More directly than to the *Didascalia* or to the *Apostolic Constitutions*, this canon could refer to the *Testamentum Domini*, which more than once mentions "the widows who sit in front," who are called "senior women."[64] Unfortunately, since the only versions that remain are in several Oriental languages and not the language of the original text, it is impossible to determine whether the word translated by "senior women" corresponds to the Greek *presbyterai* or *presbytides.*

Another text in which *presbytis* apparently means a function, or at least a dignity, in the Church is the *Martyrdom of Matthew*, an apocryphal book of the fourth or fifth century. It recounts that after the conversion of the king who had ordered the death of Matthew, the apostle appeared to him and imposed a new name on him, his wife, his son, and his daughter-in-law. According to the recension of the text supported by the majority of manuscripts, Matthew ordained the king a priest, his son a deacon, and his wife and daughter-in-law deaconesses. But according to a manuscript offering a different recension of the same text, the wife of the king would have been established, not as a deaconess, but as a "senior woman" (*presbytis*).[65] The literary genre of this book obviously makes it difficult to derive from it any reliable historical information. Outside of this case, the term *presbytis* generally has, in Greco-Christian literature, the usual meaning of "old woman";[66] sometimes, under the form *presbytera*, it designates the superior or senior women of a religious community.[67] Although Lafontaine's interpretation of Canon 9 of Laodicea has little support elsewhere, it seems that in this text the word in question can apply only to "appointed" widows.

A comparison of the two distinct series (1–9 and 20–59) which make up the canons of Laodicea reveals the presence of duplicates. For instance, Canon 45 may be a double of Canon 11: "Women should not have access to the altar"[68] (*Hoti ou dei gynaikas eis to thysiastērion eisienai*). In Canon 11 of the *Testamentum Domini*, one notices that "widows who sat in front," or the "senior women," occupied a place in the church near the bishop and the place called "front stage" (*proskēnion*?), and that during the oblation of the Eucharistic sacrifice, they took their place with the members of the clergy within the veil which was extended at that moment, it seems, to conceal the altar from the faithful.[69] Consequently, Canon 45 of Laodicea may refer to the "senior women" or "women presidents" of Canon 11, inviting them to return to the ranks.

6. The Apostolic Constitutions

The *Apostolic Constitutions* is the largest canonical and liturgical collection of antiquity. Enlarged with many additions, the first six books are a recasting of the *Didascalia Apostolorum.* The first half of Book 7 is an amplification of the *Didache*; the second half contains formularies of prayers and prescriptions regarding the instruction and baptism of catechumens. The most valuable part of the work is Book 8, which uses Hippolytus' *Apostolic Tradition* as its source. Among other things, it presents a ritual for various ordinations and a description of the Eucharistic celebration for this occasion. At the end of Book 8, there are eighty-five canons, known as the *Canons of the Apostles.* Representing the Syrian tradition, the *Constitutions* and the *Canons* go back to the end of the fourth century. The anonymous author is probably the same writer who interpolated the long collation of the Epistles of Ignatius of Antioch. A comparison of the *Apostolic Constitutions* with its sources illumines the subject and shows how the institution of widows and of deaconesses evolved during the second half of the third and the fourth century.

In the *Apostolic Constitutions*, as in the *Didascalia*, widows, because of their precarious condition, generally appear as women assisted by the Church in the same way as orphans, strangers, and the destitute.[70] The bishop was asked to be the friend of widows (*philochēros*),[71] to feed them as their husband had in the past,[72] and to see that they received their part of the offerings made for the poor.[73] Sustained by the gifts offered to God,[74] the widows were prefigured, together with the clergy, by the Levites of the Old Testament,[75] and they were presented as the altar of God.[76] Among the older women whom generous Christians entertained at charitable meals, there were probably many widows.[77] But all widows, even the younger ones, had to be assisted, lest the latter use their poverty as a pretext for remarriage.[78]

Among these widows, those who were "appointed" (*kathistasthai*) [79] enjoyed a special status; they made up the order of widows (*to chērikon*).[80] The *Constitutions* definitely state that the widow was not "ordained" (*ou cheirotoneitai*), but only admitted to the order of widows.[81] Even more than the *Didascalia*, the *Constitutions* insist on the promise of continence (*epaggelia*) which the chosen widows made to God,[82] and display more caution in admitting widows to the *chērikon*: as in First Timothy,[83] the minimum age required is sixty, whereas in the *Didascalia* it is only fifty.[84] Beginning with the first chapter of Book 3, the *Constitutions* insist that, following the example of Anna and of the "real widows" of First Timothy,[85] widows had to persevere in continuous prayer.[86] They stress some features of the "real widows" which the *Didascalia* does not emphasize: to be worthy of her name the widow had to be known for her good works, have brought up her children well, and practiced hospitality toward strangers; she must have been sober, chaste, faithful, and pious.[87] Finally, these widows were spoken of as "consecrated" to God (*Theō anakeimenōn*).[88]

Like the *Didascalia*, the *Constitutions* dissuade widows from lightly answering questions regarding their faith. It seems, however, that if they possessed the needed knowledge, the *Constitutions* do not intend absolutely to remove, as does the *Didascalia*, the right of widows to speak of truths other than the most elementary.[89] Evidently the reason is that since the writing of the earlier work, many educated women had joined the Christian faith and contributed richly, both by word and example, to the evangelization of those around them; one thinks, for example, of Olympias and her companions at

Constantinople,[90] Melania the Elder, and the Roman women corresponding with Jerome. The interdiction against teaching is retained as definitive only in church:

> We do not permit our women to teach in the Church,[91] but only to pray and hear those that teach; for our Master and Lord, Jesus Himself, when He sent us the twelve to make disciples of the people and of the nations, did nowhere send out women to preach, although He did not lack them. For there were with us the mother of our Lord and His sisters: also Mary Magdalene, and Mary the mother of James, and Martha and Mary the sisters of Lazarus, Salome, and certain others. For had it been necessary for women to teach, He Himself would have commanded these to instruct the people with us. For "if the head of the woman is the man," [92] it is not reasonable that the rest of the body should govern the head.[93]

The reasoning is the same as in the *Didascalia.*[94] The *Constitutions* add only at the end, quoting Paul, "the head of the woman is the man," and conclude that the man must command the rest of the body, and not the other way round. Here again is the idea, already expressed by Origen, that the relationship of the master to the disciples is one of the superior to the inferior, and therefore woman cannot govern man without detriment to his natural superiority.[95]

There is no striking difference between the portrait of the wicked and the good widow in the *Didascalia* and that in the *Constitutions.*[96] However, the *Constitutions*, in certain additions of their own, emphasizing the ideal of perpetual prayer, "night and day," present to widows the model of Judith [97] and stress the ascetic features of the good widow.[98] In the following chapter, a noticeable difference appears, however, in the treatment of visits made by widows to private individuals: the *Constitutions* say nothing about praying, fasting, or the imposition of the hand on the sick, which the *Didascalia* ascribes to widows, but simply forbid them to visit people without permission to "eat, drink, or receive anything." The motivation of this prohibition is similar to that of the *Didascalia*: widows would have risked accepting gifts from unworthy people.[99] Paralleling the *Didascalia,* a section of Book 4 returns to this question.[100] Some significant differences appear in the enumeration of unworthy donors; whereas the *Didascalia* includes *a priori* among them "every official of the Roman empire," [101] this category, of course, disappeared in the *Constitutions* at the end of the fourth century. Other alterations further show that relations with pagans had evolved considerably.[102]

Regarding the administration of baptism by women, the *Constitutions* are more severe and categorical than the *Didascalia*, and they have built up the rather summary reasoning of their source:

> Now, as to women's baptizing, we let you know that there is no small peril to those that undertake it. Therefore we do not advise you to it; for it is dangerous, or rather wicked and impious. For if the "man be

> the head of the woman," [103] and he be originally ordained for the priesthood, it is not just to abrogate the order of the creation, and leave the principal part to come to the extreme part of the body. For the woman is the body of the man, taken from his side,[104] and subject to him, from whom she was separated for the procreation of children. For he says, "He shall rule over you." [105] For the principal part of the woman is the man, as being her head. But if in the foregoing constitutions we have not permitted them to teach, how will anyone allow them, contrary to nature, to perform the office of a priest? For this is one of the ignorant practices of Gentile atheism, to ordain women to the female deities, not one of the constitutions of Christ. For if baptism were to be administered by women, certainly our Lord would have been baptized by His own mother, and not by John; [106] or when He sent us to baptize, He would have sent along with us women also for this purpose. But now He has nowhere, either by constitution or by writing, delivered to us any such thing; as knowing the order of nature, and the decency of the action; as being the Creator of nature, and the Legislator of the constitution.[107]

For the author of the *Constitutions*, baptism was a specifically priestly act, on the same level as the sacrificial offering, ordination, or benediction.[108] If women were not allowed to baptize, it was essentially because access to the priesthood was forbidden them. This prohibition resulted from a consideration of nature (*physis*), or, said differently, of the order of creation (*demiourgia*), which shows that woman is in a subordinate condition to man — she is the body of man, taken from his side; man is the head of woman, i.e., her lord and her master. Since the priesthood implies a superiority over those who benefit from it, it cannot be conferred on women. This is the reason why Christ, the author of nature, knowing well what conforms to it, did not entrust women with the mission to baptize. It was a characteristic aberration of pagan cults to ordain priestesses to the service of goddesses.

The *Constitutions* agree with the *Didascalia* in denouncing envy and jealousy among widows on account of gifts received.[109] They differ a little, however, where the *Didascalia* prohibits a widow who was given a gift from disclosing the name of her benefactor, whom she was supposed to know, lest she take away from him the merit of his charity and give occasion to jealous widows to disturb him; the *Constitutions* dissuade, not the widow who was favored with a gift, but the woman who was the source of the gift, from proclaiming it from the housetops. The widow was asked to pray for her benefactor, whoever he may be, knowing that God who sees in secret will reward him as he deserves; in other words, she was not supposed to know the name of her benefactor.[110]

Probably, with the increased numbers in Christian communities and centralized charities more and more in the hands of bishops and deacons, benefactors had become increasingly anonymous. There were, however, as in the time of the *Didascalia*, wicked widows who tried to find out who had given and who had received, and who, once they had discovered the giver, attacked the woman who had made the donation because another widow had been preferred and because the donor had not shouted her name from the housetops, thus preventing other widows from receiving their share.[111] Some even went so far as to utter curses, which the *Constitutions* forbid, although they do not say, as the *Didascalia* does, that widows "had been appointed to bless."[112]

The author of the *Constitutions* was manifestly offended by the sentence in the *Didascalia* which stated with one dash of the pen that neither "the bishop, nor a presbyter, nor a deacon, nor a widow should utter a curse."[113] Since, to him, this sentence associated the widow too closely with the three higher orders of the hierarchy, he substituted for widow a formula which recurs frequently in the *Canons of the Apostles*: "nor any other member of the clergy" (*mēte allos tis ek tou katalogou tou hieratikou*).[114] A few lines down, the *Didascalia* declares that the bishop must care for all,[115] but the *Constitutions* specify "clergy, virgins, widows, and laity."[116] Therefore, the *Constitutions,* which distinguish sharply between clergy and laity, point out also that widows could not in any way be assimilated with members of the clergy, but that, like virgins, they formed a special group among the laity.

The mention of widows alongside of virgins is extremely instructive. The *Didascalia* does not mention virgins; the widows seem to be the only ones to incarnate an ideal of continence. The two passages in which the *Constitutions* deal *ex professo* with virgins have no parallel in the *Didascalia.* According to these texts, since the Lord did not prescribe regarding this matter, a virgin was not ordained. She pledged herself to this state by a vow, which was not to be lightly made, for, according to the proverb of Solomon, "it is better not to make a vow than to make one and not keep it."[117]

The virgin, who was a temple of God, a house of Christ, and a dwelling of the Holy Spirit, had to be holy in body and soul. She had to demonstrate by the excellence of her life that her resolution came from her zeal for piety, and not from any contempt for marriage.[118] On four different occasions, where the *Didascalia* speaks simply of widows, the *Constitutions* mention virgins along with them: the Levites prefigure widows and virgins in that they had the right to live by the offerings of the faithful;[119] virgins and widows had to be honored as the figure of the altar;[120] virgins were granted a special place, together with widows and senior women, in the assembly of the congregation;[121] neither virgins nor widows had the right to run about or go from house to house to receive gifts.[122]

On the other hand, Book 8 mentions virgins six times alongside of widows: in the "prayer of the faithful," the same petition joined together readers, singers, virgins, widows, orphans, and married people;[123] in the Eucharistic anaphora, the priest offered the sacrifice for all those holy people who, from the beginning of the world, have pleased God, the just of the Old Testament, apostles and martyrs, members of the clergy, virgins, widows, lay people, and all whose names are known to God;[124] he prayed also for those present in the assembly, for virgins and the chaste, for the widows of the Church (*hyper tōn chērōn tēs Ekklēsias*), for the married and for children;[125] widows partook of Communion after virgins, but before children and all other people, men and women;[126] first-fruits had to sustain the bishop, the presbyters, and the deacons, but the tithes had to maintain the rest of the clergy, the virgins and widows, and those suffering from poverty.[127]

Always, virgins are mentioned before widows. The rules for the admission of virgins in Book 8 [128] also precede those regarding the admission of widows.[129] The only exception occurs in the first text, where virgins are associated with widows and where those who were prefigured by the Levites as entitled to live from the offerings of the faithful are listed.[130] Immediately after, in the typology of the Church, virgins are mentioned following widows and orphans, but what is said about them proves that the author held virgins in higher esteem: widows and orphans, he says, ought to be considered (*lelogisthōsan*) as a "type" of the altar (*thysiastērion*), i.e., as a figure of the bronze altar used for burnt offerings in the inner court of the Temple, but virgins ought to be honored (*tetimēsthōsan*) as a "type" of the *thymiatērion* and of the *thymiama*, i.e., as a figure of the golden altar for the incense offering in the holy place in the Temple, and even as a type of this offering itself.[131] The systematic association of virgins and widows, and the priority granted to the former, prove that the *Constitutions* manifest a special view of the ascetic aspect of the ideal of widowhood and that they see in it an imperfect realization of the ideal of continence realized in a perfect way in virginity.

By omitting the *Didascalia's* references to prayer, fasting, and the imposition of the hand by widows over the sick, by dropping the reference to their power of blessing, and by refusing to mention them after the bishop, presbyter, and deacon, the *Constitutions* actually strip the widow of everything which suggested the idea of an ecclesiastical function in the *Didascalia.* By insisting on the promise of continence attached to admission to the order of widows, on perpetual prayer more than on prayer for benefactors, on vigils, fasting, and other exercises of piety; by presenting widows as "consecrated to God"; and by associating them systematically with virgins, the *Constitutions* strongly accentuate the ascetic character of the ideal of widowhood, which is more succinctly developed in the *Didascalia* according to the pattern of First Timothy. Consequently, widows benefited from the extremely high esteem enjoyed by virgins toward the end of the fourth century. Whereas the *Didascalia* simply said that older women and widows had to be seated apart (*idia*) in the assembly, just as every age had its proper place (*idia*),[132] the

Constitutions prescribe that virgins, widows, and older women had to accupy the first place among women (*prōtai pasōn stēketōsan ē kathezesthōsan*).[133] One recalls also that virgins and widows received Communion before the laity, children, men, and women. In short, in more than one aspect, the image of the widow in the *Constitutions* differs noticeably from that presented in the *Didascalia.*

With regard to the position of deaconesses, except for a brief mention in the typology of the Church,[134] they appear in the *Didascalia* in only one place, where the functions for which the bishop needed their cooperation are described.[135] This passage is reworked more than once in the *Constitutions*, which also frequently mention deaconesses elsewhere. In passages in Books 2 and 3 which parallel the *Didascalia*, the term used in referring to deaconesses is *hē diakonos*, but in a chapter proper to the *Constitutions*, in Book 6 and again in Book 8, the term used is *diakonissa.*[136]

According to the *Didascalia*, the bishop chose "those who pleased him from all the people" to assist him in his pastoral ministry, and he made them deacons, the men "for the performance of the many things necessary," and the women for the service of women. According to the *Constitutions*, only male deacons should be chosen from the assembly of the people.[137] A deaconess had to be a pure virgin or a widow married only once.[138] Deaconesses were chosen, therefore, from two groups of women mentioned before: preferably virgins, otherwise widows. The first apparent advantage in their ministry is the same as in the *Didascalia*: there were houses to which the bishop could not send a male deacon to serve women without incurring gossip.[139] This reference shows that one of the chief duties of deaconesses was the assistance and the care of sick or crippled women in their homes, even though the *Constitutions*, as is frequently the case when there are reptitions in the *Didascalia*, suppressed a sentence which, a little further on, referred to this service more explicitly.[140]

Apart from this, the *Constitutions* seem to enlarge the scope of deaconesses' duties more than the *Didascalia* does. After prescribing that deaconesses ought to be sufficient in number to assist all the sick, the *Didascalia* says that it is preferable that women minister to women, and men minister to men, and that besides this work, male deacons must be ready to perform all the other missions the bishop sees fit to confide to them.[141] The ministry of deaconesses seems, therefore, to have been limited here to care of women, whereas the ministry of deacons included, besides the care of men, other tasks which the bishop entrusted to them. On the contrary, according to the *Constitutions*, men and women deacons could be asked to carry messages, on occasion beyond the city limits, and given still other tasks,[142] which the author did not specify.

One can notice only that the *Constitutions* draw a double consequence of the likening of deaconesses to the Holy Spirit proposed by the *Didascalia*. First, just as the Paraclete, according to the farewell discourse of Jesus, neither does nor says anything on his own authority but "glorifies" Christ by doing his will,[143] so deaconesses, as a "type" of the Holy Spirit, were not to do or say anything without the deacon, who was a "type" of Christ. Second, just as it is not possible to believe in Christ without being taught by the Spirit, no woman was to visit a bishop or a deacon without a deaconess.[144] The deaconess, therefore, seems to have played the role of intermediary between women and the male members of the hierarchy, and perhaps, conforming to a custom whose traces are found everywhere,[145] she was to witness the correctness of their conversation.

Concerning the liturgical role of the deaconess, the *Didascalia* mentioned only her assistance in the administration of baptism to women.[146] Here again, significant differences exist between the *Constitutions* and their source. Passing over the modifications and details attached to the ritual of baptism itself, it is of interest to note that the *Constitutions* no longer consider the case in which, if a deaconess were not available, any woman, or even the minister of the sacrament himself, would have to anoint the body of a woman.[147] The ministry of deaconesses seems, therefore, to have been widespread enough in the milieu to which the *Constitutions* were addressed. This is probably the reason that the author did not think it necessary to justify the existence of this ministry by citing the women who ministered to Christ.[148] On the other hand, the author of the *Constitutions* took offense at the idea that a woman could be entrusted with any kind of teaching in the Church. Whereas the *Didascalia* prescribed that a deaconess ought to receive women as they left the fountain and instruct them about keeping the seal of baptism unsullied in purity and holiness, the *Constitutions* prescribed that as they left the fountain of baptism, men ought to be received by deacons and women by deaconesses so that the communication of the seal, which ought to remain unsullied, might be carried out with dignity and decency.[149]

In addition to her occasional role in the celebration of baptism, the *Constitutions* assigned to the deaconess a much more regular task — welcoming women to liturgical assemblies. Just as the deacon did for men, she had to see that women arriving at church found a place, whether they were rich or poor, and that younger ones on occasion gave up their place to older ones.[150] In the prayer for the ordination of a deaconess, the allusion to women ministering at the entrance of the Tabernacle and of the Temple probably refers to this function.[151] The *Constitutions* insist that the liturgical ministry of deaconesses had to be limited to this function: "A deaconess does not bless, nor perform anything proper to the office of presbyters or deacons; she only keeps the doors and assists the presbyters in the baptism of women for reasons of decency."[152]

In spite of the similarity of names and her presentation as a feminine counterpart of the masculine deacon, the duties of deacons and deaconesses were not identical in all points. In particular, the deaconess did not assist the bishop or the priests at the altar, and she did not help with the distribution of Communion.

What position then did the deaconesses occupy in the community? First, they certainly held the highest rank among women; they were above virgins and widows who were not invested with this function. They received Communion before the other virgins and widows,[153] and they always preceded them in the enumerations.[154] Furthermore, where the *Didascalia* said that widows had to be subject to the bishops and deacons, the *Constitutions* added: "and also to the deaconesses."[155] Another fact is indisputable: deaconesses were part of the clergy. Their participation with the clergy, and with them alone, in the eulogies, i.e., in the distribution of the surplus unconsecrated loaves of bread offered by the faithful for the Eucharist, clearly supports this fact.[156] Finally, like other clerics, deaconesses received an ordination conferred by the imposition of hands and the prayer of the bishop,[157] whereas virgins and widows were not ordained.[158] This ordination was celebrated in the presence of the presbyterium, of the deacons, and of the deaconesses.[159] The text of the prayer for the ordination is revealing:

> O Eternal God, the Father of our Lord Jesus Christ,[160] the Creator of man and of woman, who replenished with the Spirit Miriam, and Deborah, and Anna, and Huldah; who did not disdain that Thy only-begotten Son should be born of a woman; who also in the tabernacle of the testimony, and in the temple, did ordain women to be keepers of Thy holy gates,[161] — do Thou now also look down upon this Thy servant who is to be ordained to the office of a deaconess, and grant her Thy Holy Spirit,[162] that she may worthily discharge the work which is committed to her to Thy glory, and the praise of Thy Christ, with whom glory and adoration be to Thee and the Holy Spirit for ever. Amen.[163]

The style of this prayer is the same as those for other ordinations, and its content is also analogous to them. It calls upon the prophetesses of the Old Testament as biblical paradigms, as women full of the Holy Spirit, and guardians of the doors of the temple; it also recalls that the only Son of God was born of a woman. Then, both for the sake of her personal holiness of life and for her work in the ministry, it asks for the gifts of the Holy Spirit. In the mind of the author, nothing in this prayer pointed to any difference between this ordination and that of male clerics.

What was the rank of deaconesses in the hierarchy of the clergy? In Book 8 of the *Constitutions*, the rite for the ordination of deaconesses follows immediately after that for the ordination of deacons, before the ordination of subdeacons and lectors.[164] In the listing of ordinations reserved to the bishop, according to a text of Book 3, deaconesses are also mentioned immediately after deacons and before the other clerics.[165] In the prayer of the faithful, they were probably included in the formula: "For all the deacons and ministers of Christ," and here again they came before lectors and cantors.[166] Similarly, in the anaphora, they were included under the term *diakonōn*.[167]

However, in other listings, the deaconess appeared, not immediately after the deacon, but after all the male members of the clergy.[168] Also she received communion only after them and after the "ascetics," i.e., monks and men vowed to continence.[169] The position of the deaconess in the hierarchy of the clergy appears, therefore, uncertain and poorly defined. On the one hand, because of the analogy of names and at least partly of their functions, one is naturally inclined to equate the deaconess with the deacon, but, on the other hand, one hesitates to grant women precedence over men. This same reluctance appeared in other documents later on.

7. The Arabic Canons of Nicaea

Since the sixteenth century, the *Arabic Canons of Nicaea* have been known in Europe in two Latin versions: one by the Jesuit Francisco Torres (Turrianus) and one by the Maronite Abraham of Hekel (Ecchellensis). The two versions, which show noticeable differences, probably represent two Arabic texts. Although the first translators of the *Canons* defended their authenticity, most scholars today do not accept it. Nor is there agreement on their place and time of origin; but it probably was in the area of influence of Antioch in the fifth century.

In the absence of a standard edition, the *Arabic Canons of Nicaea* are an extremely difficult document to utilize, particularly in regard to the canon about deaconesses. The versions of Turrianus and of Ecchellensis differ in many places, but they agree on two relevant points. First, deaconesses had to be at least sixty years old, "as prescribed by blessed Paul"; they apply, therefore, to deaconesses the rule given regarding widows in 1 Timothy 5:9. Second, the chief function (Ecchellensis), or even the only function (Turrianus), of deaconesses was to help at the baptism of women.[170]

8. Canon 15 of Chalcedon

The Council of Chalcedon treated of deaconesses in canon 15:

> A woman shall not receive the laying on of hands (*cheirotoneisthai*) as a deaconess under forty years of age, and then only after searching examination. And if, after she has had hands laid on her (*cheirotonian*, var. *cheirothesian*) and has continued for a time to minister, she should despise the grace of God and give herself in marriage, she shall be anathematized and the man united to her.[171]

One of the first things to notice is that the deaconess, as in the *Apostolic Constitutions*, received ordination with the imposition of hands; this result is evident through the use of the verb *cheirotonein* and of the substantive *cheirotonia* (or *cheirothesia*), which regularly have this meaning in the Acts and in the canons of Chalcedon.

As suggested by J. Gaudemet, the age of forty seems to be the result of a compromise.[172] Earlier legislation inclined, it seems, to be more severe and to refuse access to orders to women still relatively young, imposing a minimum of sixty years, a symbol of old age in antiquity, the same as for the admission of widows in Timothy.[173] Actually, much younger women were admitted to the ranks of deaconesses; the most outstanding of these younger deaconesses was certainly Olympias.[174] The age limit of forty, therefore, seems to have been a middle term; it was also the minimum age required for the solemn consecration of virgins in *Novella* 6 of Majorian, dated 458,[175] and the age after which, according to the same law, a widow without children was no longer obliged to remarry — in short, a term already suggesting the idea of old age.[176]

This prohibition to contract marriage applied to deaconesses as well as to clerics in major orders. If she went beyond this interdiction, she was to be anathematized for having "desecrated the grace of God." The council seems to have been more severe toward her than toward consecrated virgins unfaithful to their vows; instead of anathematizing them (*anathematizesthō*), it ruled only that they had to be "deprived of Holy Communion" (*estōsan akoinōnētoi*), and especially it authorized the bishop to show them indulgence, which was not the case for deaconesses.[177]

9. Testamentum Domini Nostri Jesu Christi

The *Testamentum Domini Nostri Jesu Christi* is a work written in the second half of the fifth century, probably in a Monophysite milieu in Syria. The original language of this book was Greek, but it survives only in Syriac, Arabic, and Ethiopic versions.[178] It is inspired by Hippolytus' *Apostolic Tradition*, which it reworks and amplifies considerably. The *Testamentum* developed chapter 11 (Dix) of the *Apostolic Tradition*[179] in a remarkable way and devoted four long chapters regarding widows to the corresponding section.[180] Just as for the bishop, the presbyter, and the deacon, the author pointed out the qualities required of deaconesses, the duties incumbent upon them, the rite of their ordination, and the prayers required of them.[181]

The *Testamentum* reveals that the author grants a far more important position to the widow than does the *Apostolic Tradition.* First, the *Testamentum* does not distinguish, as the *Apostolic Tradition* did, between "to ordain" and "to appoint." It says that the widow is "ordained" and speaks of the "ordination" of widows, using in the two instances the same word employed for clerics in major orders. The section on widows begins exactly like the previous one on deacons: "the deacon is ordained after having been chosen, . . . if he is of good conduct, etc."[182] (the qualities required of him and the duties imposed on him are enumerated); in a parallel way: "a widow is ordained after having been chosen, if she has been without a husband for a long time, etc."[183] (a similar enumeration follows). In the case of a bishop and a presbyter, the schema is the same. Regarding subdeacons, readers, and virgins,[184] however, the *Testamentum* is much shorter. The order of the *Testamentum* follows that of the Ethiopic and the Arabic versions of the *Apostolic Tradition*, which placed the widow before the reader, the virgin, and the subdeacon.[185]

As it does for presbyters, deacons, and subdeacons, the *Testamentum* also specifies the number of widows who had to be appointed in the Church: "Let twelve presbyters, seven deacons, fourteen subdeacons,[186] thirteen widows who sit in front [be appointed]"[187] According to the Syriac version, the number of widows sitting in the front was fixed at thirteen. Monsignor Rahmani suggested the reading, as in the still unedited Arabic version, of "three" instead of "thirteen." When the number is not written out in words, it is true, as he says, that a similar accident in copying is easy.[188] Rahmani argues further that the *Ecclesiastical Canons of the Apostles*, which seems sometimes to inspire the author of the *Testamentum*, fixed at three the number of widows.[189] But, since the presbyters, and, it seems, the deacons too, were also three in number,[190] the communities to which this writing referred were much less important. Whatever the exact number of widows according to the *Testamentum*, the fact that the author thought of determining it shows that their ministry was not less important in his eyes than that of presbyters, deacons, and subdeacons.

It should be noted that in this text, widows are mentioned after subdeacons, whereas in the whole of section 1, 20-47, as in chapters 2-14 of the *Apostolic Tradition*, its source, they come before them. Could it be that in the later case, the author of the *Testamentum* was following his model in these sections, whereas when he enumerated the different orders in a text of his own,[191] he spontaneously placed subdeacons before widows, revealing that in his mind the former enjoyed a higher rank? It seems that the answer to this question must be negative. Actually, the author of the *Testamentum* did not hesitate to alter the whole plan of the *Apostolic Tradition* to mention the subdeacon before the reader, and it was no more difficult to mention him before the widows.

But such was not the rank of the subdeacon. To prove this point, consider the rather short chapter of the *Testamentum* devoted to subdeacons,[192] which is about the same length as the one on readers,[193] in relation to the four notably longer chapters devoted to widows. A comparison of the rites of ordination is especially instructive. The ordination of a subdeacon, just as that of a reader, consisted of a simple nomination: "Thou, O (his name), minister and hear the Gospel in fear of God . . . Thou, O (his name), whom Christ has called to be a minister of his words, be careful and strive that you may be approved in this rule." In the case of a widow, on the contrary, the bishop said over her a prayer composed in the same style as the one for the ordination of a deacon or a presbyter.

Furthermore, the rank of widows in the hierarchy appears sufficiently in the place which they occupied in the church, adjacent to the bishop, near the place called the "front-stage." [194] During the oblation of the Eucharistic sacrifice, the widows took their place with the members of the clergy within the veil, which was spread out at that moment, it seems, to hide the altar from the view of the faithful. The bishop stood in the center; alongside of him, to the right and the left, stood the presbyters; after the presbyters came the deacons, on the right hand, and, on the left, the widows.[195] The place of the widows was, therefore, analogous to that of the deacons. After the deacons came the readers, and after the readers, the subdeacons.[196] The title of "widows that sit in the front," which is repeated no less than six times in the *Testamentum*, refers to this place of honor which belonged to ordained widows.[197]

These widows are also mentioned under the title of "senior women" in the deacon's litany, probably chanted before the offering of the Eucharistic sacrifice.[198] Here again, the title given them, which is none other than the feminine form of "presbyter," reveals the high esteem they enjoyed in the community. Finally one notices that widows received Holy Communion with the clergy, after the deacons and before the readers and the subdeacons.[199] Undeniably they were considered a part of the clergy. Indeed, no other document attributes to women a rank as high in the ecclesiastical hierarchy as that of widows who sat in front. More than once the *Apostolic Constitutions* mentioned the deaconess among the clergy, immediately after the deacon and before the subdeacon and the rest of the clergy; and above all, the deaconess of the *Constitutions* was far from enjoying the consideration that was given to the widow who sat in front.

Like a bishop, a priest, and a deacon, a widow could not be ordained unless she had been "chosen." [200] By its parallelism with the case of the bishop, the priest, and the deacon, this term must be understood as an election in good and due form, implying inquiry and examination.[201] The text does not specify who was the author of the "choice," but by way of parallelism with the other members of the clergy already cited, it must be assumed that the congregation intervened in a determinant way. The presence of the congregation is also mentioned concerning the ordination of subdeacons and the appointment of readers, but in these two cases, the term "chosen" no longer appears.[202]

The criteria for the choice of a widow are pointed out immediately. First of all, like the *Apostolic Tradition*, the *Testamentum* requires that the widow had to have been without a husband for a long time, and also adds that "she must have been frequently asked in marriage and refused for reasons of faith." [203] Then, it exacts of her three groups of qualities. First, come Christian virtues which might be called banal, in the sense that they are not characteristic of a particular function or life-style: a widow had to be pious, humble, meek, purified, "perfect in all things, ardent in spirit, with the eyes of her heart opened to all things," working in joy and without ostentation.[204]

Second, there are qualities borrowed from the portrait of the "true widow" in 1 Timothy 5:10, which were the pledge that the widow would practice the charity expected of her; she had to be examined regarding the upbringing of her children, whether she had loved and honored strangers, whether she voluntarily had gone to the aid of the afflicted, whether she had neglected the saints, whether she had done good according to her means.[205] It is not said, at least in the Syriac version, that she must have been the "wife of only one man," [206] whereas such a condition existed for the bishop and the deacon.[207] Nor is there any longer a question of age. Elsewhere, indicating that there were widows under sixty years of age,[208] the *Testamentum* prescribes that a widow who was menstruating could not receive Holy Communion nor approach the altar.

Finally, come the qualities which would help the widow live up to the ascetic ideals which had to be hers. She was questioned if she was "able to bear and endure the yoke," if she loved simplicity, if she "possessed nothing in this world, but always bore the cross," if she prayed without ceasing, if she was "attentive night and day by the altar." [209]

On the other hand, a peculiar condition, which does not appear in the case of the other members of the clergy, must be noted: "If the saints have had revelations about her." [210] This is not the only place where the *Testamentum* speaks of revelations; the bishop asked the Lord in the Eucharistic prayer to "sustain unto the end those who have gifts of revelation"; [211] the priest who was going to be ordained had to be "worthy to receive divine revelations about all that is fitting and suitable." [212] Since the text requires that "she be perfect, that she be visited by the Holy Spirit",[213] it is possible that the widow also had to be recognized as a recipient of the revelations of the Spirit. This passage recalls that, according to the *Canons*, two of the three widows had to persevere in prayer "in view of revelations." [214] In a society which esteemed private revelations and in which they did not seem to be exceptional, it is readily conceivable that a received revelation about the candidate could have been considered a criterion for election.

After enumerating the qualities required of a widow, the *Testamentum* comes to her duties. It is immediately apparent that she was invested with an extremely broad pastoral responsibility regarding women. She was expected to teach women catechumens what befitted them, to instruct the ignorant, to encourage those desiring to live in purity or in virginity, and to call them together to pray with her. She also was to rebuke those who were going astray and to try to win them back to the right way.[215] In addition, the *Testamentum* ascribes to her some of the duties which belonged to deaconesses in the *Apostolic Constitutions*: to visit sick women,[216] to anoint women being baptized, and to spread a veil hiding their nudity from the bishop.[217] They also had the responsibility to see that when women came to church,[218] they were not dressed in a provocative way. Here again, it is apparent that the widow of the *Testamentum* is not simply the counterpart of the deaconess of the *Constitutions*; she is not a subordinate minister, not just an assistant; on the contrary, she has a pastoral responsibility, being especially charged with the care of souls.

However, the chief characteristic of the widow of the *Testamentum* is not her functions, however important they may be, but her ideal of life, consisting of renunciation, prayer, and asceticism. The *Testamentum* imposes on her a total detachment as the foundation of sanctity: "She has loved no one but the God of gods, the Father who is in heaven."[219] She is released from the care of her children whom she has given to the Church, so that, living in the house of God, they may be fit for the priesthood.[220] If she possessed anything of value, she had to give it to the poor and the faithful; if she did not possess anything, the Church would assist her, just as it aided any widow.[221] She was not to do any secular work, only works of the spirit. She had to be assiduous in fasting and prayer.[222] In this regard, the *Testamentum* gives detailed rules and formulas of prayer for the "hymn of praise at night" and the "hymn of praise at dawn."[223]

The priority of the widow's ideal of life in relation to her function appears clearly in her ordination prayer, which the bishop uttered in a low voice while she prayed, eyes downcast, at the entrance of the altar.[224] In the *Apostolic Constitutions*, the prayer for the ordination of a deaconess asks God to give her His Holy Spirit and to purify her of any sin of the flesh or of the spirit so that she might worthily perform the duties entrusted to her.[225] In the *Testamentum*, the prayer for the ordination of a widow asks the Lord to give her strength to obey joyfully the precepts given her as her rule and to carry faultlessly the burden accepted as her yoke. It also asks God to bring His maidservant to perfection for the glory of His house and the edification of all believers.[226] This prayer, therefore, confirms that ordained widows were first of all "widows submitted to a rule," a title explicitly given to them.[227]

Thus it has been noted that the widows described by the *Testamentum* occupied a rank in the hierarchy analogous to that of the deaconesses presented in the *Apostolic Constitutions* (though more favorable in the latter case), and that they fulfilled most of the functions of these deaconesses. In spite of these similarities, there are in the *Testamentum* deaconessess distinct from widows, whose rank is far inferior to that of the widows. In the church, their place was near the main door.[228] During the oblation of the Eucharistic sacrifice, they stood within the veil, but in the lowest place, behind the readers and subdeacons.[229] In the deacon's litany, they were named along with readers and subdeacons, but after them.[230]

It could seem, according to these last two facts, that deaconesses, like the widows who sat in front, belonged to the clergy. But there is no evidence of an ordination or of an appointment of deaconesses; they went to Communion together with lay people, before the women but after the men, whereas widows received Communion after deacons, but before readers and subdeacons.[231] Obviously the relationship between widows and deaconesses in the hierarchy here reverses the one described in the *Apostolic Constitutions*. According to the *Constitutions*, widows were subject to deaconesses;[232] according to the *Testamentum*, widows supervised deaconesses.[233]

Since the chief functions of deaconesses in the *Apostolic Constitutions* are assumed by widows in the *Testamentum*, the ministry of deaconesses in the latter work is reduced to almost nothing. Their place at the door in church suggests that they oversaw the entrance of women, as in the *Constitutions*, but elsewhere it is apparent that the deacon indiscriminately controlled the entrance of men and women,[234] and the deacons, assisted by readers and subdeacons, maintained order among women in the assembly.[235] As he did for lay people, the deacon announced the name of a deaconess who arrived late for church.[236] Finally, the only function that the *Testamentum* clearly ascribes to deaconesses consists of taking Communion to pregnant women who, because of their state of health, could not come to church for Easter.[237]

10. The Theodosian and Post-Theodosian Legislation

Perhaps it is surprising to discover, in a chapter devoted to Greek canonical sources, a whole body of texts written exclusively in Latin. But the official language of the imperial administration, even in the Eastern Empire, remained Latin, at least until the end of the fifth century. Most of the laws which will be mentioned in this section had been promulgated in the East by Eastern emperors, and the Theodosian Code had been compiled at the order of an Eastern emperor for use in the East as well as in the West. It is also perhaps surprising to find, among "canonical" sources cited, texts which do not come from ecclesiastical authority. But, as is often the case with Christian institutions, secular legislation contains interesting references to widows and deaconesses, and undoubtedly influenced the practice of the Church in this matter as well as in many others. There is nothing surprising here for those who realize how closely the Church and the State were associated from the beginning of the fourth century and how frequently imperial authority intervened in ecclesiastical affairs. Therefore, for the purpose of this exposition, it is not illegitimate to compare imperial constitutions with canonical sources properly so-called.

It is relevant first to examine the laws grouped together in the Theodosian Code under title 25 in Book 10: "*De raptu vel matrimonio sanctimonalium virginum vel viduarum.*" According to a law of Constantius, dated September 22, 354, the raper of a widow had to be as severely punished as the attacker of a consecrated virgin, and neither the one nor the other was able to avail himself of the later consent of his victim.[238] The sentence is not indicated at this point; but ten years later, a law of Jovian threatens with death not only the kidnapper of a consecrated virgin or widow[239] but also the seducer who planned to marry his victim. This case demonstrates how closely widows were associated with consecrated virgins; it likewise echoes the same situation in the *Apostolic Constitutions*, dated about the same period.[240] Significantly, the Justinian Code and the *Lex Romana Burgundionum* repeat the law of Jovian but do not mention widows.[241] A law of the Emperors Honorius and Theodosius in 420 on the same subject mentions only the rape of virgins,[242] and the same is true of *Novella* 6 of Majorian in 458.[243]

Another group of laws worth studying concerns the succession of widows and deaconesses. On July 30, 370, Valentinian I had read in all churches of Rome a constitution addressed to Pope Damasus forbidding clerics, former clerics, and monks to visit widows and young orphaned girls, and in spite of the tribunal privilege of the Church, allowing their in-laws and relatives to prosecute transgressors before civil tribunals.

The reason for this interdict is immediately apparent. Further in the text, in fact, the emperor invalidates any donations or legacies made by a woman to a cleric or to a religious who might have won her favor under the cover of religion, and he gives to the treasury any future gifts of this nature made in violation of this prohibition.[244] This law reveals the early concern to prevent the possessions of women who were *sui juris* from falling too easily into the hands of ecclesiastics. Another law, dated June 21, 390, moved in the same direction. "Conforming to the precept of the Apostle," it prohibited admission among deaconesses of women under sixty years of age with children. The requirements of First Timothy for widows were thus applied to deaconesses.[245] According to Sozomen, the age requirement sought to exclude from this rank young women who might be the cause of scandal prejudicial to the reputation of the Church.[246]

The next part of the text formally prohibited a deaconess from bequeathing any of the possessions of her family to a church, a cleric, or a poor person, and declares null and void any such disposition in her will.[247] Since it was revoked months later, this second part of the law must have provoked loud protests.[248] However, on the basis of the law of 370, as late as 455, the last will of a wealthy widow, Hypatia, of senatorial rank, who had bequeathed part of her goods to a priest, was contested. After examining these texts, Emperor Marcian ruled that the law of August 23, 390, annulled not only the law of June 21 of the same year but also the law of the year 370; and, in consequence, he confirmed the will of Hypatia, which, besides giving many legacies to churches, the poor, monks, and the redemption of captives, also gave a part of her wealth to a priest named Anatole. And to stop all disputes in the future, the emperor declared explicitly valid all gifts and legacies made according to the law by a widow, a deaconess, a consecrated virgin, or a religious, in favor of a church, a *martyrium*, a cleric, a monk, or the poor.[249]

On the other hand, a law of Theodosius II, in 434, prescribed that when a cleric of whatever rank, a monk, or a nun died without a will and without leaving either relatives or wife, his or her possessions should go to the church or the monastery to which the deceased had belonged. This law made reservations only in regard to possessions on which the administration of taxes, patronage, or curiae had any rights. The clerics enumerated in the text of this law included the deaconess, who is cited immediately after the deacon but before the subdeacon: "*Si quis episcopus aut presbyter aut diaconus aut diaconnissa aut subdiaconus vel cuiuslibet alterius loci clericus aut monachus aut mulier quae solitaria vita dedita est*, etc.." [250] By this law, the emperor took a position regarding deaconesses exactly opposite to that of the law of June 21, 390.

Finally, a law of Majorian, dated 458, which contained severe sentiments against "young widows," is relevant. It referred to young women, without children, who preferred not to remarry, not because they loved chastity but because they wanted to enjoy without hindrance the freedom they had acquired. The emperor gave widows less than forty years old five years to contract a new marriage. If they did not remarry in this time, they had to give half of their possessions to their relatives or, if they had no relatives, to the public treasury.[251] These measures probably reduced, at least temporarily, the number of widows in the Church.

11. The Legislation of Justinian

The legislation of Justinian clearly places deaconesses among the clergy.[252] In *Novella* 3, dated March 16, 535, and addressed to Epiphanius, archbishop of Constantinople, the emperor attempted to remedy the situation created by the massive immigration of clerics who overburdened the budget of the churches of the imperial capital.[253] Consequently, he fixed the number of clerics who in the future would be attached to each of these churches, particularly the "Great Church," i.e., the cathedral of Hagia Sophia. This church could not have more than 60 priests, 100 deacons, 40 deaconesses, 90 subdeacons, 110 readers, and 25 singers, in all a total of 425 clerics, and an additional 100 janitors.[254] The 40 deaconesses were obviously included in the 425 clerics. When the laws of Justinian enumerated the different ranks of the clergy, as they did here, the deaconesses were associated with the deacons in the formula "male and female deacons" (*diakonous arrenas kai thēleias*), and given precedence over subdeacons, readers, and singers, as in the Theodosian law of 434.[255] But when the ranks of the clergy are not enumerated and the text speaks simply of clerics (*klērikoi*) or of the clergy (*klēros*) in general, a mention of deaconesses is more than once expressly added, as if it were not clear enough that they are included under the general term of "cleric" or "clergy."[256]

In the legislation of Justinian, deaconesses are compared with clerics in many regards. Like other clerics, at the moment they assumed their function they received an ordination, designated by the terms *cheirotonia, cheirotonein.*[257] Since a deaconess appears as necessarily attached to a church, either secular or monastic, this ordination, as that of other clergy, was not "absolute."[258] The minimum age for ordination to the female diaconate, which a law of 390 in the Theodosian Code[259] fixed at sixty because of an assimilation of deaconesses to the widows of First Timothy, was reduced by Justinian to fifty,[260] and finally to forty.[261] The candidates had to be virgins or widows who had been married only once.[262] A special inquiry also had to be made to assure that their life had been always above suspicion in regard to chastity.[263]

After their ordination, deaconesses like major clerics, were bound to perfect continence. At their ordination, in the presence of their sister deaconesses assembled in the church, they were solemnly reminded of this obligation in order to inspire each of them with a holy fear. As Canon 44 of Basil and Canon 15 of Chalcedon already suggested,[264] this obligation was not based on a personal engagement, but on a consecration resulting from the ordination; and, as a consequence, the transgression of this rule was considered more a profanation than a disobedience.

The penalties imposed on guilty deaconesses may seem extremely severe; however, they appear to have been tempered in relation to the deaconesses' greater or lesser consent to a union which they had not necessarily initiated. According to *Novella* 6, which does not consider any extenuating circumstances, deaconesses who "defiled their ordination," like unfaithful vestal virgins, were liable to capital punishment and their possessions were distributed to the church or monastery to which they had belonged.[265] But *Novella* 123, in chapter 43, which puts most of the blame on the ravisher or seducer of a consecrated woman and obviously reduces the responsibility of the woman in the fault committed by the two, prescribed only that the woman had to be sent to a monastery with her possessions, after her legitimate children, if there were any, had been given their share.[266] For men assaulting the chastity of a deaconess, whether she consented or not, and for their direct or indirect accomplices, in any case, the punishment was death and the confiscation of their possessions.[267]

Deaconesses who did not live in a monastery were not allowed to keep in their house a man known as "brother," "cousin," or "agapete."[268] They had to live alone, or with their parents or children, or with their blood brothers, sisters, or uncles, with whom they were not likely to be suspected of sinful relations. A deaconess who did not observe this rule had to be deposed, and *Novella* 6 threatened her and her accomplice with the same penalties as those for a deaconess and her seducer guilty of fornication, considered them *a priori* suspect of this crime.[269] According to *Novella* 123, such a deaconess had to be excluded from the ministry, deprived of her wages, stripped of her possessions, and sent to a convent.[270] Male clerics were subject to a similar rule, but the transgressors, instead of being confined to a monastery, were assigned to the curia with their possessions.[271]

Like the clergy, deaconesses benefited from a sort of tribunal privilege, in the sense that anyone who had a dispute with one of them had to first take his case before the bishop, and only afterwards, if the sentence of the bishop did not satisfy him, could he appeal to a civil court.[272] Like the clergy, deaconesses were not expected to give a small gratuity to the man who brought them a judicial summons.[273] Again like the clergy, they received their subsistence from the Church; their dependence upon the Church was the reason for Justinian's limiting, just as he did for the rest of the clergy, the number of deaconesses who could be attached to the different churches of Constantinople.[274] One of the penalties which could be imposed on a deaconess living with a man was the deprivation of her daily wages.[275] Along with clerics, convents, welfare institutions, and pious associations, deaconesses could be the beneficiaries of a pension in memory of a deceased person.[276] Like the clergy, they were not bound to the conditions implying marriage, which could have been associated with a donation or legacy destined for them; in their case, such clauses were regarded as unwritten.[277] Finally, like clerics, if deaconesses died intestate without legitimate heirs, their goods went to the church to which they were attached by their ordination.[278]

Considering the nature of this document, it is not surprising that the legislation of Justinian gives scarcely any information about the functions of deaconesses. *Novella* 6 points out that deaconesses exercised a ministry in the celebration of baptism (*tois te proskynētois hypēreteisthai baptismasi*), and then, in the vaguest terms, that they "attend to other sacred functions which they habitually perform in the most venerable mysteries" (*tois te allois pareinai tois aporrētois haper en tois sebasmiōtatois mystēriois di' autōn eiōthe prattesthai*).[279] It is difficult to see what is the intent of this rather too refined formula. The role played by deaconesses in the celebration of baptism seems to refer to their intervention to preserve the decency of the ceremony and the modesty of women in the baptismal anointing and immersion, as mentioned in other documents.[280] During the same period, the Armenian and Nestorian Churches strictly limited the ministry of deaconesses to their role at baptism,[281] whereas the Syrian Monophysite Churches granted them more extended functions.[282]

7 THEOLOGICAL WRITINGS AND OTHER GREEK DOCUMENTS FROM THE FOURTH TO THE SIXTH CENTURY

The theological writings and other Greek documents from the fourth to the sixth century confirm, by way of allusion rather than by systematic exposition, what we have found in the canonical sources of this period about widows and deaconesses. In addition, they offer elaborate considerations concerning the ministry of women in general.

1. The Anonymous Dialogue Between a Montanist and an Orthodox, A Source of Didymus the Blind

In a manuscript at the Escorial Library, G. Ficker discovered at the beginning of this century an anoymous *Dialogue* between a Montanist and an Orthodox, which dates from the second half of the fourth century.[1] A discussion of this nature naturally could not avoid the case of the Montanist prophetesses, whom Origen had already attacked in his commentary on First Corinthians.[2] Curiously enough, the author of this dialogue extended the interdiction against women's speaking in the assemblies even to their writing books; consequently he attacked the collections of oracles ascribed to Maximilla and Priscilla:

> *Montanist*: Why do you reject the holy women Maximilla and Priscilla, and say that women are not permitted to prophesy? Didn't Philip have

four daughters who prophesied? [3] And wasn't Deborah a prophetess? [4] And didn't the Apostle say: "Every woman praying or prophesying with her head uncovered . . ."? [5] If women are not permiteed to prophesy, they are not permitted to pray either. But if they pray, let them also prophesy!

Orthodox: We do not reject the prophecies of women. Blessed Mary prophesied when she said: "Henceforth all generations shall call me blessed." [6] And as you yourself say, Philip had daughters who prophesied, and Mary, the sister of Aaron, prophesied.[7] But we do not permit women to speak in the assemblies, nor to have authority over men,[8] to the point of writing books in their own name; since, such is, indeed, the implication for them of praying with uncovered head. . . .[9] Wasn't Mary, the Mother of God, able to write books in her own name? To avoid dishonoring her head by placing herself above men,[10] she did not do so.

Montanist: Do you say that to pray or to prophesy with uncovered head implies not to write books?

Orthodox: Perfectly.

Montanist: When Blessed Mary says: "Henceforth all generations shall call me blessed," does or doesn't she speak freely and openly? [11]

Orthodox: Since the Gospel is not written in her name, she has a veil in the Evangelist.

Montanist: You shouldn't take allegories for dogmas!

Orthodox: There is no doubt, indeed, that Saint Paul took allegories as confirmation of dogmas when he said: "Abraham had two wives; since these women are two covenants, he spoke in an allegorical sense." [12] If the head covering is not to be understood allegorically, you must renounce allegorical interpretations in all cases. If there is a poor woman who cannot afford to cover her head, should she abstain from praying and prophesying?

Montanist: Do you think that it is possible to be so poor that a person couldn't have a head covering?

Orthodox: We have often known women who could not afford to cover their head. But since you do not admit that there are poor women who cannot afford to cover their head, what do you do about those who are being baptized? Shouldn't these women pray? [13] And what do you say about men who frequently, on account of illness, cover their head? [14] Are you going to prevent them also from praying and prophesying?

Montanist: When he is praying or prophesying, he must uncover his head.

Orthodox: Must we not pray without ceasing, or should we disdain the teaching of the Apostle, who says: "Pray without ceasing"? [15] Do you advise a woman not to pray when she is being baptized?

Montanist: Is it because they have written books that you do not receive Priscilla and Maximilla?

Orthodox: It is not only for this reason, but also because they were false prophetesses, following their guide Montanus.

Montanist: Why do you think that they were false prophetesses?

> *Orthodox*: Didn't they say the same thing as Montanus?
>
> *Montanist*: Yes.
>
> *Orthodox*: Well, Montanus has been convicted of saying things contrary to Holy Scripture. These two, therefore, must without doubt be rejected with him.[16]

This text served as a source of a passage in the treatise of Didymus the Blind *On The Trinity*, where, among other grievances against the Montanist, he refered also to the books written by Maximilla and Priscilla:

> Scripture recognizes as prophetesses the four daughters of Philip,[17] Deborah,[18] Mary, the sister of Aaron,[19] and Mary, the mother of God, who said, as recorded in the Gospel: "Henceforth all women and all generations shall call me blessed." [20] But in Scripture there are no books written in their name. On the contrary, the Apostle says in First Timothy: "I do not permit women to teach," [21] and again in First Corinthians: "Every woman who prays or prophesies with uncovered head dishonors her head." [22] He means that he does not permit a woman to write books impudently, on her own authority, nor to teach in the assemblies, because, by doing so, she offends her head, man; for "the head of woman is man, and the head of man is Christ." [23] The reason for this silence imposed on women is obvious: woman's teaching in the beginning caused considerable havoc to the human race; for the Apostle writes: "It is not the man who was deceived, but the woman." [24]

For Didymus as well as for the anonymous author of the *Dialogue*, writing a book was a form of public teaching. Since it fell within the scope of the interdiction pronounced by Paul, any such activity had to be forbidden to women.

2. Epiphanius of Salamis

In Epiphanius' *Panarion*, the forty-ninth heresy is represented by a group of sects related to Montanism (Quintillianists, Pepuzians, Arotirites, Priscillianists, Cataphrygians,) among which the distinction, as Ephiphanius himself says, is not always easy to make. The Cataphrygians pretended that a woman named Quintilla,[25] or else Priscilla, had seen Christ visiting her in a dream at Pepuza, a city in Phrygia, Asia Minor, and sharing her bed. He had the appearance of a woman and was dressed in white. He endowed the prophetess with wisdom and revealed to her that the place she was in was holy and that the heavenly Jerusalem would descend there. This is the reason why, as late as the time of Epiphanius, men and women, hoping that Christ would appear to them also, were initiated at this place.

The members of this sect held Quintilla and Priscilla in great honor and called them "prophetesses." To justify the admission of women into the clergy, they pointed out that Eve was the first to eat of the fruit of the tree of knowledge,[26] and they referred to Mary, the sister of Aaron, and to the daughters of Philip who prophesied. Frequently a procession of seven virgins, carrying torches and dressed in white, is seen entering their assemblies. Under the power of prophetic delirium, they lamented the miseries of the human condition and surrendered themselves to noisy penitential demonstrations, so that the assistants also cried with them. But that is not all—they had women bishops and presbyters, since, as they said, they did not discriminate with regard to sex, to be in accord with the statement of Paul: "In Christ Jesus, there is neither male nor female."[27] Depending on Epiphanius, St. Augustine and St. John Damascene reported the same fact.[28]

Despite what some scholars say, there is not sufficient reason to reject this testimony.[29] It is useless to say that for Epiphanius, the uncompromising guardian of orthodoxy and canonical tradition, such aberrations showed the follies to which one is exposed when he does not attach himself firmly to the "anchor of truth." Wishing to admit women to the episcopacy or to the priesthood in consideration of Eve is forgetting the word of the Lord to her: "Your desire shall be for your husband, yet he shall rule over you."[30] It is to ignore the statement of the Apostle: "I permit no woman to teach or to have authority over men."[31] And again: "Man was not created for woman, but woman for man."[32] And finally: "Adam was not deceived, but the woman was deceived and became a transgressor."[33]

Epiphanius returned at greater length to the question of the ministry of women in relation to the heresy of the Collyridian women.[34] These women honored the Blessed Virgin as a deity and, on a certain day of the year, offered her, on an improvised altar, a small loaf of bread, which they afterwards consumed as communion.[35] Although the origins of this custom are of small importance to this study, its confutation by Epiphanius is interesting.[36] His first concern was not to insist on Mary's creaturehood, but to denounce women's claim to exercise a sacred function.[37] Women, he said, are weak, fickle, and only moderately intelligent; and once more the devil used them as instruments to spread error, just as he did with Quintilla, Maximilla, and Priscilla, just as he did with Eve at the beginning of the human race.[38]

Never since the beginning of the world did a woman exercise the priesthood. Even though she was guilty of an enormous fault, Eve herself did not dare to go to this point of impiety. In the Old Testament the sacrifices were always offered by men, and only men were admitted to the priesthood.[39] In the New Testament, access to the priesthood is not an option open to women either. If that had been the case, no one would have been more worthy of this function than the Blessed Virgin. But God did not decide that way; and since Jesus received baptism from the hand of John, the son of Zechariah,[40] neither did he permit her to baptize. And none of the other holy women mentioned in Scripture was granted priestly dignity: neither Salome,[41] nor the mother of Rufus,[42] nor those who followed Jesus from Galilee,[43] nor Martha, the sister of Lazarus and Mary,[44] nor any of those women who obtained their salvation through the coming of Jesus and helped him with their goods,[45] nor the Canaanite woman,[46] nor the woman afflicted with hemorrhage.[47] The Apostles all had to be men, and the succession of bishops and presbyters, which originated from the Apostles, likewise includes men only.

Scripture says that the four daughters of Philip prophesied, not that they exercised sacred functions.[48] In the same way, the prophetess Anna, Phanuel's daughter, was not invested with any priestly dignity.[49] There were, indeed, deaconesses in the Church, but they did not perform any sacerdotal acts. No more than deacons did they exercise any priestly tasks; like them, they were but servants. Their ministry, which was confined to women only, was destined to safeguard decency, preventing men, when they performed the sacred rites, from seeing the naked bodies of women at the moment of baptism or during illness.

These were the limits of a deaconess' minstry, and Epiphanius recalled that Scripture does not allow women to speak in church or to have authority over men.[50] He admitted, however, that deaconesses belonged to the "ecclesiastical order" (*to ekklēsiastikon tagma*), i.e., to the clergy. In the enumeration of the different orders contained in chapter 21 of the *Summary of Faith*, first came the priestly hierarchy (*hē hierōsynē*), which today is called "major" or "sacred" orders, from bishop to subdeacon.[51] Next came the order of readers, which did not belong to the "priestly hierarchy";[52] then deaconesses;[53] and, finally, exorcists, interpreters, grave-diggers, and janitors.[54]

The conditions imposed on deaconesses regarding marriage were the same as those for the members of the "priestly hierarchy": they had to be virgins, or widows of one husband, or have promised to be continent in marriage. These conditions were more severe than those for readers, who, if they were married, were not obliged to live continent, and who, in case of necessity, could be chosen from among remarried men. This text said that deaconesses were "established" (*kathistantai*)[55] for the service of women; but the Epistle of Epiphanius to John of Jerusalem, preserved only in a Latin translation, contained the following sentence: "I have never ordained (*ordinavi*) deaconesses to send to other provinces."[56] Since it has a very general sense and is not here expressly opposed to *cheirotonein*, as in the *Apostolic Tradition* and texts derived from it,[57] the first term (*kathistantai*) does not necessarily exclude deaconesses from receiving ordination. On the other hand, since this document is only a translation whose accuracy has been contested,[58] and since the meaning of *ordinare* is less clearly defined *a priori* than that of *cheirotonein*, the second term (*ordinavi*) does not prove with certitude that Epiphanius actually ordained deaconesses whom he destined to minister within the limits of his own province. Since the practice of ordaining deaconesses, noted earlier, tended to be generalized in the East from the beginning of the second half of the fourth century, it is probable, however, that Epiphanius did ordain deaconesses.

Epiphanius did not speak of widows, except to note in an allusion to the Epistle to Titus that the elder among them were called "senior women" (*presbytidas*).[59] He never mentioned "presbyteresses" (*presbyteridas*) nor "priestesses" (*hierissas*). From the writings of Epiphanius, it is apparent that, in contrast to deaconesses, widows were not a part of the clergy.[60]

3. John Chrysostom

John Chrysostom dealt with the ministry of women principally in his homilies on Scripture. Romans 16 mentions a number of women whom the Apostle asked his correspondents to greet. The first is Phoebe, "deaconess" of the church of Cenchreae.[61] Chrysostom remarked that the Apostle added to her name recognition of her dignity (*kai to axiōma prosethēke, diakonon eipōn*); but he did not feel the need to speak about the institution of deaconesses and limited himself to putting in relief the excellence of the praise accorded to Phoebe.[62]

Nor does Chrysostom enlarge any further on the diaconate of women elsewhere, even though this institution was then in its golden age and he himself was in close contact with many deaconesses.[63] For only an instant he lingered with the women in the passage on deacons in First Timothy.[64] For him, undoubtedly, the women whom the Apostle wished to be "serious, not slanderers, but temperate, faithful in all things" were those who had the "dignity of the diaconate" (*tōn to axiōma tēs diakonias echousōn*). Some claim, he said, that the Apostle spoke here of women in general, but this assertion is not true; for why would Paul have inserted a sentence concerning women in general in this context dealing with deacons? When he came to the next verse: "Let deacons be the husband of one wife,"[65] he added that it was fitting to say the same thing of women deacons (*peri gynaikōn diakonōn*), whose parallel state was in the highest degree necessary, useful, and fitting in the Church.[66]

After Phoebe come the couple Priscilla and Aquila.[67] Chrysostom ascribed to the woman all the merit of having instructed Apollos in the correct Christian faith; and although Luke did not make any distinction between the two spouses,[68] Chrysostom made use of the testimony of Luke in the Acts of the Apostles to affirm his own position. Priscilla, he continued, was one of the noble women whose nature has not prevented them from running in the way of virtue. The "vessel of election" was not ashamed to call a woman a "collaborator in his ministry"; he even made it an honor; he did not pay attention to nature, but he prizes resolution of will.[69] In Homily 40 on Acts, on account of the similar work of Priscilla and Aquila, Chrysostom noted the fact that a woman did the same thing as a man and taught.[70] The reason he ascribed a special role to Priscilla was certainly the unusual mention of the woman before her husband when the couple was presented.[71] In Homily 10 on First Timothy, he definitely called attention to the situation in regard to the words "Greet Priscilla and Aquila": [72]

> These are they whom Paul continually mentions, with whom too he had lodged, and who had taken Apollos to him. If he names the woman first, it is, it seems to me, because she showed more zeal and faith; for she had already received Apollos. At least, Paul did not act thus without some specific reason.[73]

But in a homily on the salutation in Romans addressed to Priscilla and Aquila, which is separate from the series of homilies forming the commentary on this Epistle,[74] Chrysostom enlarged extensively on this point:

> It is worth examining Paul's motive, when he greets them, for putting Priscilla before her husband. Indeed, he did not say: "Salute Aquila and Priscilla," but rather, "Salute Priscilla and Aquila." [75] He did not do so without reason: the wife must have had, I think, greater piety than her husband. This is not a simple conjecture; its confirmation is evident in the Acts. Apollos was an eloquent man, well versed in Scripture, but he knew only the baptism of John; this woman took him, instructed him in the way of God, and made of him an accomplished teacher.[76]
>
> The women who lived at the time of the Apostles did not have the same concerns as women today. The latter dream only of dressing in lavish clothing, of greasing and painting their face to give themselves a borrowed beauty, of fatiguing their husbands to buy finery to eclipse their neighbors and rivals, white slippers with golden bands, a retinue of eunuchs, a swarm of servants, and all the accoutrements of a ridiculous luxury. The others, on the contrary, put aside all these things, stamped under foot the vanities of the world, and desired only to be associated with the Apostles and to share in the same reward.
>
> Priscilla was not, then, the only one animated with these ideals; they were held by all the others. About a woman named Persis, Paul also says: "She has worked hard for us." [77] He also praises Mary and Tryphaena for having endured the same hardships, since they labored diligently with the Apostles and shared in the same struggles.[78]
>
> How, then, can he afterwards say, when he writes to Timothy: "I do not permit a woman to teach or to have authority over men"? [79] This posture refers to the case of a man who is pious, professes the same faith, practices the same wisdom; but, when the man is not a believer and the plaything of error, Paul does not exclude a woman's superiority, even when it involves teaching. Writing to the Corinthians, he says: "If any woman has a husband who is an unbeliever, she should not divorce him. Wife, do you not know that you might save your husband?" [80] But how can the believing woman save her unbelieving husband? By instructing, obviously, by teaching, by trying to lead him to the faith, as Priscilla did with Apollos.
>
> The matter is not the same when he says: "I permit no woman to

> teach." This declaration concerns teaching from the pulpit and giving speeches in public, which belongs to priestly duties. But he does not forbid exhorting and advising in private. Indeed, if that were forbidden, he would not have eulogized this woman who had conducted herself in this way.[81]

Here again, Chrysostom, at the expense of the role Priscilla exercised jointly with her husband, put in relief the part she played in the instruction of Apollos. This position led him to ask how this role could be reconciled with the interdict in First Timothy against women's teaching. His answer was twofold: first, this prohibition concerns only the case where the husband and wife are both believers; and, second, it concerns only instruction given in public, such as priests give from the pulpit, not exhortations and advice given in private.

In a series of homilies on the Epistle to the Romans, Chrysostom raised the same question and gave a similar answer about this Mary who "worked hard" for the recipients of the Epistle:

> How is this? A woman again is honored and proclaimed victorious! Again are we men put to shame. Or rather, we are not put to shame only, but have even an honor conferred upon us. For an honor we have, in that there are such women among us, but we are put to shame, in that we men are left so far behind by them. But if we come to know whence it comes that they are so adorned, we too shall speedily overtake them.
>
> Whence then is their adorning? Let both men and women listen. It is not from bracelets, or from necklaces, nor from their eunuchs either, and their maidservants, and gold-embroidered dresses, but from their toils in behalf of the truth. For he says, "Who bestowed much labor on us," [82] that is, not on herself only, nor upon their own advancement (for this many women of the present day do, by fasting and sleeping on the floor), but upon others also, so carrying on the race Apostles and Evangelists ran.
>
> In what sense then does he say, "I suffer not a woman to teach"? [83] He means to hinder her from publicly coming forward, and from the seat on the bema, not from the word of teaching. Since if this were the case, how would he have said to the woman that had an uneblieving husband, "How do you know, O woman, if you shall save your husband?" [84] Or how came he to suffer her to admonish children, when he says, "but she shall be saved by childbearing if they continue in faith, and charity, and holiness, with sobriety"? [85] How came Priscilla to instruct even Apollos?
>
> It was not, then, to prohibit private conversation for advantage that he said this, but that which it was the teacher's duty to give in the public assembly; or again, in case the husband be believing and thoroughly instructed, able also to instruct her. When she is the wiser, then he does not forbid her teaching and improving him. And he does not say, "who taught much," but "who bestowed much labor," because along with teaching she performs other ministries besides, those in the way of dan-

> gers, in the way of money, in the way of travels. For the women of those days were more spirited than lions, sharing with the Apostles their labors for the gospel's sake. In this way they went traveling with them, and also performed all other ministries. And even in Christ's day women followed him, "which ministered unto him of their substance," and waited upon the Teacher." [86]

In this passage, as in the preceding one, by distinguishing public teaching from private teaching, John Chrysostom easily reconciled what Paul said about women's sharing the work of the Apostles with his interdict against women's teaching. He also insisted that the alleged collaboration of women with the Apostles did not consist so much in teaching as in giving the preachers of the gospel all necessary services. A third time, Chrysostom resolved the same type of difficulty in regard to the "senior women" who were invited, according to the Epistle to Titus, to "teach what is good, and so train the young women to love their husbands and children": [87]

> And yet you forbid a woman to teach; how do you command it here, when elsewhere you say, "I suffer not a woman to teach"? [88] But mark what he has added: "nor to usurp authority over the man." [89] For at the beginning it was permitted to men to teach both men and women. But to women it is allowed to instruct by discourse at home. But they are nowhere permitted to preside, nor to extend their speech to great length, wherfore he adds: "nor to usurp authority over the man." [90]

Again this time, the distinction between public and private teaching provides the key to the problem.

It is perhaps surprising that, regarding the teaching performed by women, there has been no citation of the classic text of First Corinthians: "Women should keep silence in the churches" [91] The reason for this absence appears in Chrysostom's homilies on First Corinthians. According to him, this text does not concern the claim of women to teach publicly, but rather the disorder caused by women chattering in church. He noted that Paul relied on the Law to forbid women to open their mouths in the assembly; he believed that the text to which Paul referred is the sentence in Genesis: "Your desire shall be for your husband, and he shall rule over you." [92]

The silence demanded of women is the respectful silence of a servant. The reason for this restriction is that woman is weak, unstable, and giddy.[93] Commenting in his homilies on First Timothy about the command, "Let a woman learn in silence with all submissiveness," [94] Chrysostom compared it to a similar precept in First Corinthians, and also complained of the disorder caused by women in the liturgical assemblies — they talked without restraint, even more than at the public markets or baths; they seemed to come only to gossip; how could people learn anything good in such confusion? The following verse, "I permit no woman to teach," [95] is explained through extension of the preceding one. To deprive women of all claim to speak, Paul forbade them to teach and ordered them to remain among those who receive instruction; their silence was to be a sign of their submission.

Chrysostom developed the justification of this defense, which is contained in the continuation of the text: "Adam was formed first, then Eve." [96] This sentence, just like the other ("Man was not created for woman, but woman for man" [97]), shows that at the moment of creation, man enjoyed a greater dignity, a primacy over woman. Certainly, the inferior dignity of woman, implicit in her being created second, does not preclude that in the beginning she was essentially equal to man; man was then only a *primus inter pares*. But the leading part that woman played in original sin turned man's primacy of honor into authority properly speaking. "Adam was not deceived, but the woman was deceived and became a transgressor." [98] Woman tried once to teach man and led him to disobey God; consequently, God subjected her to man: "Your desire shall be for your husband." [99] For this reason God forbade her to teach. It is not valid to say that only Eve deserved this treatment; the whole feminine race is weak and fickle.[100]

After all that has been presented, it is evident that women are excluded from the priesthood. Without feeling the necessity of giving other reasons, John Chrysostom quietly affirmed this point. In his treatise *On the Priesthood*, he said:

> But when one is required to preside over the Church, and to be entrusted with the care of many souls, the whole female sex must retire before the magnitude of the task, and the majority of men also; and we must bring forward those who to a large extent surpass all others, and soar as much above them in excellence of spirit as Saul overtopped the whole Hebrew nation in bodily stature, or rather far more.[101]

Elsewhere in the same work, denouncing the dangers arising from the search for vainglory, he said:

> For all these wild beasts, and more than these, are bred upon that rock of which I have spoken, and those whom they have once captured are inevitably dragged down into such a depth of servitude that even to please women they often do many things which it is well not to mention. The divine law indeed has excluded women from the sanctuary, but they endeavor to thrust themselves into it; and since they can effect nothing of themselves, they do all through the agency of others; and they have become invested with so much power that they can appoint or eject priests at their will. Things in fact are turned upside down, and the proverbial saying may be realized: "The ruled shall lead the rulers"; and would that it were men who do this instead of women, who have not received a commission to teach. Why do I say "teach"? For the blessed Paul did not suffer them even to speak in the church.[102] But I have heard some say that they have obtained such a large privilege of free speech as even to rebuke the prelates of the Churches, and censure them more severely than masters do their own domestics.[103]

Not only, therefore, are women not admitted into the sanctuary, but they are not supposed to interfere in any way in ecclesiastical affairs.

On various occasions John Chrysostom spoke a great deal about widows. Besides the series of homilies on First Timothy,[104] a long homily on 1 Timothy 5:9-10 has been preserved.[105] It is Chrysostom's most instructive text on this subject. Reading it, one gets the impression that the widow described by Paul, the one who made profession of widowhood (*tēs helomenēs chēreian*), was an institution of the past. "Just as there are choirs of virgins," Chrysostem said "there were *formerly* (*to palaion*) choirs of widows." [106]

The profession of virginity seemed to have substituted, as a state of perfection, for the profession of widowhood, so that to explain what constituted the life of widows to whom Paul referred in 1 Timothy 5:9-10, Chrysostom had no better explanation than to compare them to the "choirs of virgins" of his own time. The "list of widows" (*ho katalogos tōn chērōn*) was no longer a list of women who had made profession of widowhood and had consequently reached a particular dignity, but only a list of needy widows who were assisted by the Church.[107] At Antioch, for instance, the Christian community provided for the needs of about three thousand virgins and widows.[108] Relying on the texts of St. Paul already cited, John Chrysostom, nevertheless, still recommended the ideal of a widowhood consecrated to God in asceticism and prayer, and he attested that a number of widows, like Anna, praised God night and day in church.[109]

4. Theodore of Mopsuestia

The commentary of Theodore of Mopsuestia on First Timothy contains some interesting passages on this subject. First, there is the explanation which he gave of 1 Timothy 2:12 "I permit no woman to teach." It immediately appears that Theodore viewed these words in the same way as Chrysostom. Theodore said that it was evident that by pointing out that women should not teach in church, Paul referred to their public behavior. He expained this interdict by the fact that women, in the time of Paul, enjoyed the charism of prophecy and, as a consequence, had great assurance about speaking before the whole world; the Apostle, therefore, warned them not to abuse the spiritual gift which they had received, to disturb the order in the assembly.

But Paul never meant this interdict against teaching to extend to private life, as if women were forbidden to instruct their husbands who were not of the faith or to criticize those who did not behave correctly. How could he have then said: "If you are a wife, it may be your part to save your husband"? [110] This prohibition was, therefore, a matter of public order only. Since Paul seriously wanted this order to be enforced, he began with a reason taken from nature: "Adam was formed first, then Eve"; [111] he continued with a reason taken from history: "Adam was not deceived, but the woman was deceived and became a transgressor."[112]

Theodore declared that 1 Timothy 3:11 did not deal with the wives of deacons but with women who performed the duty of deacons (*mulieres quae diaconi officium implere statuuntur, de mulieribus diaconiae officium fungentibus*). These women had to possess virtues similar to those of the male deacons; in particular, since their position brought them many confidences from other women, they had to be discreet, and if they lacked this quality, the inevitable consequence was quarrels and divisions.[113] Theodore added that some people considered a necessary requirement for deaconesses the minimum age of sixty, which Paul prescribed for inscription among the widows;[114] in effect, he said that this order was superior to that of widows.

But if such were the opinion of Paul, Theodore answered, he should have, with even more reason, fixed a similar limit for admission to the priesthood and to the episcopacy. But he did nothing of the sort. When Paul conferred a function, he paid attention, not to age, but to excellence. The reason for the age limit imposed on widows was that without such a rule, young widows would have had themselves listed, not for the love of virtue, but for benefits from the Church and for an easy life, sheltered from material worry. The bad consequences of such a practice would be that without anything else to do, these women would gossip, tell one another what they heard in confidence, and occasion hatred; then, free from any responsibility, they would think about marriage and be in danger of breaking their promise. Better, then, that young widows worked for their living, and, if such was their wish, remarry. Since the requirement of having been "the wife of one husband," just as its counterpart "the husband of one wife,"[115] which applied to the bishop, the presbyter, and the deacon, meant conjugal fidelity, not a prohibition to remarry, these young widows did not need to fear that later on their right to assistance from the Church would be taken away from them.

5. Theodoret of Cyrus

The commentaries of Theodoret of Cyrus on the Pauline Epistles are less developed, less rich, and less original than those of Theodore of Mopsuestia or of John Chrysostom. Regarding 1 Corinthians 14:34-25, he noted simply that the text of the law to which Paul alluded is Genesis 3:16, "Your desire shall be for your husband, and he shall rule over you." This opinion was already identified as John Chrysostom's position.[116] Regarding 1 Timothy 2:12, Theodoret referred, like John Chrysostom and Theodore of Mopsuestia, to First Corinthians: "If you are a wife, it may be your part to save your husband, for all you know."[117] But he gave an interpretation quite different from, and even opposite to, theirs. Whereas Chrysostom and Theodore of Mopsuestia, believing the question called for a positive answer, discovered in this quotation a justification of a wife's teaching privately her unbelieving husband, Theodoret, thinking that the question demanded a negative response, used this quotation as a confirmation of the interdiction against women's teaching in church. In his opinion, Paul's reason for enacting this prohibition was the fact that women also possessed the charism of prophecy.[118]

Theodoret's position resulted from the discussion in First Corinthians relative to women who pray and prophesy. According to him, the first verse of this passage: "The head of every man is Christ, the head of a woman is her husband, and the head of Christ is God,"[119] supports the idea that women should not usurp the function of teaching, which from the beginning had been given as a prerogative to men.[120] In his commentary on First Timothy, Theodoret suggested that the prohibition against woman rested on her inferiority, or, more exactly, on her "natural" posteriority — Adam was created first[121] — and also on the leading part she took in original sin — Adam was not deceived, but Eve was.[122]

Just as for John Chrysostom and Theodore of Mopsuestia, for Theodoret of Cyrus there was no doubt that the women discussed in 1 Timothy 3:11 are deaconesses. He noticed the similarity of the requirements imposed on them and on deacons:

> "The women likewise," i.e., the (women) deacons, "must be serious, no slanderers, but temperate, faithful in all things." What he prescribes for the men, he prescribes also and in about the same terms for the women. Since he says that the deacons must be "serious,"[123] he also says that the woman must be "serious." Just as he forbids the men to be "double-tongued," so too he forbids the women to be "slanderers." And, as he forbids the men to be addicted to much wine, so also he commands the women to be "temperate."[124]

In his commentary on Romans, Theodoret remarked that since a deaconess by the name of Phoebe is mentioned there, the Christian community of Cenchreae, a village near Corinth, had early reached some importance. He viewed her presence as an indication of the rapid success of evangelical preaching.[125]

Concerning widows, Theodoret insisted in his commentary on First Timothy that only a widow who could not hope for help from anywhere else had a right to benefit from Church assistance. The widow who had a family obviously had to care for it and was entitled in return to expect material help from it. Of course, widows in both categories were expected to live an irreproachable life.

Theodoret considered the minimum age of sixty a wise limit. The youngest were able to earn their own living, and working helped them subdue the passions of the flesh; idleness, on the other hand, would only encourage vice. There was no obstacle to prevent their remarrying. Faithful to the interpretation of Theodore of Mopsuestia, Theodoret presented "the wife of one man" as denoting conjugal fidelity, not a prohibition against remarriage. Therefore, provided her conduct had always been honest, a woman was not to be refused eventual admission among the assisted widows because she had been married several times. But whether she had educated her children well, practiced hospitality, as Lydia and Phoebe had for the Apostles,[126] helped the destitute according to her means, and accomplished all the good works possible had to be investigated. Then, free from all cares, she had only one duty: to pray without ceasing.[127]

6. Greek Deaconesses from the Fourth to the Sixth Century

Historical documents record the names of some Eastern deaconesses from the fourth to the sixth century. The most celebrated of these is undoubtedly Olympias, a deaconess of Constantinople and a friend of John Chrysostom. Seventeen letters of the saint to Olympias, written during the painful years of his exile, are preserved.[128] Palladius, in his biography of Chrysostom, mentions her on several occasions.[129] His *Lausiac History* gives a most eulogistic portrait of her.[130] The data of these two sources are combined in a *Life of Deaconess Olympias*, written shortly after 450, which gives other valuable information about her.[131] Sozomen speaks of Olympias twice in his *Ecclesiastical History*.[132]

These documents give abundant information about this outstanding woman. Olympias, born between 360 and 370 of an illustrious family, was related to kings and emperors. In 384 or 385, she was given in marriage to Nebridios, a prefect of Constantinople, but according to her life, death quickly took her husband before she lost her virginity. Her noble birth, her beauty, and her fortune made her a highly enviable match; more than once the Emperor Theodosius tried to have her marry Elpidius, a member of the imperial family in a second marriage. Since she categorically refused, her wealth was impounded, but in 391 she recovered the free disposition of it and from then on multiplied her gifts to the Church and the poor.

In spite of her youth, Bishop Nectarius ordained her a deaconess because of her exemplary life. Next to the Great Church she built a monastery, to which she brought her housemaids, about fifty in number, her relative Elisanthia, and her sisters, Martyria and Palladia. The latter three were also ordained deaconesses; later on Elisanthia became the third superior of the monastery, after Olympias and Marina. The number of nuns soon reached two hundred fifty.

When Chrysostom arrived at Constantinople, a close friendship developed between him and Olympias. She considered it an honor to care for him until the end of his life. One of the reasons why John made enemies in his episcopal city was his advice to her to reserve her liberality to the poor and not to give without regard to the person of the solicitor, as her disdain of riches had led her to do until that time. When Theophilus of Alexandria visited her in Constantinople, he could obtain nothing from her except room and board, which she gave graciously to all traveling ecclesiastics.

At the tragic moment of his departure into exile, Chrysostom did not want to leave without bidding farewell to Olympias. He asked for her, along with Pentadia and Procla, two other deaconesses, and he exhorted all three not to depart from their usual kindness to the Church and to submit to his future successor. From the epistles he later wrote to them, it is evident that their fidelity to the exiled bishop occasioned for them, as for all his supporters, many painful experiences.[133] Finally, Olympias also had to leave the city of Constantinople and died in exile a few months after Chrysostom. To complete this review of deaconesses of Contantinople at the time of Chrysostom, one must mention Sabiniana, who, according to the *Lausiac History*, was his aunt and who did not hesitate, in spite of her old age, to join him in his distant exile.[134]

Besides those around Chrysostom, other deaconesses are known; but information regarding them is less detailed, and frequently no more than a name is preserved. In 360 the Council of Constantinople deposed Elpidius, bishop of Satala in First Armenia, for, among other reasons, admitting to the diaconate a woman called Nectaria, who, according to the Church laws, was not eligible for this dignity; charged with breaking oaths and agreements,[135] she had been excommunicated. Theodoret tells how, under Julian the Apostate, a pious woman who had merited the grace of the diaconate (*tou tēs diakonias ēxiōmenē charismatos*) converted the son of a pagan priest to Christianity. When he was still a small child, as a friend of his mother she always exhorted him to join the true faith. When his mother died, she persuaded him to leave his father, who was a friend of the emperor, and helped him to flee from his anger.[136]

An epistle which St. Basil addressed "to the deaconesses, daughters of Count Terentius" (*diakonis thygatrasi Terentiou kometos*) in 372, encouraging them to remain firm in the orthodox faith in the Father, the Son, and the Holy Spirit, is also preserved.[137] When Dionysia, mother of St. Euthymius the Great, entrusted her son to Otreus, bishop of Melitene in Second Armenia in 378, at the same time that he made the child a reader he ordained the mother a deaconess in his church.[138] Sozomen also mentioned a deaconess of the Macedonian sect, Eusebia, who looked after the relics of the forty martyrs of Sebaste.[139] Among the correspondents of Theodoret of Cyrus appear the names of three deaconesses: Axia, Casiana, and Celerina. The epistles addressed to the first two were letters of condolence; to the third, Theodoret briefly explained his Christology, asking her to do everything in her power on behalf of the true faith and peace in the Church.[140] All these details, however, provide little information on the status and the function of deaconesses.

There is proof that during this same period some deaconesses ruled over a monastery. Besides Olympias and Elisanthia,[141] mentioned earlier, there were: Lampadia, a friend of Macrina the Younger;[142] Theodula, a superior of the Egyptian monastery where St. Euphrasia lived;[143] Marthana, a friend of Etheria, whom she met while the latter was returning from her pilgrimage to Jerusalem;[144] and Manaris, a deaconess of Gaza under the episcopacy of Porphyrius.[145] A reader is also mentioned who, although he was falsely accused by a fallen virgin as her seducer, resolved, with exemplary generosity, in spite of the injustice of which he was the victim, to take her as his wife. Palladius, who reported this story in his *Lausiac History*, added that the reader put the future mother in a monastery of women and begged the deaconess of the community (*tēn autothi diakonon tēs adelphotētos*) to take charge of her until the birth of the child.[146]

7. The Testimony of the Inscriptions

Although Greek epitaphs give the names of quite a few deaconesses, again they do not reveal much information about them. The most interesting text is the epitaph of a deaconess named Mary, who, according to the Apostle, raised children, practiced hospitality, washed the feet of the saints, and distributed bread to the needy. This eulogy was obviously inspired by 1 Timothy 5:10 and manifests, consequently, the inclination at that time to assimilate deaconesses to the Pauline widows, a tendency for which other evidence abounds.[147]

A funeral inscription found in Jerusalem describing deaconess Sophia as a "servant and spouse of Christ" and presenting her as a "second Phoebe" suggests that, according to the example of her illustrious forebear, she helped many people.[148] Another inscription found near Jerusalem reads: "Tomb of Eneon, daughter of Neoiketes, deaconess at this hospital."[149] Since one of the chief functions of this order was the care of sick women, the fact that a deaconess was attached to a hospital is not surprising. At Delphi, the tomb of deaconess Athanasia indicates that she was "established" (*katastatheisa*) by Bishop Pantamianos,[150] who lived in the first half of the fifth century. At a time when *cheirotonein* seems to have been used commonly for the rite performed at the admission of a deaconess to her office, the use here of the verb *kathistasthai* is notable.

Most of the other Greek inscriptions which mention deaconesses belong to Asia Minor: for instance, deaconesses Nunes, Strateges, Pribu, and Matrona, at Axylos (Eastern Phrygia);[151] deaconesses Masa, Aurelia Faustina, and Paula, at Laodicea Combusta (Cilicia;)[152] Elaphia, deaconess of the Encratite sect in Nevinne;[153] Timothea, at Korykos in Cilicia;[154] and Arete, in Aphrodisias in Caria.[155] There is also in the monastery of Karea, on Mount Hymetta, near Athens, the epitaph of a deaconess named Nicagora,[156] and on the island of Melos (one of the Cyclades), a funeral inscription of the first half of the fourth century mentioning, among other persons, the deaconess Agaliasis.[157] Finally, two Latin inscriptions dating from the Byzantine reconquest in Italy and Dalmatia in the sixth century attest to the existence of deaconesses in this culture.[158]

8 TWO LATIN EXEGETES OF THE END OF THE FOURTH CENTURY: AMBROSIASTER AND PELAGIUS

Proceeding now from the East to the West, and reversing the order used in the last two chapters, this chapter begins with the commentaries of two Latin exegetes of the end of the fourth century, Ambrosiaster and Pelagius, on the Pauline texts relative to the ministry of women. This chapter proves that the Latin West totally ignored at this period the institution of deaconesses which flourished in the East.

1. Ambrosiaster

The commentary of Ambrosiaster on 1 Corinthians 14:34-35 is extremely harsh toward women:

> "Women should keep silence in the churches." [1] He is now teaching what he omitted before; he had, indeed, prescribed that women should be veiled in church.[2] Now he explains that unless they are quiet and reserved, there is no purpose in their being veiled. For, if the image of God is man, and not women, and if she is subject to man on account of natural law, how much more in church should she be submissive through respect for him who is the representative of (Christ), who Himself is the head of man.[3] "For they are not permitted to speak, but should keep silence as the Law says." [4] What does the Law say? "Your desire shall be for your husband, and he shall rule over you." [5] This law is for

> the whole species. Therefore, Sarah called her husband Abraham her "lord." [6] Women are commanded to keep silent so as not to empty the prescription of this law, on account of which Sarah was subject to her husband, as has been said.
>
> Although she (the wife) is one flesh (with her husband), there are two reasons why she is, nevertheless, ordered to be submissive: [7] because she originated from man,[8] and because through her sin entered the world.[9] "If there is anything they desire to know, let them ask their husbands at home. For it is shameful for a woman to speak in church" [10] Since it would be contrary to the rule that in the house of God, who ordered them to be subject to their husbands, they ought to be silent, their pretending to speak about the law would be shameful.
>
> Women know, indeed, that in the house of God men have the first place and that women there ought to pray, keeping their tongues quiet, but opening their ears to learn how the mercy of God has triumphed through Christ over death, which established its reign through Eve. Since they are veiled to manifest their subjection, if they dare to speak in church it would be a shame, for in this action they would show their lack of humility! Since in the arrogance of women their husbands are also exposed to blame, this situation would be equally a cause of criticism for them.[11]

The same idea echoes through the commentary on 1 Timothy 2:11-14:

> "Let a woman learn in silence, with all submissiveness; a woman is not permitted to teach, or to have authority over men, but she is to keep silence." [12] Woman must not only dress modestly;[13] but (the Apostle) also prescribes that she be refused authority and that she be subject to man, so that as well by her dress as by her obedience she be under the power of man from whom she draws her origin. "For Adam was formed first, then Eve; and Adam was not deceived, but the woman was deceived and became a transgressor." [14] Since man was created first, Paul places him before woman; also since she was created after man and from him, he considers woman inferior. He adds yet another reason: it was not man that the devil deceived, but the woman, and man was duped by her intervening; therefore, no concessions should be made to her audacity, but instead since through her death entered the world, she ought to remain in submission.[15]

The key word of these two passages is "submission." Since they would undermine the submission they owe to man, women must not open their mouth in church. This subjection, imposed on woman in virtue of the natural law, is explicitly confirmed in Scripture; the word spoken to Eve, "He shall be your master," applies to the entire species. This word was spoken after original sin, for which woman carries a particularly heavy responsibility. But, from the moment of creation, since man was created first and he only is an image of God, she appears as inferior to man. Since woman had been brought forth from man, the first place belongs naturally to him and he alone may assume the exercise of authority.

And if woman must be submissive to all men, with all the more reason must she show respect to the bishop, who presides over the Christian assembly as the representative of Christ. According to the commentary of Ambrosiaster on 1 Corinthians 11, the veil which Paul prescribed for women to wear in the assembly "because of the angels" [16] is exactly the symbol of the respect which they owe to the bishop, since the "angels" here are the bishops, to whom this title was given in letters to the churches of the Apocalypse.[17]

A little earlier in the commentary on this same chapter 11, concerning verse 7b, "Woman is the glory of man," there is the same affirmation that the image of God is man, not woman:

> It is man who has been made to the image of God, not woman. The image of God in man consists in this, that a unique God has made a unique man; just as all things come from a unique God, all men come from a unique man; a unique visible man carries the image on earth of a unique invisible God; therefore, a unique God safeguards in a manifest way the authority of a unique principle in the person of a unique man, to the confusion of the devil, who, despising the unique God, pretended to usurp sovereignty and deity.[18]

This idea is developed at greater length in the twenty-first section of *Questions on the Old and the New Testament*, which is entirely devoted to the following problem: "What does the creation of man in the image and likeness of God signify; and, by implication, is woman created in the image of God?" The author answers the second question negatively and gives the prohibition against women teaching as a consequence of this fact:

> That man was made in the "image of God" means that a unique (God) made a unique (man); just as all things come from a unique God, likewise the whole human race comes from a unique man. The "likeness" consists in this, that just as the Son proceeds from the Father, likewise the woman proceeds from man, so that the authority of a unique principle may be safeguarded. But the Son is born of God the Father in an ineffable and incomprehensible manner, whereas woman was made from man, as we read, in a corporeal manner,[19] so that, through her, men might begin to be born. The Son of God himself was born so that, through his intervention, creation could be accomplished.
>
> The difference, therefore, consists of the following: from God, a God is born; from man, a woman; for in (God) all is simplicity. A simple being can be born only from a simple being, a spirit from a spirit, a God from a God. Therefore, man is the image of God; for it is written: "God created man in his own image, in the image of God he created him." [20] For this reason the Apostle says: "A man ought not to cover his head, since he is the image and glory of God." [21] On the other hand, he says: "Let her wear a veil." [22] Why? Because she is not the image of God. For this reason, the Apostle repeats: "I permit no woman to teach or to have authority over men." [23]

The same interpretation of the notion of the image of God reappeared in the same work in question 45, entitled simply, "Regarding the Image":

> Since, whether it is a question of the Father or the Son or the Holy Spirit, God is unique, the image of the three is unique. Therefore, according to the image of a unique God, a unique man was made. Man is the image of God in that, just as there is in heaven a unique God from whom all spiritual beings receive their existence, so also there is on earth a unique man from whom all others derive their existence according to the flesh.
>
> However, some think that it is in receiving domination that man was made in the image of God, since it is written: "Have dominion over the fish of the sea and over the birds of the air and over every living thing that moves upon the earth."[24] However, it is not to man only but also to woman that they are subjected, though it is obvious that the latter is not the image of God.
>
> Therefore, for two reasons this interpretation is ungrounded. On the one hand, it would appear that it is not to the Son that God said: "Let us make man in our image, after our likeness,"[25] but to heavenly Dominions of whom the Apostle speaks[26] — if it is true that man possesses the image of God in his domineering power. On the other hand, woman would have to be recognized as the image of God, which is absurd. When it is clear that she is subject to the power of man and that she has no authority whatever, how can we say then that woman is the image of God? Since she may be neither a teacher nor a witness nor a guarantee nor a judge, how much less can she exercise authority![27]

In this last text Ambrosiaster stood up resolutely against the interpretation which represents man as the image of God because of his dominion over the rest of creation. In this case, he said, since the animals and the whole of creation are subject to woman as well, it is apparent that woman as well as man is the image of God. But since she is subject to the power of man, this conclusion is absurd. Even if she shares with man domination over other creatures, this fundamental subordination of woman in the framework of social life precludes one's thinking of her as an image of God. To illustrate this social inferiority of woman, the author enumerated different incapacities which flaw her: she is forbidden to teach; she cannot be a witness, nor a warrant, nor a judge, and still less exercise leadership. In short, all functions or all acts implying any authority or responsibility are forbidden her.

It is in the name of this same imperative of submission, of which the law of silence is one expression, that Ambrosiaster discarded the possibility of a diaconate for a woman. For him, the precepts contained in 1 Timothy 3:11 refer to women in general, and there can be no question of deaconesses:

> "The women likewise must be serious, no slanderers, but temperate, faithful in all things." Since (the Apostle) ordered that one who is chosen to be a bishop, and similarly a deacon, must be holy, he wants the people to be in no way different from them, according to the Lord's imperative: "You shall be holy; for I the Lord your God am holy."[28] Therefore, since the Church must be pure, he wants even women, who seem inferior, to be without reproach.

> But the Cataphrygians, taking this opportunity to fall into error, under the pretext that Paul addresses women after deacons, maintain in their foolish audacity that deaconesses also should be ordained. They know, however, that the Apostle chose seven deacons.[29] When it is written that in the midst of the twelve Apostles there were holy women, is it possible that no woman was found capable at that moment? [30]
>
> As is the way with heretics, who try to build their opinions on words and not on the meaning of the law, they invoke the words of the Apostle to go against the thought of the Apostle. Whereas the latter orders a woman to keep silent in church,[31] they, on the contrary, demand for her the authority which the diaconate confers in the Church.[32]

According to Ambrosiaster, the women warned in this text to be serious, temperate, etc., are Christian women in general. The Apostle wished that, like the bishop and the deacon, the entire Christian people practice an exemplary life. Ambrosiaster heard, though, that because these women are mentioned immediately after deacons, some people believed that the text here refers to deaconesses. Such is actually the interpretation most frequently given by Eastern exegetes, who knew the institution of deaconesses in their own Churches.

But Ambrosiaster had an extremely poor knowledge of Eastern customs. For him, deaconesses were an invention of the Cataphrygians, i.e., of the Montanists, who inclined from their beginning to give women an inordinate place in their communities. Even though holy women were not lacking in the primitive Church, he answered that the Apostles chose only men as deacons. Since Paul imposed silence on women in church, on account of their inferiority to man and to the submission they owe to him, he could not think of conferring the diaconate on women; he taught, as already mentioned, that they should be denied all authority.[33] How could he then later admit their claiming for themselves the authority which the diaconate confers in the Church?

This last remark is no doubt surprising. But it must be remembered that the seven deacons at Rome enjoyed a prestige and considerable authority, superior even to that of presbyters, who were more numerous. It is a known fact that the dispute about the priesthood originated in the excessive pretensions of the Roman deacons. In Rome, deacons were not in any way subaltern ministers; they were invested with important responsibilities. In the mind of Ambrosiaster, therefore, a woman could not accede to this function without giving up the submission to which her "inferior" condition bound her.

These reasons might suggest that Ambrosiaster found difficulty with the text of Romans where Paul commended to his correspondents Phoebe, a "deaconess" of the church of Cenchreae.[34] It was no problem for him, however, because where the Greek read *diakonos*, his Latin text read *ministra*, and he understood this term in a non-technical sense: this woman ministered to the church of Cenchreae by helping numerous people.[35] A little further on, referring to Mary, Tryphaena, Tryphosa, and Persis, who "worked hard in the Lord,"[36] Ambrosiaster explained that "this work consisted of exhortation, service of the saints (*in ministerio sanctorum*), tribulation and poverty suffered for the cause of Christ."[37] Unless the commentator totally contradicted himself, the "service of the saints" must certainly be understood in the same sense as applied to Phoebe, and "exhortation" can refer, in the present case, only to words of comfort and encouragement said privately.

In his comment on 1 Timothy 5:3-16, Ambrosiaster dealt at length with widows. From reading these commentaries, it is obvious that in Rome at the end of the fourth century there was, just as in the communities mentioned in the Pastoral Epistles, a special group of widows, "widows of the Church" (*vidua Ecclesiae*[38]), whose names were written on the lists of the Church,[39] who were "received" (*suscipi*) by the Church.[40] These widows made a formal promise to renounce marriage (*profiteri, professio*[41]), to devote themselves totally to God, in a life of fasting and perpetual prayer, after the example of Anna, the daughter of Phanuel.[42] As a result, they enjoyed a particular consideration (*honorari, honor*[43]) and they received material aid from the Church.[44]

As in the beginning and at the time of the *Didascalia Apostolorum*, this institution occasioned some abuses. To prevent them, Ambrosiaster could do nothing better than paraphrase the rules already fixed by the author of the Pastoral Epistles. Among widows he admitted only those who had already fulfilled all their duties toward their neighbor and practiced good works.[45] For fear that they might break their promise[46] or take advantage of their position to visit the houses of the rich and live in idleness,[47] he excluded young widows. In this case they would do better to remarry than to live unfaithful to the ideals that ought to have been theirs.[48]

On the other hand, instead of reducing widows to a bare living because their advanced age no longer permitted them to take their part in domestic work, the well-to-do faithful were to take care of their kindred widows. Their failure to do so obliged the Church to support a considerable number of widows, and the congregation got tired of hearing about giving the necessary contribution.[49] The rule which prescribed admitting only widows married only once was poorly observed; there were maintained among the widows of the Church not only women who had had two or more husbands, but also others whose lives had been shameful. They were able to get in either by taking advantage of the negligence of those in charge or because they benefited from influential references.[50]

2. Pelagius

The commentaries of Pelagius on the Pauline texts relative to the ministry of women are less negative than those of Ambrosiaster. Instead they recall those of Chrysostom and of Theodore of Mopsuestia:

> "Women should keep silence in the churches. For they are not permitted to speak." [51] It is contrary to the order of nature and of the law that women speak in an assembly of men. But how can Paul say elsewhere that women must teach prudence and chastity? [52] They must teach their sex. Just as he points out the place where they must be silent, he permits them to speak elsewhere.
>
> "But they should be subordinate, as even the law says," [53] since man was created first,[54] and since Sarah called Abraham "lord." [55] "If there is anything they desire to know, let them ask their husbands at home. For it is shameful for a woman to speak in church." [56] So as not to seem to forbid them to be instructed, he enjoined them to do at home that which was not suitable to do in public.[57]

Because their doing so would be contrary to the order of nature and to the law of Moses, women are not permitted to speak in an assembly of men; according to Scripture, man was created first and Sarah called her husband "lord." But women are not absolutely forbidden to teach; nothing prevents them from instructing other women. Paul explicitly prescribes in his Epistle to Titus that older women teach younger ones prudence and chastity. In his commentary on the Epistle to Titus, Pelagius makes the same remark: " 'Let them teach chastity and prudence.' [58] He [Paul] permits them to teach, but women only, and that not in church but in private." [59] Furthermore, provided that she does so in private, a woman may even teach a man. Pelagius expressly indicated in his commentary on First Timothy: " 'I permit no woman to teach.' [60] He [Paul] does not permit her to teach in public; for it is in private that she must teach a son or a brother." [61] In the same sense again, concerning the rule that a woman must have her head veiled when she prays or prophesies, Pelagius specified that "to prophesy" must be understood "*in suo sexu et in domo*"—among persons of her own sex and at home.[62]

Pelagius knew about the existence of deaconesses in the East, and, in his opinion, they were the women exhorted by Paul in 1 Timothy 3:11,

> "The women likewise must be chaste." He commands that they must be chosen in the same way as deacons. One may deduce from this that he is talking about those who still today in the East are called "deaconesses." [63]

Significantly, to clarify his text Pelagius had to refer to the Eastern deaconesses; but if he had been acquainted with a similar institution in the West, this reference would have been superfluous. What were the duties of these Eastern deaconesses? Relevant here is the refernce in Romans to Phoebe:

> ". . . a deaconess of the church at Cenchrea." [64] Just as now, in the Eastern regions, one sees women deaconesses ministering to those of their sex at baptism or in the ministry of the word; for one finds women who have taught in private, like Priscilla, whose husband was called Aquila.[65]

In the first place Pelagius mentioned the role of deaconesses in the administration of baptism to women, which was actually their function most frequently attested to in the East. He suggested also that their service may have been a service of the word, similar to that which Priscilla performed — of course privately — at the side of her husband Aquila:

> "Greet Prisca and Aquila, my fellow workers in Christ Jesus." [66] One reads about them that they confirmed Apollos in the faith.[67] Paul calls them his helpers, because in the work of teaching to which he gave himself, they also aided him.[68]

On the other hand, Pelagius believed that deaconesses also are referred to in 1 Timothy 5:3-16 (the text about the true widows):

> "Let a widow be enrolled if she is not less than sixty years of age, having been the wife of one husband." [69] He wants deaconesses to be chosen in such a way that they might be for all examples of a good life. . . . "But refuse to enroll younger widows." [70] For fear that they might give a bad example rather than a good one, avoid placing them in charge of others in the ministry of the diaconate.[71]

Here again one finds the tendency to assimilate deaconesses to the Pauline widows, a tendency which has already appeared in two or three examples in the Greek sources.

9 THE LATIN CANONICAL SOURCES OF THE FOURTH TO THE SIXTH CENTURY

In the Latin canonical sources, after the end of the fourth century, we come across references to "deaconesses" rather often, but we soon discover that this dignity did not represent a true function, as in the East, but rather an honorary title of the "professed widows."

1. Texts of the Fourth Century

We know through the historian Sulpicius Severus that Priscillian propaganda was particularly successful with women.[1] Among the chief charges which motivated Priscillian's condemnation by the imperial power was the accusation that he "organized nightly meetings of dissolute women." [2] Among his followers who were executed at the same time that he was, there was a woman named Euchrotia, the wife of Rhetor Delphidius of Bordeaux, who was attached to Priscillian with her daughter Procula when he came from Spain to Aquitaine. It is not therefore surprising that the councils opposing Priscillianism enacted certain canons forbidding any usurpation of ecclesiastical functions by women. At the First Council of Saragossa in 380, this move was already evident:

> Let all believing women belonging to the Catholic Church keep away from lectures and meetings conducted by foreign men; neither let them

> join women who give lectures, neither to teach nor to be instructed, for such is the command of the Apostle.[3]

According to the historical context, the "foreign men" referred to in this canon are the Priscillianists. According to Augustine, in their meetings they proclaimed a twofold teaching: one founded on the canonical Scriptures for those who reasoned according to the flesh and another contained in apocryphal Scriptures for those who reasoned "according to the spirit and the truth of God." [4] It seems from this canon that since they were expressly forbidden to frequent the meetings of the sect, women were especially fond of this esoteric teaching. It seems also that women organized special meetings for women at which they made readings and gave speeches. When the council forbade this practice as contrary to the commands of the Apostle, it certainly was referring to 1 Corinthians 14:34-35 and Timothy 2:12.

The Priscillians were probably the first who, wanting to provide some of the women joining the sect with an official function, imported from the East the title of "deaconess," which until then was unknown in the West.[5] Consequently, in 394 (or 396), the Council of Nîmes (also an anti-Priscillian assembly) condemned the admission of women to the diaconate.

> It has been reported (*suggestum est*) by certain ones that, contrary to apostolic discipline and unknown until today, women seem to have been, one knows not where, admitted to the Levitical ministry. Since it is improper, the ecclesiastical rule does not permit this innovation. Made contrary to reason, an ordination of this type must be annulled, and care must be taken that no one in the future shows a similar audacity.[6]

It is not a question here of a "suggestion" made by some people, as more than one author has understood it,[7] but of "rumors" coming to the council; *suggerere* does not mean in this context "to suggest," but has the technical sense of "to give an account, to report." The events had already taken place and the council was passing judgment on them. Actually, these deeds were not absolutely established, and the reports about them were quite vague; women seemed to have been admitted to the ministry of the diaconate (*videantur adsumptae*), but where they were received remained unknown (*nescio quo loco*).

This lack of specification, however, did not prevent the council from reacting with the greatest vigor. Such an innovation, it declared, was contrary to the discipline which the Church had received from the Apostles. This, therefore, is a rule which, according to the Council, goes back to the beginning. They had no example that it had been violated up to their time. Therefore, the Fathers of this council had no knowledge at all of the existence of deaconesses in the East; they ignored even what Ambrosiaster seemed to know, i.e., that the Montanists fell into a similar error. They denounced this practice as "indecent" (*indecens*); this term recalls the one used in First Corinthians to stigmatize women who did not cover their heads or who dared to speak in church (*aischron*).[8] They also declared it contrary to reason. Paul, in like fashion, referred to the teachings of nature (*physis*) in connection with the veil of women.[9]

Since the Fathers of Nîmes were extremely uninformed regarding the abuse which they denounced (actually the words "deaconess" and "diaconate" were not used), one cannot expect from them a clear notion of the "Levitical ministry" to which women were admitted. Was it a question of a true feminine diaconate, i.e., of women exercising, as in the East, a liturgical and social ministry similar, at least in part, to that of deacons, and entitled to exercise this ministry by an ordination similar to that of their male colleagues, as in the *Apostolic Constitutions*? There is no evidence that such deaconesses ever existed in the West. Apparently, as was the case more than once when titles were borrowed from the East by the West (e.g., the Carolingian *chorepiscopus*), the Latins, not having a corresponding institution, took the term from the Greeks. Here "deaconess" was probably an honorary title, associated with a particular liturgical blessing rather than with a real function. In any case, the documents of the following centuries suggest this interpretation.

2. Texts of the Fifth Century

Fifty years later, in canon 25 of the First Council of Orange, "deaconesses" reappear — this time with the term itself: "Deaconesses are absolutely not to be ordained; and if there are still any of them, let them bow their head under the benediction which is given to the congregation."[10] The Fathers of Orange did not provide more precise information than the Fathers of Nîmes had. They apparently believed that deaconesses had been ordained in the past, yet they were uncertain whether any of them still existed. When the Council took place, this abuse seemed to be, therefore, neither really widespread nor truly actual.

Canon 25 categorically prohibited this practice. In no way, nor under any pretext, could deaconesses be ordained. The Fathers did not judge it necessary to justify this interdiction. The very brief text does not provide further information about what these deaconesses really were. The only detail that it gives is the fact that these deaconesses claimed a privileged position in the Church, since the canon ordered them to submit to the blessing given to the laity. The clergy, therefore, seem to have been granted a blessing apart from the laity, or, at least, not to have bowed during the benediction given to the congregation. Deaconesses followed the example of the clergy; but the Council forbade this custom and ordered them to act as the assembly did.

But even this prohibition does not tell exactly what these deaconesses were. Apparently they were widows who received at their profession a particularly solemn blessing, which, according to the West's extremely vague knowledge of Eastern ecclesiastical institutions, resembled the ordination of deaconesses in the East. This leads us to a better picture of what the institution of widows in the West was like at this peroid, and to see how the hypothesis presented above can be justified.

As already seen, Ambrosiaster laid emphasis on the ascetical features of the "real widow" of First Timothy, and in this context often employed the words *profiteri, professio*, which are also the technical terms designating the vow of perpetual virginity or of entrance into monastic life.[11] The condition of the widows of the Church was, consequently, considered more and more as parallel to that of virgins and monks; it was a "state of perfection," essentially characterized by continence, prayer, and mortification. In many of his epistles, St. Jerome extolled the ideal of the Christian widow,[12] and St. Ambrose wrote an entire treatise on widows.[13] The First Council of Toledo, in 400, associated the consecrated virgin (*professa*) and the widow, forbidding both of them, in the absence of the bishop or a priest, to recite the Office at home with a religious or with a servant.[14]

From this time on, a special dress distinguished widows. Although there was already some evidence for this distinctive dress in St. Jerome, it is not absolutely conclusive, for the texts in question simply suggest modest clothes, manifesting a resolution to renounce the attractions of the world, without necessarily pointing out a true "uniform" characteristic of widows.[15] On the other hand, in canon 26 of the First Council of Orange, it is clear that there is a question of a "uniform":

> The profession (*professionem*) to persevere in widowhood, made before the bishop in the *secretarium*, will be marked by the clothing of the widow imposed by the bishop. Anyone who abducts one of these women, or she who violates such an engagement, must be punished.[16]

From this text it appears that widows who decided to persevere in their state made this promise before the bishop. Since this ceremony did not take place in the church but in an adjacent room, the *secretarium*, which can be compared to the modern sacristy, it was not, properly speaking, a liturgical ceremony. This room, though, was not only a place where liturgical vestments were stored and where clerics vested, but it was also a place where the bishop and the priests received the faithful, settled conflicts, etc. The promise of the widow was made manifest by a particular dress (*vestis vidualis*) imposed on her by the bishop.

It is probable that the juxtaposition of canon 26 of Orange with canon 25 of the same council, which forbade the ordination of deaconesses, is not accidental, but that the two canons form a logical sequence and clarify each other. Obviously, as is frequently the case in such documents, the canons of the First Council of Orange were not arranged in an indifferent order, but instead they were grouped more or less according to the subject they treated. Thus, canons 1 and 2 deal with the chrismation and the post-baptismal "blessing," which were equivalent to the present sacrament of confirmation; canons 3 and 4, with penance; canons 5 and 6, with particular privileges of the churches; canon 7 and 10, with the necessary respect that bishops have for the jurisdiction belonging to their colleagues over their subjects and their territories; canons 11 and 15, with the administration of the sacraments to the abnormal and possessed; canons 17 to 19, with catechumens; and canons 21 to 24, with clerical continence. Because of this ordering, one may assume that canons 25 and 26 are logically connected and that they can, therefore, be interpreted in the following way: deaconesses could not be ordained; the profession of widowhood had to be made in the *secretarium*, and it had to be uniquely marked by the imposition of the widow's garment. Widows did not receive a type of ordination in church which would have placed them apart from the laity and exempted them from having to submit to the blessing given to the assembly.

Widows, called this time "professed widows" (*professas viduas*), appear in a canonical collection compiled in Gaul during the second half of the fifth century and presented as the "Second Council of Arles." Canon 46 of this collection, which calls to mind the second part of canon 26 of Orange, prescribed that "professed widows" who eventually complied with their ravishers had to be punished along with them.[17]

Widows appear again in the *Statuta Ecclesiae antiqua*, the work of a priest, Gennadius of Marseilles (died *ca.* 500), who used the *Apostolic Constitutions* as his chief source.[18] Like the *Constitutions*, more than once the *Statuta* associate widows with consecrated virgins, whom they call *sanctimoniales*.[19] Since, in the West as well as in the East, these two sacred engagements demanded a similar program of spiritual life, this linking is, indeed, in keeping with the comparison of these two *professiones*. Widows had a right to benefit from the material assistance of the Church; this right was also granted to young widows, at least if they were in poor health.[20] This concern recalls that the *Constitutions*, following the *Didascalia*, were already particularly interested in young widows.[21] If, to meet the demands of life, young widows or consecrated virgins were forced to suffer intimacies with members of the clergy,[22] the *Statuta* made the bishop or the priest in charge of a parish responsible for these women. The bishop, however, did not have to care directly for widows, orphans, or strangers; he could entrust the archpriest or the archdeacon with this mission.[23] In return, the widows assisted by the Church had to support it with their prayers and other good works.[24] The

Constitutions especially insisted that widows had the obligation of praying for their benefactors and for the entire Church.[25]

Other than that, following the *Constitutions*, the *Statuta* tried to prevent all kinds of abusive zeal on the part of women. Canon 37 declared that "a woman, as learned and as holy as she might be, should not be bold enough to instruct men in the assembly."[26] The *Constitutions* had already voiced this prohibition,[27] which echoed the *Didascalia* and the Pauline epistles.[28] In addition, "a woman must not have the audacity to baptize."[29] This prohibition is also found in the *Didascalia* and is developed in greater length in the *Constitutions*.[30] This interdict did not prevent widows and consecrated virgins from being chosen to assist women at baptism (*ad ministerium baptizandarum mulierum*). Their functions partially paralleled those the *Didascalia* assigned to deaconesses in the same circumstances:[31] they had to instruct women how to answer the questions asked of them in the celebration of baptism and how to live after receiving this sacrament; but no explicit mention was made concerning their intervening in the sacrament itself.[32]

Canons 25 and 26 of Orange seem to lead to the conclusion that occasionally in Gaul attempts were made to solemnize the profession of widows by conferring on them some sort of diaconal ordination. There is no evidence that this practice was ever introduced elsewhere. Apparently in Italy some people sought the same result by other means. The similarity between the situation of widows and that of virgins, which, as shown above, became more and more marked in details of vocabulary and in the canonical prescriptions themselves, suggested a solemn consecration of widows, like that of virgins, by the imposition of the veil and a *benedictio* of the bishop. We know this from a letter to the Italian bishops in which Pope Gelasius formally condemned this practice.[33]

Another abuse against which the Pope protested in the same letter was that, with the explicit agreement of some bishops and the silent complicity of others who neglected to denounce this situation, "women discharged altar service" and "performed all the other things which had been assigned to the ministry of men only." The Pope did not give any other details but hastened to emphasize in impressive terms the enormity of this fault.[34] In the absence of precise information, it is difficult to form an idea of the situation which Pope Gelasius opposed. Since this geographic region had always been closely connected with the East, did the problem concern deaconesses? But the text spoke of women who "serve at the altar," a function which Eastern deaconesses never performed. And the following sentence had an even broader meaning: these women "performed all the other things which had been assigned to the ministry of men only." It is regrettable that more details regarding this question are not available.

3. Texts of the Sixth Century

If it were not for the distance of time and especially of place, there would be a temptation to compare the letter of Pope Gelasius to the bishops of southern Italy with the one which three bishops of northern Gaul, Licinius of Tours, Melanius of Rennes, and Eustochius of Angers, addressed to the Breton priests Lovocatus and Catihernus in 511.[35] Visiting the countryside, these priests celebrated Mass in the cabins of peasants on *tabulae* made especially for that purpose, which they carried with them wherever they went. They were assisted in the celebration of the Holy Sacrifice by women whom they called *conhospitae*, i.e., women sharing the life of a man vowed to continence without having carnal relations with him.

Ecclesiastical authorities had always looked on this practice with mistrust. The third canon of Nicaea had expressly forbidden clerics to keep under their roof a woman who was not a close relative, and many councils since then renewed this decree. When the bishops notified the Breton priests to separate themselves from their women assistants, the authors of the present epistle made allusion to this decree. But their case was even worse — these women assisted the priests in the celebration of the Eucharist and, in their presence, took the chalice in hand and distributed the Blood of Christ to the people.

This practice provoked the bishops to the height of indignation. They saw in it a resurgence of a sect formerly condemned in the East; the Pepodian sect, named after Pepodius, its founder, had not until then been noticed in Gaul. Ecclesiastical history knows of no person by this name, which is probably a corruption of Pepuza, the name of a city of Phrygia which had been one of the cradles of Montanism; furthermore, in some documents the Montanists are called *Pepuzitae*,[36] after the name of this city. The Gallic bishops vaguely knew that an Eastern sect had earlier been condemned for granting women an abusive importance in the Church; regarding this sect, they had heard or read names like *Pepuza* and *Pepuzitae*, distorted into *Pepodius* and *Pepodianus*. Consequently, what had been the name of a city became in their minds the name of a man.

Since the Montanists granted women a choice place in their sect, there is some foundation for the comparison by the bishops of Gaul.[37] As for the rest, these bishops did not judge it useful to justify their condemnation otherwise. They consider this trend an innovation in Gaul, an unprecedented superstition, an illicit ministry, which soiled the divine sacraments; they needed no more explicit explanation to order these practices to cease without delay.

The canons of the Gallic councils of the sixth century confirm the interpretation suggested above for canons 25 and 26 of the First Council of Orange. They also prove that the interdiction formulated at Orange had not been operative. This lack of enforcement is clearly evident in canon 21 of the Council of Epaon, which assembled the bishops of the Burgundian kingdom in 517:

> We completely suppress throughout our territory the consecration of those widows who are often called "deaconesses"; if they wish to convert, only penitential benediction may be conferred on them.[38]

This statement shows that at that time widows were still consecrated with a solemn rite which gave them a right to the title of "deaconesses." This rite was certainly similar to what canon 25 of Orange signified by the term "to ordain" (*ordinare*). The bishops wanted this practice to disappear completely from their territory. Widows who wished "to convert," i.e., according to the meaning of this term at that time, to embrace the ascetic life, should receive only the blessing given to penitents at their entrance into repentance. Frequently in fifth-century Gaul, Christians who wished to subject themselves freely to the harsh demands imposed on "public" penitents asked for a laying on of hands similar to the one given to the latter.[39] It was only this imposition of hands that widows were allowed to receive.

The Second Council of Orleans, in 533, handled a new question concerning women who had received a diaconal ordination:

> Women who, in spite of its interdiction by the canons, have before this time received the benediction of the diaconate must, if it is proven that they indulged again in marriage, be excluded from communion. But if, having been admonished by the bishop, they admit their fault and put an end to this kind of concubinage, after doing penance, they may recover the grace of communion.[40] Besides, it has been decided that, henceforth, no woman may any longer receive diaconal benediction due to the frailty of her sex.[41]

Once more, the issue involved widows, as a word of the text indicates: "If . . . they indulged *again* (*iterum*) in marriage." In spite of the prohibition of the canons — the only ones known on this subject are those of Orange and of Epaon mentioned above — there again were widows who had received the "benediction of diaconate" (*benedictionem diaconatus*). The terms *benedictio* and *consecratio*, and their corresponding verbs, appear frequently as synonyms of *ordinatio* and *ordinare* in texts of this period.

Once more, therefore, the same kind of rite is pointed out, but the perspective seems different from that of the former councils. At Orange and at Epaon, the rite itself appeared incongruous to the bishops. But the Fathers of these councils did not oppose the engagement sanctioned by the rite; they wished only that it be sanctioned in a different way. At Orléans, on the contrary, the rite seemed to be opposed as implying an engagement of a particular gravity, which, owing to the frailty of womankind, they judged imprudent to consecrate. No other rite was suggested as a substitute, and apparently they refused purely and simply to recognize a commitment of this kind. It must be remembered that since "conversion" was in principle an ideal way of life practiced in the world, not in a convent, it required a will more strongly tempered than that needed for monastic life, and that since this was a period when the general morality was on the downgrade, the Church was reluctant to endorse such a dangerous engagement. In the years that followed, however, "deaconesses" of one kind or another appeared. Helaria, St. Remi's daughter, possessed this title.[42] When St. Radegunda, the wife of King Chlothar I, renounced conjugal life, St. Médard, bishop of Noyon, consecrated her a deaconess by a laying on of the hand (*manu superposita consecravit diaconam*).[43]

At the Second Council of Tours, in 567, the question was raised why a widow who had not received the benediction (*quae benedicta non fuit*) could not contract marriage. The answer was that the canonical texts never mentioned a benediction for the widow "because the engagement alone had to suffice for her" (*quia solus propositus illi sufficere debet*). Canon 21 of Epaon and canon 46 of the pseudo-Council of Arles were cited in support of this.[44] Actually, the Third Council of Orléans, in 538, spoke only of *viduae in proposito manentes* and excommunicated those who failed in this duty.[45] The same penalty was indicated by the Fifth Council of Orléans, in 549; by the Second Council of Tours, in 567; and by the Second Council of Paris, between 556 and 573.[46] In these documents, reminiscent of canon 26 of the First Council of Orange, profession was followed by the imposition of a distinctive habit. In the last four texts cited, the position of widows was assimilated in all points with that of consecrated virgins.

CONCLUSION

From the beginnings of Christianity, women assumed an important role and enjoyed a place of choice in the Christian community. Paul praised several women who assisted him in his apostolic works. Women also possessed the charism of prophecy. There is no evidence, however, that they exercised leadership roles in the community. Even though several women followed Jesus from the onset of his ministry in Galilee and figured among the privileged witnesses of his resurrection, no women appeared among the Twelve or even among the other apostles. As Epiphanius of Salamis pointed out, the successors of the Apostles were all men, and in the Catholic Church there have never been women presbyters. The only duty with which women have been invested is the diaconate, but two centuries had to pass before the female diaconate took a distinct shape.

Before the *Didascalia Apostolorum*, there were only three references to women "ministers," but the brevity of these allusions and some ambiguity in their meaning make it difficult to affirm that a regular diaconate of women existed in the first two centuries. The author of the *Didascalia* himself emphasized the usefulness of a ministry of deaconesses in a way which suggests that it was an innovation. He assigned to deaconesses two tasks: caring for sick women and assisting at the baptism of women.

From the fourth century on, references to deaconesses multiplied in the East, except in Egypt, where no traces of them appear. To the two tasks already mentioned, the *Apostolic Constitutions* added welcoming women at the doors of the church and acting as an intermediary between women and male members of the hierarchy; but this document is the only one that mentions these new duties, and the first two tasks, especially assistance at the baptism of women, are cited far more often.

In the beginning of the fourth century, deaconesses were certainly not considered part of the clergy, and such a position seems still to have been the case in the canons of St. Basil. But from the end of the fourth century, they were definitely counted among the clergy. Like clerics, with a laying on of hands (*cheirotonia*), they received ordination under precise juridical conditions. They had to be virgins or widows of one husband; and, although Epiphanius also admitted women who had practiced continency in marriage, there is no reference to this exception in later documents. A preliminary investigation must have established their moral integrity. Finally, a minimum age was required, which after much hesitation was set at forty; but this condition, as some famous examples prove, was not always observed in practice.

Furthermore, after their ordination, deaconesses were under the same rules regarding marriage as major clerics: Basil and Epiphanius, who still admitted married women, required perfect continence of them. Later, deaconesses, virgins, and widows were sternly forbidden to remarry, and every transgression of this rule, the same as any carnal sin, was punished with the utmost rigor. The institution of the feminine diaconate, as it has been briefly described, remained a characteristic feature of the East. Although they diminished and limited the feminine diaconate to a mere dignity or an honorific title, the attempts to introduce this practice in the West in the fourth and fifth centuries were not successful.

Up to the end of the nineteenth century, historians of the early Church often identified deaconesses and widows, as if these two different titles corresponded, for those who held them, to the same function. Even if they were assimilated in some marginal documents, such as the Theodosian Code or the commentaries of a Latin writer like Pelagius, since deaconesses and widows obviously corresponded to quite different institutions, one can only wonder, after a close study of all the evidence, at the persistence of such an error.

Widowhood was not a function but a state of life, sublimated within the framework of a spiritual ideal and organized for older widows, under the form of an "order of widows" (*chērikon, viduatus*), which was a kind of religious order or, more exactly what we would today call a secular institute. Except in Tertullian and in the particular case of the *Testamentum Domini*, widows do not seem to have belonged to the clergy. Since the widows in the latter source were practically the equivalent of the deaconesses of the *Apostolic Constitutions*, the *Testamentum* is excluded from the general considerations which follow. Concerning the *Testamentum*, a document representative of the Syrian Monophysite Church at the end of the fifth century, the reader is referred to the detailed analysis of it earlier in this study.

Widows were not "ordained," but simply "enrolled" or "established"; several documents make an explicit difference between "to ordain" and "to establish," a distinction which the *Apostolic Tradition* justifies by the fact that the widow had no liturgical service. The chief condition given for the admission of a widow was that she had to have been married only once; and, except for Theodore of Mopsuestia and Theodoret of Cyrus, who interpreted "the wife of one husband" in the sense of the "wife who has never betrayed conjugal faith," this condition was required in all the documents. The chief demand, which no document compromised, was the prohibition against remarriage.

The vow of perpetual continence was truly the basic ideal of Christian widowhood; consequently, it illumines the other conditions required for the admission of a widow: an advanced age (generally sixty years, but the rule was, nonetheless, transgressed sometimes), a time of probation after the death of her husband, etc.. These conditions explain why widows, after serving as a paradigm for virgins (second-century documents refer to "virgins called widows" and "virgins admitted among the widows") were often associated later on with virgins, because they fulfilled, though imperfectly, the ideal of Christian continence incarnated at its height in virgins.

After the duty of continence, the duty of prayer was demanded of widows with the greatest insistence. Although prayer is, indeed, an obligation common to all Christians, it was imposed on widows in a particular way. The vigils and fasts mentioned in the *Apostolic Constitutions* also reveal the outline of an ideal whose ascetic character appeared stronger and stronger toward the end of the fourth century. At this moment, the rise of monastic life seems to have occasioned the progressive disappearance of the order of widows, and the ideal which they had lived in the world was then lived by preference in conventual settings.

The *Didascalia* attached a particular value to the prayer and fasting of a widow, accompanied by imposition of hands, at the bedside of the sick. This, however, was not the exercise of a function, but a charismatic type of intervention which, because of the holiness of their life, was recognized as their due privilege. Neither must one see the exercise of a function in the counsels and exhortations which the widows, as elder women in general, were urged to impart to younger ones; this was nothing but a very human and natural response. The same caution is true for the care of the sick which was entrusted to the third widow of the *Ecclesiastical Canons of the Apostles* and to widows in general in the *Canons of Hippolytus.* And, since these texts are Egyptian, and Egypt ignored the ministry of deaconesses, it is obvious that this indispensable charitable activity had to be accomplished by someone, and preferably by elderly women such as widows, who had been relieved of the charge of a family. All these responsibilities were not enough to constitute a function properly speaking, and the duties which they may have eventually assumed did not define widows. Finally, it appears quite clearly that the feminine diaconate was essentially a function, whereas widowhood was a way of life with a canonical status.

It is obvious, therefore, that the only function exercised by women in the Church is the diaconate. Women bishops or women priests have never been known in the Catholic Church. Neither is there any evidence of women's exercising an official ministry of teaching. There have been prophetesses among Catholics, but only a small number; outside of those mentioned in the New Testament, Eusebius of Caesarea knew of only Ammia of Philadelphia in the second century. Women have not baptized, except perhaps in case of necessity, nor offered the Eucharist. Only in heretical sects more or less marginal to the Church, especially among the Montanists, have women taught, baptized, consecrated the Eucharist, and functioned as bishops and presbyters. Obviously, this intrusion of women in ecclesiastical functions among heretics, and all the abuses following from it—at least the fact that such a zeal was put to the service of heterodox doctrines—did not encourage the Church to entrust similar functions to women and contributed in part to a certain distrust of women.

It does not seem, however, that the concern of the Catholic Church to distinguish herself from heresy was the determining reason why she believed in the necessity of excluding women from public teaching and priestly office. Neither does it seem logical to incriminate, at least at first glance, the influence of the Greco-Roman world, where women, in fact, had access to many priestly offices, some of which were even exclusively reserved for them. The *Apostolic Constitutions* present the ordination of priestesses as a characteristic aberration of pagan cults. The fundamental arguments advanced by theologians of the early Church to justify this interdiction against women are the scriptural argument and the argument from tradition. Never in the Jewish-Christian economy, Epiphanius observed, had women been admitted to the priesthood, and the sacrifices had always been offered by men. And above all, even though there were among his followers women not less worthy than men to exercise these functions, Jesus never appointed women to teach, to baptize, or to offer the Eucharist.

Jesus, therefore, had made a deliberate choice in this matter, a choice which the early Church did not believe it had the power to question. In regard to the prohibition against teaching, the famous verse of First Corinthians, "The women should keep silence in the churches" (14:34), whose authenticity was not suspected at that time, though it seems to have been an interpolation of Jewish-Christian origin, exercised a determining influence. Undoubtedly, in this verse the notion of "submission," inherited from the laws of the Old Testament, played an important role. Also, the considerations which supported the traditional argument in the ancient writers often reflect an anthropology which could not be unanimously admitted today. To these men, who had an extremely vivid sense of the domineering power of the orator over his audience and of the superiority of the teacher over his disciples, it was unbecoming for a woman to teach publicly.

Analogously, the priesthood, since it was a ministry of salvation, in their opinion implied mental superiority in the one exercising the ministry over those for whom it is exercised, and for this reason they felt it right, as the *Ecclesiastical Canons of the Apostles* says, that "the weak should be saved by the strong," i.e., woman by man, and not the reverse. Underlying this line of argument, and more than once explicitly affirmed, is the idea of the natural superiority or primacy of man over woman, which appears frequently and approvingly in the quoted biblical verses, such as Genesis: "Your desire shall be for your husband, and he shall rule over you," and St. Paul: "The head of a woman is her husband," whose meaning was probably forced to make it, as in the *Apostolic Constitutions*, the decisive slogan in this matter. To this background one should add — details no doubt, but relevant details nonetheless — unkind references to the "female race" which present it as weak, fickle, lightheaded, of mediocre intelligence, a chosen instrument of the devil in his desire to establish his reign in the world.

As a conclusion, what can one make of all of this? From a doctrinal point of view, since for several centuries a large portion of the Church followed this practice without raising a theoretical problem, it is perfectly conceivable to confer on women a diaconal type of ministry. Women deacons then receive a true ordination, with nothing distinguishing it formally from the ordination of their male colleagues. Their functions, however, were less extensive and less important, and the most regularly attested one, which was their assistance at the baptism of women for reasons of decency, has no reason to exist today. Consequently, unless it were given an object different from the ancient female diaconate, it is not certain that the restoration of the feminine diaconate today would make much sense.

About the admission of women to the priestly ministry, the conclusion is less clear. The main obstacle is that, even though there were among Jesus' disciples women who, according to all evidence, possessed the qualities needed to accomplish this mission, he did not mandate women to preach the gospel with apostolic authority. It is not out of place, though, to ask whether the Jewish mentality at that period was ready to listen to the preaching of a woman. Rabbinical tradition generally manifested a profound contempt for woman and stipulated more than once that her witness could not be received. If this was already the common opinion at the time of Jesus, would it have been wise to choose women as official witnesses of the Resurrection? In renouncing this option, did Christ wish expressly to forbid women access to the ministries which sought to carry on in the post-apostolic Church the work of the Apostles? This is, in any case, the way the tradition of the early

Church has understood it. In her refusal to admit women to teach publicly and to exercise priestly functions, the Church is guided essentially, according to her explicit declarations, by her desire to be faithful to the example of Jesus.

It must be conceded, however, if some provisional generalizations may be admitted, that the status women had in the Greco-Roman world ought to cause Christian scholars to question whether the absence of women among the ministers of the primitive community was not a fact tied up with time and place, and whether it implied, without a possibility of doubt, a rule binding in a definitive way the Church of all times. Certainly, the condition of women seems generally to have been better in the Greco-Roman milieu where the Church spread during the first centuries than in the Church's native Palestine. Particularly, in the Greco-Roman world there were women priests, which was not the case in the Old Testament. But the ministry of the apostles, bishops, and presbyters was not at first considered a priestly office; and when the title "priest" was given to them, it was still true that their ministry was more than a priesthood, or, if one prefers, that their priesthood was more inclusive than the purely cultural one of the pagans; it also included — and perhaps first of all — the direction of the community and the task of teaching.

Therefore, one may ask once more whether the Fathers, sharing in a civilization which accorded women little place in the exercise of public duties, could envision with sufficient freedom of spirit the possibility of admitting women to a priestly ministry. These are the reasons why, in the eyes of many, the scriptural argument, as well as the traditional one, in the present state of their elaboration, are not sufficient to invalidate the issue of women priests and require, instead, to be put to good scholarly use to solve the prejudiced issues implicit in them.

To answer, first, the question about the attitude of Jesus himself, and second, the question, depending on the first, about the discipline of the early Church, requires, as the Introduction of this work points out, a serious study of the image and the juridical status of woman in the different milieus of ancient society where the Church was born and developed. Then a parallel study needs to be devoted to the understanding of woman herself in the primitive Church. This is certainly an enterprise of great breadth, but without it, it is impossible to respond on solid ground to the question of women priests.

Meanwhile, I will be happy if the present study has at least presented the facts clearly, indicated precisely how the problem should be formulated, and pointed the research in the right direction. I also hope that my book suggests some prudence and conveys some solicitude for the nuances of the problem to those whose zeal or unawareness of the complexity of the problems involved may sometimes lead them too quickly, either in one direction or the other, to make peremptory statements which cannot be in the kindest sense, anything but premature, because not sufficiently substantiated.

APPENDIX

The Ordination of Deaconesses According to the *Apostolic Constitutions**

In a note on my book *Le ministère des femmes dans l'Église ancienne*, M. Martimort makes some remarks which I consider require an answer, concerning the ordination of deaconesses in the *Apostolic Constitutions*.[1] I wrote that, according to this text, deaconesses received "an ordination similar to that of their male colleagues" (p. 113). According to M. Martimort, if an abstraction is made from a later evolution, the reality is different. First, one must be aware, he says, that the *Apostolic Constitutions* are a private compilation springing from a milieu of questionable orthodoxy, that this compilation represents only imperfectly the Syrian discipline, and that its liturgical formularies did not come from the actual practice of a Church.

Although these statements are true, they do not mean that everything was fabricated in this kind of writing. On the contrary, an apocryphal, pseudo-apostolic book, to be accepted, could not depart far from contemporaneous usage, which the ancient mind-set, lacking a historical perspective, readily likened, even in details, to the apostolic tradition; if he did not want to be identified, the author could include his own notions only through discreet touches. The heterodoxy of the compiler of the *Constitutions* pertains to Trinitarian and Christological doctrine, not to the structure of the ecclesiastical institution or to sacramental theology. Therefore, because of the apocryphal and "hardly orthodox" character of the book, everything pertaining to these two latter areas cannot be considered *a priori* as suspect. In-

*Translated from an article which appeared in *Mélanges de science religieuse*, Vol. 31, No. 1 (March, 1974), pp. 41–45.

deed, a liturgical formula affirming, more or less openly, the inferiority of the Word to the Father probably was recast or completely forged by the pseudepigraphist. But this type of alteration does not mean that he invented an entirely new liturgy and an absolutely new law for the Church.

When it is necessary to distinguish more precisely and more rigorously between fictional matter and historical truth, one cannot reasonably, M. Martimort seems to suggest, "make an abstraction from a later evolution." But, in my opinion, it is this evolution which, in the absence of contemporaneous testimonies, provides the major criterion for separating the true from the false. When one has to evaluate the historicity of a practice attested to by a pseudepigraphist, such as the author of the *Apostolic Constitutions*, three circumstances ought to be considered. First, whether the practice is attested to by other contemporary documents in the same milieu; in this case, there is no problem — the pseudepigraphist simply confirms these attestations. Second, whether there is any trace of the practice in question in either contemporary testimonies or later tradition; in this case, even if this practice had nothing to do with the special ideas of the pseudepigraphist, his testimony must be considered insufficient and unreliable. Third, whether the practice mentioned is not attested to by other contemporary sources but is found in later tradition; in this case, if one can discard the hypothesis of a direct influence of the pseudepigraphist on this later tradition, one must acknowledge that the pseudepigraphist witnesses to the fact that this practice was already in existence in his own time. Otherwise beings are multiplied without reason: i.e., to maintain, on the one hand, that this practice was successively and independently invented by the pseudepigraphist, and moreover, was introduced into actual use by custom or a legitimate authority. Such a coincidence is too improbable to be proposed as a rule of interpretation; it could be admitted on the contrary, only after demonstration in a particular case.

Take an example. The Byzantine prayerbooks of the Middle Ages, from the period of the tenth–eleventh centuries, mention as the rite for the ordination of a subdeacon the tradition of the ewer together with the pitcher and towel. Since in the period where one finds it clearly attested to, the washing of the hands had already disappeared from the eucharistic liturgy, the origin of this rite was certainly very old. The Barberini prayerbook (eighth century), which says that the subdeacon "gives to wash" to the pontiff who ordained him, presupposes that these objects were delivered to him or that he took them in his hands. But is it possible to go farther back? Yes, for the *Statuta Ecclesiae antiquae* (southern Gaul at the end of the fifth century) prescribe for the ordination of the subdeacon a twofold rite: the tradition of the paten and chalice, which was the ancient Roman rite, then the tradition of the pitcher, ewer, and towel.

Now, one knows that the author of the *Statuta* used Eastern sources. He certainly did not invent this rite of the tradition of the pitcher, ewer, and towel, which was completely foreign to Western tradition; he found it in his Eastern sources. Therefore, although the first direct attestation of the ritual of the pitcher, ewer, and towel for the ordination of the subdeacon is found only in the East in the tenth century, the *Statuta Ecclesiae antiquae* witness to the use of this rite already at the end of the fifth century.

Similarly, if the rite of ordination for deaconesses present in the Barberini prayerbook (eighth century) and in later Byzantine ones contains all the features of a sacramental ordination, analagous to that of the male deacons; and if the Byzantine sources of the fifth and sixth centuries attest that their status was analogous to that of the deacons, and, particularly, if they use the same word to designate the two ordinations; and if the examination of the *Apostolic Constitutions*, at the end of the fourth century, suggests already the same conclusions, it seems logical to me, even if the only witness to this situation at that time was a "compilation of a private character coming from a milieu of questionable orthodoxy," to conclude that the situation described by the documents from the fifth century on went back at least to the end of the fourth century.

Actually, the apochryphal character of the *Apostolic Constitutions* had been recognized rather early by the Byzantine theologians, and it is not conceivable that the ordination of deaconesses, which before would have been non-sacramental, would have been transformed into a sacramental ordination on the basis of this text. Therefore, it had to be considered sacramental before appearing as such in the authentic liturgical sources, and the testimony of the *Constitutions* on this point corresponds to the practice and to the mentality of the time in which this apochryphal book was written.

But is the ordination of deaconesses presented as sacramental in the *Apostolic Constitutions*? M. Martimort contests this point also. Certainly, he says, the *Constitutions* prescribe for the ordination of deaconesses the laying on of hands by the bishop, and the prayer of ordination asks on behalf of the elected women a gift of the Holy Spirit. But one must consider the totality of the rites of ordination in the *Constitutions*, in comparison with the corresponding sections of the *Apostolic Tradition* of which they are a reworking. One then notices that the subdeacons and readers were also ordained, according to the *Constitutions*, by the laying on of hands by the bishop, who called down a gift of the Holy Spirit upon them. In the mind of the compiler of the *Constitutions*, all ordinations, without exception, therefore, were sacramental — not only that of deaconesses but also that of subdeacons and readers.

"On this point," M. Martimort comments, "and according to the concepts of our modern theology, the *Apostolic Constitutions* show a decadence in regard to the firm principles of the *Apostolic Tradition* of Hippolytus, who clearly distinguished the three ordinations which we consider sacramental and which included the laying on of hands, from the institution of the inferior categories, which were refused even the vocabulary of ordination."

I believe that "the concepts of our modern theology" have nothing to do with determining how the *Apostolic Constitutions* regarded the ordination of deaconesses. One cannot say that because our theology is reluctant to accept this ordination as sacramental, the same as that of the male deacons, the *Apostolic Constitutions* could not consider it such. And I will not say, in the name of "the concepts of our modern theology," that the *Constitutions* "show a decadence in regard to the firm principles of the *Apostolic Tradition* of Hippolytus." But I will say that they strictly applied the principle, formulated by Hippolytus concerning widows, that those who accomplish a liturgical service ought to receive ordination. According to the author of the *Constitutions*, such was the case of the deaconess, the subdeacon, and the reader. For this reason he prescribed that they, like the bishop, the priest, and the deacon, be ordained by the imposition of hands.

M. Martimort states that the *Constitutions* preserved at least a trace of the distinction introduced by Hippolytus between the functions for which people were "ordained" (*cheirotonein*) and those for which they were only "appointed" (*kathistasthai*); the three ordinations of the bishop, priest, and deacons were announced by the word *cheirotonein* or *cheirotonia*, whereas these words do not appear in the beginning of the ritual for the ordination of deaconesses, subdeacons, and readers. However, since it did not prevent the author of the *Constitutions* from using the term *cheirotonein* later on for the subdeacon, he concedes that it is "an extremely weak point."

When I made the comparative analysis required for this research, the detail noted by M. Martimort did not escape my attention. I had also noticed the contradiction between the apparent refusal to use the term *cheirotonia* in the beginning of chapters 19, 21, and 22 and the fact that the author did not hesitate, however, to use the term *cheirotonein* in the body of one of these chapters. Moreover, it cannot be contested that the rite for the ordination of deaconesses, subdeacons, and readers consisted actually of the laying on of hands. At this time an attentive analysis of the critical apparatus led me to conclude that the formulas in question *peri de cheirotonias presbyterōn* and others were wrongly inserted by Funk in the current text, and that in fact, these titles had been introduced later on into part of the mansucript tradition. Whatever their interest, they do not provide information concerning the thought of the compiler of the *Constitutions*. For this reason I did not take account of them.

In conclusion, M. Martimort writes that "if we recognize the ordination of a deaconess according to the *Apostolic Constitutions* as a sacramental act in the modern sense of the term, the consequence would be that we must equally affirm the ordination of the subdeacons and readers as such." I subscribe to this affirmation without hesitation. Since, it is evident that for him the ordination of subdeacons and especially of readers was obviously not sacramental, I realize that in M. Martimort's opinion this is an argument against the sacramental character of the ordination of deaconesses in the *Constitutions.*

But these are "the concepts of our modern theology." If there is no proof that the author of the *Constitutions* himself made a distinction between the various rites of ordination, one cannot ascribe to him the concepts of our modern theology. We have already noted that he did not restrict the use of *cheirotonein* to the first three ordinations.

M. Martimort further notes three more pecularities which distinguish the ordination of deaconesses from that of deacons. First, the prayer for the ordination of the deaconess, unlike that of the deacon, which mentions St. Stephen, "does not offer any paradigm referring the deaconess to an institution of the New Testament, nor a properly liturgical ministry." Actually, all the prayers of the *Constitutions* refer almost exclusively to paradigms from the Old Testament. There is a passing allusion to the Apostles in the prayer for the ordination of the bishop, but the "paradigms," strictly speaking, are the sacrificers of the Old Testament. There is no allusion to people of the New Testament in the prayer for the ordination of a presbyter, but only to the elders elected by Moses as his assistants in the government of the Chosen People. Because of the *per transennam* mention of the apostles, ought one to infer that the ordination of the bishop was sacramental, and that that of a presbyter was not? The notion of "a properly liturgical ministry" demands at least more precision. Can the reading of the Gospel by a deacon be a ministry properly liturgical, but not that of prophetic writings by a reader? Can the oil of exorcism placed on a man by a deacon be properly liturgical, but not the same unction placed on a woman by a deaconess?

M. Martimort notes, moreover, that the prayer for the ordination of a deaconess, unlike that of a deacon, does not point to the possibility of acceding to a higher degree in the hierarchy, but since the *Constitutions* strongly reject the idea of the priesthood of women, this rationale is meaningless. Finally, he notes that the deacon must, according to the prayer of ordination, liturgically accomplish the ministry to which he has been ordained *leitourgein tēn egcheiristheisan autō diakonian,* while the deaconess performs the works to which she has been ordained, *epitelein to egcheiristhen autē ergon.* Certainly, just as I clearly state in my book, the ministry of the deaconess did not have the same extent as that of the deacon; but the ministry of deacons was also different from that of presbyters, a difference which did not prevent the two kinds of ordinations from being sacramental.

Furthermore, one notices that since they do not occupy the same position in the prayer ritual, the two formulas quoted above are not parallel, and therefore cannot strictly be contrasted formally with each other. In any case, this slight discrepancy in vocabulary is truly extremely unimportant in comparison with the two basic coincidences which one can observe: the first in the "rubric," and the second in the text of the prayer. The ordination of a deacon and that of a deaconess were performed by the same rite — the laying on of hands by the bishop — and with the same solemnity — in the presence of the presbyterium and the deacons; the bishop asked God to look upon his servant (or his female servant) who had been appointed to the diaconate and to confer on him (or her) the gift of the Holy Spirit. Therefore, after examining all that M. Martimort contends, I find no reason to change my opinion, namely, that, according to the *Apostolic Constitutions*, deaconesses received an ordination similar to that of their male colleagues.

Finally, M. Martimort points out that "to be sure of the exact meaning of a liturgical fact is a delicate task for the historian," and that "to evaluate it theologically is even more risky, especially when one tries to infer from it an orientation toward future development." I readily subscribe to these wise warnings, but I do not think I missed the prudence required in this matter. Concerning the exact meaning of the liturgical fact, I think that I explained my own position fully enough above. Concerning the theological appreciation, I certainly would never have hazarded a conclusion on the sole basis of the testimony of the *Constitutions*. But actually, this evidence is not isolated; it appears in a series of concordant testimonies tending to prove that, in the milieu termed "Syrian-Byzantine," from the end of the fourth century in any case, women deacons received an ordination analogous to that of men deacons, and, as a consequence, if one refers to the "concepts of our modern theology," it was a sacramental ordination. Since this is not a marginal fact or a fantasy rejected by legitimate authority, but, on the contrary, an institution peacefully accepted by a large part of Christianity for several centuries, one can deduce from it, it seems to me, that when the Church judges it relevant, women can receive the sacrament of orders for a ministry of the diaconal type, whose limits the Church can establish.[2]

So much for the theological point of view. As for the prospective, i.e., the question as to whether similar opportunities exist today and what would be the mission of a renewed feminine diaconate, a different problem is involved which calls for diverse considerations, concerning which the present dialogue with M. Martimort does not oblige me to take a position. I only wanted to say that if the *Apostolic Constitutions* alone cannot provide the basis for a theological argument concerning the ordination of deaconess, it is excessive, in my opinion, to conclude, as M. Martimort does, that "one is not able to infer any argument [about this issue] from the *Apostolic Constitutions*."

Louvain R. Gryson

BIBLIOGRAPHY

This bibliography lists works referred to several times, as well as works cited which are closely related to the subject matter of this book. After the first citation, reference is made by the simple mention of the author's name and the abridged title of his work.

ACHELIS, H., "Diakonissen (Altkirchliche)," *Realenzyklopädie für protestantische Theologie und Kirche*, IV, pp. 616–620.

ALLWORTHY, T.B., *Women in the Apostolic Church*, Cambridge, 1917.

BAUER, J.B., "Uxores circumducere (1 Kor. 9, 5)," *Biblische Zeitschrift* (new series), III (1959), pp. 94–102.

BLUM, G.G., "Das Amt der Frau im Neuen Testament," *Novum Testamentum*, VII (1964), pp. 142–161.

BOPP, L., *Das Witwentum als organische Gliedschaft im Gemeinschaftsleben der alten Kirche. Ein geschichtlicher Beitrag zur Grundlegung der Witwenseelsorge*, Mannheim, 1950.

BORSINGER, H., *Rechtsstellung der Frau in der katholischen Kirche*, Borna–Leipzig, 1930.

COLSON, J., *La fonction diaconale aux origines de l'Église*, s. 1, 1960.

DANIELOU, J., *The Ministry of Women in the Early Church*, tr. Glyn Simon, London: The Faith Press.

DAVIES, J.G., "Deacons, Deaconesses and the Minor Orders in the Patristic Period," *Journal of Ecclesiastical History*, XIV (1963), pp. 1–15.

DE LABRIOLLE, P.," 'Mulieres in Ecclesia taceant'. Un aspect de la lutte anti-montaniste," *Bulletin d'ancienne littérature et d'archéologie chrétiennes*, I (1911), pp. 1–24, 103–122.

DIECKHOFF, A.W., "Die Diakonissen der alten Kirche," *Monatsschrift für Diakonie und innere Mission*, I (1876–1877), pp. 289–309, 348–357, 394–408.

FITZER, G., *"Das Weib schweige in der Gemeinde". Ueber den unpaulinischen Charakter der Mulier-taceat-Verse in 1. Korinther 14* (Theologische Existenz heute, new series, 110), Munich, 1963.

FORGET, J., "Diaconesses," *Dictionnaire de théologie catholique*, 4, 685–703.

GAUDEMET, J., *L'Église dans l'Empire romain (IV*[e]*–V*[e] *siècles)*, Paris, 1958.

GRYSON, R., *Les origines du célibat ecclésiastique du premier au septième siècle* (Recherches et synthèses de sciences religieuses, section d'histoire, 2), Gembloux, 1970.

HANSSENS, J.M., *La liturgie d'Hippolyte. Document et études*, Rome, 1970.

HEILER, F., "Wertung und Wirksamkeit der Frau in der christlichen Kirche," *Veritati. Festgabe für Joh. Hessen*, Munich, 1949, pp. 116–140.

HULS, G., "De dienst der vrouw in de Kerk. Een onderzoek naar de plaats der vrouw in een presbyteriale Kerkorde" (doctoral thesis, Utrecht), Wageningen, 1951.

KAEHLER, E., *Die Frau in den Paulinischen Briefen*, Zürich, 1960.

KALSBACH, A., "Die altkirchliche Einrichtung der Diakonissen biz zu ihrem Erlöschen," *Römische Quartalschrift*, Suppl. 22, Freiburg-im-Breisgau, 1926.

———, "Diakonisse," *Reallexikon für Antike und Christentum*, III, cols. 917–928.

LAFONTAINE, P.H., *Les conditions positives de l'accession aux ordres dans la première législation ecclésiastique (300–492)*, Ottawa, 1963.

———, "Le sexe masculin, condition de l'accession aux ordres aux IV et Ve siècles, *Revue de l'Université d'Ottawa*, XXXI (1961), pp. 137*–182*.

LECLERCQ, H., "Diaconesse," *Dictionnaire d'archéologie chrétienne et de liturgie*, 4, 725–733.

———, "Femme," *Dictionnaire d'archéologie chrétienne et de liturgie*, 5, 1300–1353.

LEIPOLDT, J., *Die Frau in der antiken Welt und im Urchristentum*, Leipzig, 1954.

LUDWIG, A.F., "Weibliche Kleriker in der altchristlichen und frühmittelalterlichen Kirche," *Passauer theologische Monatsschrift*, XX (1910), pp. 548–557; XXI 1911), pp. 609–617.

Monumenta de viduis, diaconissis virginibusque tractantia, ed. J. Mayer (Florilegium patristicum, 42), Bonn, 1938.

ODELEM, J.P., *Dissertatio de diaconissis primitivae Ecclesiae*, Leipzig, 1700.

OEPKE, A., "Gynē," *Theological Dictionary of the New Testament*, I, pp. 776–790.

"On the Early History and Modern Revival of Deaconesses," *Church Quarterly Review*, XLVIII (1898–1899), pp. 302–340.

PANKOWSKI, A.J.C., *De diaconissis*, Ratisbon, 1866.

PARIS, P., "Quatenus feminae res publicas in Asia Minore Romanis imperantibus attigerint" (doctoral thesis, Paris), Paris, 1891.

PARISOT, J., "Les diaconesses," *Revue des sciences ecclésiastiques*, LXXIX (1899), pp. 289–304, 481–496; LXXX, pp. 193–209.

PINIUS, J., "Tractatus praeliminaris de Ecclesiae diaconissis," *Acta Sanctorum Septembris*, I (1746), Antwerp, pp. i–xxviii.

ROBINSON, C., *The Ministry of Deaconesses*, London, 1898.

ROSAMBERT, A., *La veuve en droit canonique jusqu'au XIVe siècle*, Paris, 1923.

SCHAEFER, K.H., *Die Kanonissenstifter im deutschen Mittelalter. Ihre Entwicklung und innere Einrichtung im Zusammenhang mit dem altchristlichen Sanktimonialentum* (Kirchenrechtliche Abhandlungen, 43–44), Stuttgart, 1907.

———, "Kanonissen und Diakonissen. Ergänzungen und Erläuterungen," *Römische Quartalschrift*, XXIV (1910), pp. 49–90.

SCHAEFER, P., "Der Dienst der Frau in der alten Kirche," *Eine Heilige Kirche*, XXI (1939), pp. 49–57.

SCHAEFER, T., *Die weibliche Diakonie in ihrem ganzen Umfang*, 3 vols., 2nd ed., Potsdam, 1887–1894.

SPICQ, C., *Saint Paul. Les Épîtres pastorales* (Études bibliques), I, 4th ed., Paris, 1969.

STOECKER, L., *Die Frau in der alten Kirche* (Sammlung gemeinverständlicher Vorträge und Schriften aus dem Gebiet der Theologie und Religionsgeschichte, 47), Tübingen, 1907.

THEODOROS, E.D., "He 'cheirotonia' ē 'cheirothesia' tōn diakonissōn," *Theologia*, XXV (1954), pp. 430–469, 576–601; XXVI (1955), pp. 57–76.

TURNER, C.H., "Ministries of Women in the Primitive Church. Widow, Deaconess and Virgin in the First Four Christian Centuries," *Catholic and Apostolic. Collected Papers*, ed. H.N. Bate, London, 1931, pp. 316–351.

VAESSEN, C.J.H., "Die Stellung der Frau. Theologische Betrachtungen nach der Lehre der Heiligen Schrift und der kirchlichen Lehramtes" (doctoral thesis, Angelicum, Rome), Rome, 1956.

VAN DER MEER, H., *Priestertum der Frau?* (Quaestiones disputatae, 42), Freiburg-im-Breisgau, 1969.

VON DER GOLTZ, E., *Der Dienst der Frau in der christlichen Kirche*, 2nd ed., Potsdam, 1914.

VOS, C. J., "Women in Old Testament Worship" (doctoral thesis, Free University, Amsterdam), Delft, 1968.

WAHL, J. A., *The Exclusion of Women from Holy Orders* (The Catholic University of America. Studies in Sacred Theology, 2nd series, 110), Washington, D.C., 1959.

WIECHERT, F., "Die Geschichte der Diakonissenweihe," *Eine heilige Kirche*, XXI (1939), pp. 57–79.

WIELAND, F., "Die genetische Entwicklung der sogenannten Ordines minores," *Römische Quartalschrift*, Suppl. 7, Rome, 1897.

ZAHN, T., *Ignatius von Antiochien*, Gotha, 1873.

ZIEGLER, C., *De diaconis et diaconissis veteris Ecclesiae*, Wittenberg, 1678.

ZSCHARNACK, L., *Der Dienst der Frau in den ersten Jahrhunderten der christlichen Kirche*, Göttingen, 1902.

NOTES

Introduction — pages xi–xvi

[1] See, for instance, J. Goar, *Euchologion, sive Rituale Graecorum . . .*, Paris, 1647; 2nd ed., Paris, 1730, pp. 218–222; J. Morinus, *Commentarius de sacris Ecclesiae ordinationibus . . .*, Paris, 1655, 3rd part, pp. 182–192; C. Ziegler, *De diaconis et diaconissis veteris Ecclesiae*, Wittenberg, 1678, pp. 347–366; L. Thomassin, *Ancienne et nouvelle discipline de l'Église . . .*, I, 2nd ed., Paris, 1679, pp. 164–167; J.C. Suicerus, *Thesaurus ecclesiasticus . . .*, II, Amsterdam, 1682, cols. 864–869; J.P. Odelem, *Dissertatio de diaconissis primitivae Ecclesiae*, Leipzig, 1700; J.A. Bingham, "The Antiquities of the Christian Church," 1, II, ch. 22, in *The Works of the Learned Joseph Bingham*, I, London, 1726, pp. 96–101; J. Pinius (= Pien), "Tractatus praeliminaris de Ecclesiae diaconissis," in *Acta Sanctorum Septembris*, I, Antwerp, 1746, pp. i-xxviii; A.J. Binterim, *Die vorzüglichsten Denkwürdigkeiten der christ-katholischen Kirche*, I, Mainz, 1825, pp. 434–455; A.J. Pankowski, *De diaconissis*, Ratisbon 1866.

[2] T. Zahn, *Ignatius von Antiochien*, Gotha, 1873, pp. 580–585. In the same sense: A.W. Dieckhoff, "Die Diakonissen der alten Kirche," in *Monatsschrift für Diakonie und innere Mission*, I (1876–1877), pp. 289–309, 348–352, 394–408; G. Uhlhorn, *Die christliche Liebesthätigkeit in der alten Kirche*, 2nd ed., Stuttgart, 1882, pp. 159–171; T. Schaefer, *Die weibliche Diakonie in ihrem ganzen Umfang*, I, 2nd ed., Potsdam, 1887, pp. 1–61; E. von der Goltz, *Der Dienst der Frau in der christlichen Kirche*, 2nd ed., Potsdam, 1914, pp. 5–48.

[3] L. Zscharnack, *Der Dienst der Frau in den ersten Jahrhunderten der christlichen Kirche*, Göttingen, 1902. In the same sense: L. Stoecker, *Die Frau in der alten Kirche* (Sammlung gemeinverständlicher Vorträge und Schriften aus dem Gebiet der Theologie und Religionsgeschichte, 47), Tübingen, 1907; T.B. Allworthy, *Women in the Apostolic Church*, Cambridge, 1917, pp. 124–130, 142.

[4] See, for instance, F. Wieland, "Die genetische Entwicklung der sogenannten Ordines minores," (in *Römische Quartalschrift*, Suppl. 7), Rome, 1897, pp. 60–65; K.H. Schaefer, *Die Kanonissenstifter im deutschen Mittelalter. Ihre Entwicklung und innere Einrichtung im Zusammenhang mit dem altchristlichen Sanktimonialentum* (Kirchenrechtliche Abhandlungen, 43–44), Stuttgart, 1907, pp. 46–49; *Idem*,"Kanonissen und Diakonissen. Ergänzungen und Erläuterungen," in *Römische Quartalschrift*, XXIV (1910), pp. 49–90; A.F. Ludwig, "Weibliche Kleriker in der altchristlichen und frühmittelalterlichen Kirche," in *Passauer theologische Monatsschrift*, XX (1910), pp. 548–557; XXI (1911), pp. 609–617.

[5] This theory is given the clearest ex-

pression by H. Achelis, "Diakonissen (Altkirchliche)," in *Realenzklopädie für prot. Theol. und Kirche*, IV, pp. 616–620.

6 See particularly C. Robinson, *The Ministry of Deaconesses*, London, 1898; J. Parisot, "Les diaconesses," in *Revue des sciences ecclésiastiques*, LXXIX (1899), pp. 289–304, 481–496; LXXX, pp. 193–209.

7 In *Römische Quartalschrift*, Suppl. 22, Freiburg im Breisgau, 1926. Let us mention two important reviews, that of W. Voelker in *Theologische Literaturzeitung*, LII (1927), cols. 582–584, and that of O. Casel, in *Jahrbuch für Liturgiewissenschaft*, XI (1931), pp. 273–278. Kalsbach gives a résumé of his own book in the article "Diakonisse," in *Reallexikon für Antike und Christentum*, III, cols. 917–928.

8 For instance, the articles "Diaconesses" and "Veuves" in *Dictionnaire des antiquités chrétiennes*; "Deaconesses" and "Widow" in *The Catholic Encyclopedia*; "Deaconess" and "Widows" in *Dictionary of Christian Antiquities*; see also S. Many, *Praelectiones de sacra ordinatione*, Paris, 1905, pp. 176–183 (he supports the original distinction between widows and deaconesses); and C. Pesch, *Praelectiones dogmaticae*, VII, 5th ed., Freiburg im Breisgau, 1920, pp. 302–303 (the theory of identity).

9 J. Forget, "Diaconesses," in DTC 4, 685–703; H. Leclercq, "Diaconesse," in DACL 4, 725–733.

10 A. Rosambert, *La veuve en droit canonique jusqu'au XIVe siècle*, Paris, 1923.

11 See the review by G. Le Bras in *Revue des sciences religieuses*, VI, (1926), pp. 281–288.

12 "On the Early History and Modern Revival of Deaconesses," in *Church Quarterly Review*, XLVIII (1898–1899), pp. 302–340.

13 *Monumenta de viduis, diaconissis virginibusque tractantia*, ed. J. Mayer (Florilegium patristicum, 42), Bonn, 1938.

14 For instance, the articles "Diaconessa" and "Vedovanza," in *Enciclopedia cattolica*; "Diakonissen" and "Witve," in *Lexikon für Theologie und Kirche*; "Deaconess" and "Widow," in *The New Catholic Encyclopedia*; "Diaconesse(s)," in *Catholicisme* and in *Dictionnaire de droit canonique*; see also B. Kurtscheid, *Historia iuris canonici. Historia institutionum. I: Ab Ecclesiae fundatione usque ad Gratianum*, Rome, 1941, pp. 49–52.

15 C.H. Turner, "Ministries of Women in the Primitive Church. Widow, Deaconess and Virgin in the First Four Centuries," in *Catholic and Apostolic. Collected Papers*, ed. H.N. Bate, 1931, pp. 316–351.

16 L. Bopp, *Das Witwentum als organische Gliedschaft im Gemeinschaftsleben der alten Kirche. Ein geschichtlicher Beitrag zur Grundlegung der Witwenseelsorge*, Mannheim, 1950.

17 E.D. Theodorou, "He 'cheirotonia' ē 'cheirothesia' tōn diakonissōn," in *Theologia*, XXV (1954), pp. 430–469, 576–601; XXVI (1955), pp. 57–76.

18 J. Colson, *La fonction diaconale aux origines de l'Église*, s. 1 (1960), pp. 121–139.

19 J.G. Davies, "Deacons, Deaconesses and the Minor Orders in the Patristic Period," in *Journal of Ecclesiastical History*, XIV (1963), pp. 1–15 (see pp. 1–5).

20 P. de Labriolle, "'Mulieres in Ecclesia taceant'. Un aspect de la lutte antimontaniste," in *Bulletin d'ancienne littérature et d'archéologie chrétienne*, I (1911), pp. 1–24, 103–122 (see also pp. 292–293). The article "Femme" by H. Leclercq, in DACL 5, 1300–1353, is mainly a recasting of this article of P. de Labriolle.

21 P. Schaefer, "Der Dienst der Frau in der alten Kirche," in *Eine heilige Kirche*, XXI (1939), pp. 49–57; F. Wiechert, "Die Geschichte der Diakonissenweihe," *ibid.*, pp. 57–79.

22 J. Daniélou, "Le ministère des femmes dans l'Église ancienne," in *La Maison-Dieu*, 61 (1960), pp. 70–96 (English translation by Glyn Simon, *The Ministry of Women in the Early Church* [London: The Faith Press]).

23 P.H. Lafontaine, *Les conditions positives de l'accession aux ordres dans la première législation ecclésiastique* (300–492), Ottawa, 1963, pp. 7–55. This chapter was

first published separately as "Le sexe masculin, condition de l'accession aux ordres aux IVe et Ve siècles," in *Revue de l'Université d'Ottawa*, XXXI (1961), pp. 137–182*.

[24] H. Borsinger, *Rechtsstellung der Frau in der katholischen Kirche*, Borna-Leipzig, 1930; F. Heiler, "Wertung und Wirksamkeit der Frau in der christlichen Kirche," in *Veritati. Festgabe für Joh. Hessen*, Munich, 1949, pp. 116–140; G. Huls, "De dienst der vrouw in de Kerk. Een onderzoek naar de plaats der vrouw in een presbyteriale kerkorde," (doctoral thesis, Utrecht), Wageningen, 1951; J. Leipoldt, *Die Frau in der antiken Welt und im Urchristentum*, Leipzig, 1954; H. van der Meer, *Priestertum der Frau*? (Quaestiones disputatae, 42), Freiburg im Breisgau, 1969.

[25] C.J.H. Vaessen, "Die Stellung der Frau. Theologische Betrachtungen nach der Lehre der Heiligen Schrift und der kirchlichen Lehramtes" (extract from doctoral thesis, Angelicum), Rome, 1956.

[26] *Op. cit.*, pp. 25–57.

[27] J.A. Wahl, *The Exclusion of Women from Holy Orders* (Washington, D.C.: The Catholic University of America. Studies in Sacred Theology, 2nd series, 110), 1959.

[28] This comment does not mean that nothing has been done in this area. There are, for instance, the well-known studies of H. Dacier on woman according to St. Ambrose and St. John Chrysostom. But many more inquiries are necessary before a sufficiently balanced and accurate synthesis can be reached.

[29] In this area also one can rely on some existing studies for a future synthesis. The best items however are not necessarily the most recent ones. Note particularly the doctoral thesis of P. Paris, "Quatenus feminae res publicas in Asia Minore Romanis imperantibus attigerint" (doctoral thesis), Paris, 1891.

Chapter One — pages 1–10

[1] The Old Testament is not within the chronological limits of the present inquiry; therefore, it shall be referred to only in so far as it may have influenced Christian practice and theology. For more detail, see the recent study by C.J. Vos, "Women in Old Testament Worship" (doctoral thesis, Free University, Amsterdam), Delft, 1968 (with extensive bibliography). I am inclined, though, to agree with E. Osswald (*Theologische Literaturzeitung*, XCIV [1969], col. 115) that this work, in spite of its merit, should be used cautiously because more than once the author interpreted the Old Testament references in a way that is more favorable to women than the letter of the text allows.

[2] A text of Exodus (38:8) mentions "the ministering women who ministered at the door of the tent of meeting." This formula reappears in a gloss of 1 Samuel 2:22 which is absent from the Greek. There is no other reference to these women in the Bible. In the absence of other information, it is impossible to explain exactly to what these texts are referring. See R. de Vaux, *Ancient Israel: Its Life and Institutions*, II (New York: McGraw-Hill, 1961), pp. 383–384.

[3] Exod. 15:20.

[4] Judg 4:4.

[5] 2 Kings 22:14.

[6] Neh. 6:14.

[7] Luke 2:36.

[8] Joel 3:1-2.

[9] In Luke 23:2, after *keleuonta phorous mē dounai* (= *kōluonta phorous Kaisari didonai* in the received text), the text of Marcion adds the following words: *kai apostrephonta tas gynaikas kai ta tekna* (Ephiphanius of Salamis, *Adv. haer.* 42, 11, 6, 70; GCS 31, 116, 13-14, 42, 11, 15, 70, p. 152, 1-2).

[10] Luke 8:1-3. Our biblical quotations are generally taken from the *Revised Standard Version: An Ecumenical Edition* (New York: Collins, 1973).

[11] Mark 15:40-41.

[12] Matthew 27:56: Mary Magdalene, Mary the mother of James and Joseph, and the mother of the sons of Zebedee; 27:61 and 28:1: Mary Magdalene and the other Mary. Mark 15:40: Mary Magdalene, Mary the mother of James the younger and of Joses, and Salome: 15:47: Mary Magdalene and Mary the mother of Joses; 16:1: Mary Magdalene, Mary

the mother of James, and Salome. Luke 8:2-3: Mary Magdalene, Joanna, the wife of Chuza, Herod's steward, and Susanna; 24:10: Mary Magdalene, Joanna, and Mary the mother of James. John 19:25: the mother of Jesus, and his mother's sister, Mary the wife of Clopas, and Mary Magdalene. The differences between one list and another are explainable in the context of the history of the Gospel tradition. Notice that the name of Mary Magdalene is found everywhere and, except in John, always comes first.

[13] See G.G. Blum, "Das Amt der Frau im Neuen Testament," in *Novum Testamentum,* VII (1964), pp. 142–161 at pp. 143–144.

[14] Matthew 28:1-10; Mark 16:1-11; Luke 24:1-11; John 20:1-2, 11-18.

[15] Acts 1:14.

[16] Acts 5:14; 8:3; 9:2; 17:4, 12, 34.

[17] Acts 9:36, 39.

[18] Acts 12:12.

[19] Acts 16:14-15.

[20] The question whether this list was part of an Epistle addressed to the church of Rome or whether it came from a copy of this document addressed to the church of Ephesus is unimportant for the present purpose; see A. Robert and A. Feuillet, *Introduction to the New Testament,* New York, 1965, pp. 451–452.

[21] Rom. 16:1-2.

[22] In this sense, see Forget, "Diaconesses," 686; Leclercq, "Diaconesse," 725, with the reservation "vraisemblablement"; Leipoldt, *Frau in antiken Welt,* 133; Blum, "Amt der Frau," 145–146. [Translator's note: The Jerusalem Bible and the New American Bible also use "deaconess"].

[23] Kalsbach, "Altkirchliche Einrichtung," pp. 9–10; *Idem,* "Diakonisse," col. 917; Daniélou, *The Ministry of Women,* pp. 7–8; Davies, "Deacons, Deaconesses and Minor Orders, p. 1.

[24] Rom. 11:13; 1 Cor. 3:5; 2 Cor. 3:4–6:13; etc.

[25] 1 Cor. 16:15.

[26] Rom. 12:7.

[27] Cf. 1 Cor. 16:15. The formula *diakonon tēs ekklēsias tēs en Kegchreais* (minister of the church at Cenchreae) is similar to *tous presbyterous tēs ekklēsias* in Acts 20:17 and John 5:14. Two other arguments produced by G. Huls ("Dienst der vrouw," p. 50) to prove that here *diakonos* should be taken in a very inclusive sense are not tenable, in my opinion. The participle *ousa* does not necessarily mean that the following term is a title referring to a known function. None of the references given to that effect ("Dienst der vrouw, p. 50, n. 1) is specific. In John 10:12, no name of function is given. In John 11:49, the participle has a causal connotation (cf. v. 51). In Acts 18:12, there is an absolute genitive. In Acts 24: 10, the participle has a completive function. In Romans 13:1, *ousai* means "those that are existing." And the authenticity of *kai* after *ousan* in Rom. 16:1, seems to be questionable according to the critical apparatus.

[28] Zscharnack, *Dienst der Frau,* pp. 45–47.

[29] At this time, Christian communities certainly met in private houses. Earlier this study referred to the community meeting in the house of John-Mark's mother in Jerusalem (Acts 12:12; above, p. 3). There is also mention of a community meeting in the house of Prisca and Aquila (Rom. 16:5; 1 Cor. 16:19), in that of Philemon (Philemon 2), and in that of Nympha at Laodicea (Col. 4: 15). In this last reference, the Nestle edition preferred the reading of Nympha as a woman (*Nymphan* instead of *Nymphān, tēn kat'oikon autēs ekklēsian*), though most manuscripts read the masculine.

[30] 1 Cor. 12:11.

[31] A. Oepke, "Gynē," in TDNT, I (English ed., p. 787), "The description of Phebe as the *diákonos* of the church at Cenchrea indicates the point where the original charisma is becoming an office."

[32] Rom. 16:3.

[33] Rom. 16:21.

[34] 2 Cor. 8:23.

[35] Phil. 2:25.

[36] Phil. 4:3.

[37] Philemon 1:24.

[38] Rom. 16:4.

[39] Acts 19:23-40.

[40] Acts 18:1-3.

[41] Acts 18:18-19.

[42] Acts 18:24–19:1; cf. 1 Cor. 1:12; 3:4-6, 22: 4:6.

[43] Acts 18:18, 26; Rom. 16:3. The same in 2 Tim. 4:19. However, in 1 Cor. 16:19, Aquila is mentioned before Prisca. In Acts 18:26, many manuscripts restore the "natural" order, but the other reading seems to be better.

[44] See later on, pp. 80–83.

[45] Rom. 16:5; 1 Cor. 16:19.

[46] Rom. 16:6.

[47] Rom 16:12.

[48] Rom. 16:13.

[49] Rom. 16:15.

[50] Phil. 4:2-3.

[51] Acts 21:9. A menologic manuscript of the fourteenth century (*cod. Paris. gr.* 1551) mentions their names: Hermione, Charitina, Irais, and Eutychiana (according to R.A. Lipsius, *Die apokryphen Apostelgeschichten und Apostellegenden*, II, 2nd part, Braunschweig, 1887, p. 3, footnote); this information is late and unreliable. According to the Epistle of Polycrates of Ephesus to Victor, the bishop of Rome (189–199), partly preserved in Eusebius' *Ecclesiastical History*, two of Philip's daughters, who "grew old in virginity," are buried at Hierapolis together with their father (who is confused with the Apostle Philip), and the third, "who lived in the Holy Spirit" (which probably also means the profession of virginity), is buried at Ephesus (*Eccl. Hist.* 3, 31:3; GCS 9-1, 264, 13-16; the same text is quoted again, *ibid.*, 5, 24:2, p. 490, 16-19). Eusebius continues with a sentence from the *Dialogue* of Caius against Proclus (from the episcopate of Zephyrinus in Rome; therefore between 199 and 217), which, he says, agrees with what was said before: "After him there were four prophetesses, the daughters of Philip, at Hierapolis in Asia. Their tomb is there and the tomb of their father" (*ibid.*, 3, 31:4; GCS 9-1, 266, 3-5.)

As is evident, Polycrates' statement does not agree with that of Caius, in spite of Eusebius' allegation. Polycrates mentions only three daughters of Philip, but Caius mentions four of them, as the Acts of the Apostles does. According to Caius, the four daughters rest in Hierapolis, whereas according to Polycrates, two of them are buried there and the third at Ephesus. Papias of Hierapolis reports a miracle of their time, the resurrection of a dead person, but Eusebius does not preserve this story (*ibid.*, 3, 39:9; GCS 9-1, 288, 17-25).

Clement of Alexandria contradicts Polycrates' testimony, mentioned above, when he says that Philip (confused here with the Apostle Philip again) gave his daughters in marriage, which, according to Clement, proves that the Apostles, who themselves were married, considered marriage as good and permitted, contrary to the contention of some Gnostic sects (*Stromata* 3, 6, 52, 5; GCS 52, 220, 15-16; see R. Gryson, *Les origines du célibat ecclésiastique du premier au septième siècle*, Gembloux, 1970, pp. 8–12).

An anonymous anti-Montanist writing, quoted by Eusebius, mentions Philip's daughters among the genuine prophetesses whom the Montanists claimed as theirs (*Eccl. Hist.* 5, 17:3; GCS 9-1, 470, 15). All of this witnesses to the high consideration of the early Church for Philip's daughters. The anonymous anti-Montanist writing also mentions, among "those who prophesied according to the New Testament," Ammia, a Philadelphian woman, who is not known otherwise (*ibid.*, 5, 17:2-4; GCS 9-1, 470, 8, 15-16, 19).

[52] 1 Cor. 11:4-5.

[53] Gal. 3:28.

[54] 1 Cor. 11:10.

[55] 1 Cor. 11:3.

[56] *Ibid.*

[57] See E. Kaehler, *Die Frau in den Paulinischen Briefen*, Zürich, 1960, pp. 43-70, who combines the contributions of the best commentaries on this difficult text.

[58] 1 Cor. 14:34-35.

[59] See Blum, "Amt der Frau," p. 150.

[60] For a detailed study of these different points, see G. Fitzer, *"Das Weib schweige in der Gemeinde". Ueber den unpaulinischen Charakter der Mulier-taceat-Verse in I Korinther 14* (Theologische Existenz heute, new ser., 110), Munich, 1963. H. Conzelmann (*Der erste Brief an die Korinther*, Göttingen, 1969, pp. 289–290) thinks that the interpolation extends from verses 33b to 36. In my opinion, the reasons of G. Fitzer, who limits

the interpolation to verses 34-35, are more convincing. Except for this remark, I agree completely with Conzelmann when he writes, "Wer den Text als ursprünglich verteidigt, ist zu Hilfskonstruktionen genötigt" (p. 290). He refutes some of these *Hilfskonstruktionen*, p. 290, n. 58.

61 1 Tim. 2:11-14.

62 1 Tim. 2:12.

63 1 Tim. 3:2-5; 5:17.

64 1 Tim. 3:11.

65 C. Spicq, *Saint Paul. Les Épitres pastorales* (Études bibliques), I, 4th ed., Paris, 1969, p. 456.

66 *Ibid.*, p. 575, about 1 Tim. 6:17-19.

67 *Ibid.*, p. 549, about 1 Tim. 5:23.

68 Davies, "Deacons, Deaconesses and the Minor Orders," p. 2. Ambrosiaster also agrees. See later, pp. 95–97.

69 This is the opinion of Thomas Aquinas and of Luther, among others.

70 *Diakonous hōsautōs semnous . . . Gynaikas hōsautōs semnas.*

71 The adjective *semnos* is found in the two instances; to *mē dilogous* corresponds *mē diabolous; to mē oinō pollō prosechontas, nephalious*; finally, *mē aischrokerdeis, echontas to mystērion tēs pisteōs en kathara syneidēsei* seems to be summarized in the concise formula *pistas en pasin.*

72 This is the opinion of Zscharnack, *Dienst der Frau*, pp. 103–104; Forget "Diaconesses," 686; Kalsbach, "Altkirchliche Einrichtung," pp. 10–11; *Idem*, "Diakonisse," p. 917; Huls, "Dienst der vrouw," pp. 51–52; Leipoldt, *Frau in antiken Welt*, pp. 133–134; Colson, *Fonction diaconale*, p. 64; Daniélou, *The Ministry of Women*, p. 14; Spicq, *Épitres pastorales*, pp. 460–461.

73 1 Tim. 5:3-16.

74 The strongest expression is that of F. Wieland ("Ordinaes minores," p. 60): "Eine eigene kirchliche Berufsklasse mit klerikalen Prärogativen." J. Daniélou (*The Ministry of Women*, p. 14), speaks of "an order of Widows, parallel to the other orders"; and P. Schaefer ("Dienst der Frau," p. 50) discovers in 1 Timothy 5:9-10, after Romans 16:1-2, "eine zweite Spur eines kirchlichen Frauenamtes." J. Forget ("Diaconesses," 686) is inclined to think that this text refers to a college of widows devoted to God who assist the clergy in their social ministry. According to Zscharnack (*Dienst der Frau*, p. 101), nothing prevents the affirmation of a clerical character of the ministry of widows, but there is no positive certitude in this interpretation. G. Blum ("Amt der Frau," p. 159) is more hesitant: it is difficult to decide with certainty solely in favor of a *Witwenstand* or of a true *Witwenamt* with clearly defined duties and rights. A. Oepke ("Gynē," TDNT, p. 788) uses the adjective "semi-clerical" with regard to widows. This kind of formula disagrees with Huls ("Dienst der vrow," p. 54), who asks that those who use them explain clearly the reason for which they deem it right to introduce a distinction of principle between the ministries of men and those of women.

75 C.H. Turner ("Ministries of Women," p. 319) wonders at the supposition that widows could be "anything else, from the beginning to the end of these verses, than the recipients of the official poor relief of the Church." According to J. Davies ("Deacons, Deaconesses and the Minor Orders," p. 5), "they were . . . in no sense an active order, rather . . . an organised group of Church pensioners, and to be on the 'roll' was to be the recipient of charity."

76 Acts 6:1.

77 1 Tim. 5:3.

78 Spicq, *Épitres pastorales*, pp. 524–525.

79 Deut. 14:29; 16:11, 14; 24:19-21; 26:12-13; Job 29:12-13; 31:16-20; Is. 1:17; etc.

80 James 1:27.

81 1 Tim. 5:4, 8, 16.

82 1 Tim. 5:5.

83 1 Tim. 5:6-7.

84 1 Tim. 5:9-10.

85 1 Tim. 5:11-15.

86 1 Tim. 5:10.

87 Titus 2:3-5: "Bid the older women likewise to be reverent in behavior, not to be slanderers or slaves to drink; they are to teach what is good, and so train the young women to love their husbands and children, to be sensible, chaste, domestic,

kind, and submissive to their husbands, that the word of God may not de discredited." The text does not actually refer to widows (chērai), but to older women (*presbytides*). This term refers to age, not to a function, as the context shows, which mentions successively older men (*presbytai*, v. 2), older women (*presbytides*, v. 3), young women (*neai*, v. 4) and young men (*neōteroi*, v. 6).

88 This exegesis agrees substantially with that of A. Kalsbach ("Altkirchliche Einrichtung," pp. 11–16).

Chapter Two — pages 11–16

1 Is. 1:17, quoted in Clement of Rome, *Ep. to Corinthians* 8, 4 (AV 1, 39, 18-27).

2 *Ep. of Barnabas* 20, 2 (AV 1, 33, 7-8).

3 Ignatius of Antioch, *Ep. to Symrneans* 6, 2 (AV 1, 108, 2-4).

4 *Idem, Ep. to Polycarp* 4, 1 (AV 1, 111, 25-26).

5 Polycarp of Smyrna, *Ep. to Philippians* 6, 1 (AV 1, 116, 27-29, *Early Christian Fathers*, tr. C.C. Richardson, New York 1970, p. 133).

6 Justin, *First Apology* 67, 6 (Goodspeed, 75-76).

7 Hermas, *The Shepherd* 38, 10 (SC 53, 180).

8 Ibid., 56, 7.

9 *Ibid.*, 50, 8-9; *The Apostolic Fathers*, II (Loeb), tr. K. Lake, p. 141.

10 *Ibid.*, 103, 1-2, p. 281.

11 *Ibid.*, 104, 1-2, p. 285.

12 Polycarp of Smyrna, *Ep. to Philippians* 4, 3 (AV 1, 116, 4-9), tr. C. Richardson, *op. cit.*, p. 133.

13 The verb *mōmoskopeō*, translated above by "examine," is a technical term for the examination of the victims destined to be sacrificed to make sure they are free from all impurity.

14 Kalsbach "Altkirchliche Einrichtung," pp. 17-18.

15 Daniélou, *The Ministry of Women*, p. 18.

16 Huls, "Dienst der vrouw," p. 63; Colson, *Fonction diaconale*, p. 121.

17 Ignatius of Antioch, *Ep. to Smyrneans* 13, 1 (AV 1, 110, 9-10).

18 Zahn, *Ignatius von Antiochien*, pp. 336, 585; Achelis, "Diakonissen," p. 617; Colson, *Fonction diaconale*, p. 121.

19 Ignatius of Antioch, *Ep. to Smyrneans* 12, 2 (AV 1, 110, 3-4).

20 1 Tim. 5:11-12.

21 Ignatius of Antioch, *Ep. to Polycarp* 5, 2 (AV 1, 112, 9-10).

22 Hermas, *The Shepherd* 8, 2-3 (SC 53, 96), tr. K. Lake, *op. cit.*, p. 25.

23 Lucian of Samosata, *The Death of Peregrinus* 12 (Loeb, V, p. 12). Peregrinus died in 165 A.D.; the event referred to in the text took place in Palestine.

24 Pliny the Younger, *Ep.* 10, 96, 8 (Durry, 74).

25 Pliny was governor of Bithynia, a Greek-speaking province of Asis Minor; one may, therefore, assume that he transposes a Greek term into Latin.

26 See Zscharnack, *Dienst der Frau*, pp. 160–162.

27 Epiphanius of Salamis, *Panarion* 26, 1, 3 (GCS 25, 275, 12-18); Philaster of Brescia, *Liber de haeresibus* 33, 3 (CCL 9, 231, 9).

28 Hippolytus of Rome, *Philosophoumena* 5, 7, 1 (GCS 26, 78, 22-79, 6); 10, 9, 3 (268, 22-23).

29 *Acts of Philip* 94 (Lipsius-Bonnet, 2-2, 36, 29ff.), etc. (see the index of the edition quoted, p. 339, for *Mariammē* and *Mariamnē*).

30 See later on, p. 18.

31 Apoc. 2:20-24.

32 Justin, *First Apology* 26, 3 (Goodspeed, 43); Irenaeus, *Adv. haer.* 1, 16, 2 (1, 23, 2; Harvey, 1, 191).

33 Irenaeus, *Adv. haer.* 1, 16, 3 (1, 23, 4; Harvey, 1, 194).

34 Jerome, *Ep.* 133, 4, 2 (CSEL 56, 248, 3-4).

35 Tertullian, *De praescriptione* 6, 6 (CCL 1, 191, 17-20); 30, 6 (211, 20-24); Hippolytus of Rome, *Philosophoumena* 7, 38, 2 (GCS 26, 224, 8-9).

36 Irenaeus, *Adv. haer.* 1, 7 (1, 13; Harvey, 1, 114-127). See also Hippolytus of Rome, *Philosophoumena* 6, 40, 1-4 (GCS 26, 171, 12–172, 13).

[37] Hippolytus, *Philosophoumena* 8, 19, 1 (GCS 26, 238, 4-8) mentions Priscilla and Maximilla in first place among the leaders of the sect, noticing however that Montanus appeared before the two women. See also *ibid.* 10, 25, 1 (282, 15-17).

[38] See Origen, *Fragments on 1 Cor.* 74, quoted later, pp. 28–29; Epiphanius, *Panarion* 49, 1-3, summarized later, pp. 77–79. Historians have often connected with the Montanists a prophetess of Cappadocia who, according to the Epistle of Firmilian of Caesarea to Cyprian, dared to offer the Eucharist, following every detail of the rites of the Church; see Cyprian, *Ep.* 75, 10, 5 (Bayard, 2, 297-298). But it is not certain that this woman belonged to the Montanist sect; see Lafontaine, *Conditions positives*, pp. 11-12.

Chapter Three — pages 17–24

[1] *De praescriptione* 41, 5 (CCL 1, 221, 12-15), translated in *Ante-Nicene Fathers* (ANF), Grand Rapids, Mich.: Eerdmans, III, p. 263. All the translations from ANF and LNPF have been slightly altered to conform to modern usage.

[2] The Confessors' Letter to Cyprian, in Cyprian, *Ep.* 23 (Bayard, 1, 62); Letter of Cornelius of Rome to Fabius of Antioch, in Eusebius, *Eccl. Hist.* 6, 43, 11 (GCS 9-2, 618, 16).

[3] See *Apologeticum*, 23, *passim* (CCL 1, 130, 1–133, 95), especially 23, 4 (131, 22-25): "Let a person be brought before your tribunals who is plainly under demoniacal possession. The wicked spirit, bidden to speak by a follower of Christ (*a quolibet christiano*), will as readily make the truthful confession that he is a demon as elsewhere he has falsely asserted that he is a god." See also *De corona* 11, 3 (CCL 2, 1056, 17-18); *De idolatria* 11, 7 (CCL 2, 1111, 21-25). I borrow these remarks about exorcism from de Labriolle, "Mulieres . . . taceant," pp. 106–107.

[4] About this Gnostic sect, which does not seem to have been important, see G. Bareille, "Caïnites," in DTC 2, 1307–1309.

[5] *De baptismo* 1, 3 (CCL 1, 277, 13-14): "Thus it was that portent of a woman, who had no right to teach even correctly . . . (*cui nec integre quidem docendi ius erat*)."

[6] *Ibid.*, 17, 1-3 (291, 1-19).

[7] Cf. 1 Cor. 14:34-35. *De baptismo* 17, 4 (CCL 1, 291, 20–292, 31); tr. E. Evans, *Tertullian's Homily on Baptism* (London: S.P.C.K., 1964), p. 37.

[8] *Acts of Paul and Thecla* 41 (Lipsius-Bonnet, 1, 267, 4-6): "And Thecla arose and said to Paul: I go unto Iconium. And Paul said: Go, and teach (*didaske*) the word of God" (tr. M.R. James, *The Apocryphal New Testament*, Oxford, 1953, p. 281).

[9] *Ibid.*, 39 (265, 4-8), "Thecla therefore went in with her and rested in her house eight days, teaching (*katēchēsasa*) her the word of God, so that most of the maid-servants also believed, and there was great joy in the house" (tr. James, *op. cit.*, p. 280).

[10] *Ibid.*, 43 (269, 6-7), "She departed unto Seleucia, and after she had enlightened many with the word of God (*phōtisasa tō logō tou theou*), she slept a good sleep" (tr. James, *op. cit.*, p. 281).

[11] *Ibid.*, 34 (260, 3–261, 4), "Then did they put in many beasts, while she stood and stretched out her hands and prayed. And when she had ended her prayer, she turned and saw a great tank full of water, and said: Now is it time that I should wash myself (*lousasthai*) on the last day. And she cast herself in, saying: In the name of Jesus Christ do I baptize myself (*baptizomai*) on the last day" (tr. James, *op. cit.*, p. 279).

[12] *De resurrectione carnis* 11, 2 (CCL 2, 933, 4-6); *De exhortatione castitatis*, 10, 5 (CCL 2, 1030, 30-34).

[13] Cf. 1 Cor. 14:34-35.

[14] *De virginibus velandis* 9, 1 (CCL 2, 1218, 4–1219, 6).

[15] "Sacerdotes pudicitiae," *De cultu feminarum* 2, 12, 1 (CCL 1, 367, 2-3).

[16] Cf. 1 Cor. 14:34-35.

[17] Cf. 1 Cor. 11:5.

[18] Cf. 1 Cor. 14:34.

[19] *Adv. Marc.* 5, 8, 11 (CCL 1, 688, 7-13), tr. E. Evans, *Tertullian Adversus Marcionem*, Oxford, 1972, p. 561.

[20] *Ibid.*, 5, 8, 12 (688, 18-27), "So then let Marcion put in evidence any gifts there are of his god, any prophets, provided they have spoken not by human emotion but by God's spirit, who have foretold things to come, and also made manifest the secrets of the heart; let him produce some psalm, some vision, some prayer, so long as it is a spiritual one, in ecstasy, which means abeyance of mind, if there is added also an interpretation of the tongue; let him also prove to me that in his presence some woman has prophesied, some great speaker from among those more saintly females of his. If all such proofs are more readily put in evidence by me, and are in full concord with the rules and ordinances and regulations of the Creator, without doubt both Christ and the Spirit and the apostle will belong to my God" (tr. E. Evans, *op. cit.*, p. 263).

[21] *De anima* 9, 4 (CCL 2, 792, 24–793, 38), tr. ANF, III, p. 188.

[22] See P. van Beneden "Ordo, Ueber den Ursprung einer kirchlichen Terminologie," in *Vigiliae christianae*, XXIII (1969), p. 161–176.

[23] *De exhortatione castitatis* 13, 4 (CCL 2, 1035, 35-39).

[24] Cf. 1 Tim. 3:2; Titus 1:6.

[25] Cf. 1 Tim. 5:9.

[26] *Ad uxorem* 1, 7, 4 (CCL 1, 381, 19-25), tr. ANF, IV, p. 43.

[27] Some evidence in this sense seems to be found in the following text: "But again, writing to Timotheus, he 'wills the very young (women) to marry, bear children, act the housewife' (1 Tim. 5:14). He is (here) directing (his speech) to such as he denotes above, 'very young widows,' who, after being 'apprehended' in widowhood, and subsequently, wooed for some length of time, after they have had Christ in their affections, 'wish to marry, having judgment, because they have rescinded the first faith'; cf. 1 Tim. 5:11-13), that (faith), to wit, by which they were 'found' in widowhood, and, after professing it, do not persevere. For this reason he 'wills' them to 'marry,' for fear of their subsequently rescinding the first faith of professed widowhood" (*De monogamia* 13, 1; CCL 2, 1248, 1-7; tr. ANF, IV, p. 70). But this text comments on 1 Timothy and does not refer to a formal profession of widowhood.

[28] See *De exhortatione castitatis* 12, 2, (CCL 2, 1032, 11-15): "If a consort in domestic works is necessary, (then) take some spiritual wife. Take to yourself from among the widows one fair in faith, dowered with poverty, sealed with age. You will (thus) make a good marriage. A plurality of such wives is pleasing to God"; *De monogamia* 16, 3 (CCL 2, 1251, 14-18): "What if he plead the loneliness of his home? As if the woman afforded company to a man ever on the eve of flight! He has, of course, a widow (at hand), whom it will be lawful for him to take. Not one such wife, but even a plurality, is permissible to have." The practice of "spiritual marriage" seems to have been very frequent in the early Church: see H. Achelis, *Virgines subintroductae. Ein Beitrag zum VII. Kapitel des I. Korintherbriefs*, Leipzig, 1902, with the distinctions found in P. de Labriolle, "Le mariage spiritual dans l'antiquité chrétienne," in *Revue historique*, XLVI (1921), pp. 204–225. Ecclesiastical authority generally frowned at this custom because of the risks involved, and from the middle of the third century positively forbade it for clerics, since their life was to be free from any suspicion. "Spiritual unions" with widows were forbidden in Africa by the Council of Carthage, 345 (can. 4; Bruns, 1, 113).

[29] *De monogamia* 11, 1 (CCL 2, 1244, 1-5).

[30] Kalsbach "Altkirchliche Einrichtung," p. 73; Huls, "Dienst der vrouw," p. 72; Daniélou, *The Ministry of Women*, p. 17.

[31] *De pudicitia* 13, 7 (CCL 1, 1304, 24-31).

[32] Cf. 1 Tim. 5:9-10.

[33] *De virginibus velandis* 9, 2-3 (CCL 2, 1219, 15-29), tr. ANF, IV p. 33.

[34] *Ep. to Smyrneans* 13, 1, quoted above, p. 13.

[35] Forget, "Diaconesses," 687, 691, 194; Colson, *Fonction diaconale*, p. 122. See also J. Gaudemet, *L'Église dans l'empire romain* (IVe-Ve siècles), Paris, 1958, p. 123, n. 4.

[36] *Apost. Trad.* 20 (Botte, 43), tr. G. Dix, *The Apostolic Tradition of Hypoly-*

tus (London: S.P.C.K., 1968), XX, 1, p. 30.

[37] J.M. Hanssens, *La liturgie d'Hippolyte. Documents et études*, pp. 129-131.

[38] *Apost. Trad.* 24, tr. Dix, *op. cit.*, XXV, p. 49.

[39] *Apost. Trad.* 30, tr. Dix, *op. cit.*, XXVII, p. 53.

[40] The Ethiopic version, which obviously tried to give a meaning to a difficult text, reads here, "because of the clerics who are invited."

[41] It is known from a letter of Pope Cornelius to Fabius of Antioch that in the middle of the third century, there were more than fifteen hundred widows and poor people assisted by the church of Rome (see Eusebius, *Eccl. Hist.* 6, 43, 11; GCS 9-2, 618, 17-18).

[42] *Apost. Trad.* 10, tr. Dix *op. cit.*, XI, p. 20.

[43] *Ibid.*, 2-3, 7 and 8.

[44] Cf. *ibid.*, 13.

[45] *Ibid.*, 12.

[46] *Ibid.*, 23, tr. Dix, *op. cit.*, XXV, p. 44. In the following, one reads: "And having risen after supper, the children and virgins having prayed, they shall sing psalms" (*Apost. Trad.* 25; Dix, p. 51). Botte notes (65, n. 1) that this sentence is obviously not in its place, and it is difficult to say what its original setting was. It proves, though, that virgins were entrusted with a special mission of prayer.

Chapter Four — pages 25–34

[1] Clement of Alexandria, *Pedagogue* 3, 12, 97, 1 (GCS 12, 289, 18-20), tr. ANF, II, p. 294.

[2] Origen *On Prayer* 28, 4 (GSC 3, 377, 17-21), tr. J.J. O'Meara, *Prayer, Exhortation to Martyrdom,* Ancient Christian Writers, XIX, p. 108.

[3] Origen, *Homilies on Luke* 17 (GCS 49, 110, 3-5).

[4] 1 Tim. 3:1-2.

[5] 1 Tim. 3:12.

[6] 1 Tim. 5:9.

[7] Titus 1:5-6.

[8] Origen, *Commentary on Matthew* 14, 22 (GCS 40, 336, 26–337, 19).

[9] 1 Tim. 5:10.

[10] Titus 2:3; cf. Titus 1:9. – Origen, *Commentary on John* 32, 12 (7) (GCS 10, 144, 18-26. J. Daniélou (*The Ministry of Women*, p. 17), does not give the exact meaning of this text when he writes: "It is the same with Origen. There he states that if the role of the widow consisted solely of feet-washing, which could be done by servants and domestics, there would have been no reason for ranking them with those enjoying a definite ecclesiastical status."

[11] Titus 1:5.

[12] Titus 1:7.

[13] Titus 1:9.

[14] Cf. 1 Tim. 5:10.

[15] Cf. Titus 2:3-4.

[16] 1 Tim. 2:12.

[17] Origen, *Homilies on Isaiah* 6, 3 (GCS 33, 273, 9-19).

[18] G. Huls ("Dienst der vrouw," p. 66, n. 6) wrongly states: "In this instance it is surprising that Origen gives as a reason for forbidding the instruction of men, not a reference to Paul, but the fact that it is not becoming (*indecens*) for a woman to be a teacher of men." Probably he makes this mistake because he read the text of the *Commentary on Isaiah* in Migne, which reads: "For he does not permit (*permittit*) a woman to teach, or to govern a man," whereas the text chosen by the editor of the Corpus of Berlin, which should be preferred as more difficult, reads: "For I do not permit (*permitto*) a woman to teach, or to govern a man," which is a literal quote of 1 Timothy 2:12. Anyway, the reference to Paul is certain in the fragment of the commentary on 1 Corinthians 14:34-35, which is quoted later on.

[19] Rom. 16:6.

[20] The word "too" probably refers to what was said above about Phoebe in the commentary on Romans (Rom. 16:1-2); this text is discussed later on, p. 31.

[21] Cf. Titus 2:3-5.

[22] Cf. 1 Tim. 5:10.

[23] Origen, *Commentary on Romans* 10, 20 (PG 14, 1279 D–1280 A).

[24] 1 Cor. 14:34.

[25] Cf. Apoc. 21:2, "*Hōs nymphēn kekosmēmenēn tō andri autēs.*"

[26] Acts 21:9.

[27] Judg. 4:4.

[28] Exod. 15:20-21.

[29] 2 Kings 22:14-20. Actually, the messengers of the king who visited Huldah were five.

[30] Luke 2:36.

[31] 1 Cor. 14:35.

[32] 1 Tim. 2:12.

[33] Titus 2:3-4.

[34] 1 Cor. 14:35.

[35] Origen, *Fragments on 1 Corinthians* 74 (JTS 10, 41-42).

[36] 2 Cor. 12:12.

[37] See, for instance *Didache* 11-12 (AV 1, 6, 28–7, 26).

[38] Clement of Alexandria, *Stromata* 3, 6, 53, 3-4 (GCS 52, 220, 20-25). tr. J.E.L. Oulton and H. Chadwick, *Alexandrian Christianity*, The Library of Christian Classics, II, p. 65.

[39] "Altkirchliche Einrichtung," pp. 32-33.

[40] See Gryson, *Origines du célibat*, pp. 8–12.

[41] At least according to the standard text, the one which Clement gives: "*Mē ouk echomen exousian adelphēn gynaika periagein.*" But an important part of the textual tradition reads simply *gynaikas* (or *gynaika*) instead of *adelphēn gynaika*, which led some exegetes to suppose that it was the original reading, and that *adelphēn* was an interpolation explained by the intention to make clear that the Apostles did not live in wedlock with their wives; see J.B. Bauer, "Uxores circumducere (1 Kor. 9, 5)," in *Biblische Zeitschrift*, III (1959), pp. 94-102.

[42] Rom. 16:1-2.

[43] "Hic locus apostolica auctoritate docet etiam feminas in ministerio Ecclesiae constitui." Since in the lemma, *ousa diakonos tēs Ekklēsias tēs en Kegchreais* is translated ". . . quae est in ministerio Ecclesiae quae est in Cenchris," one can suppose that the Greek text of the commentary read ". . . *kai gynaikas diakonous tēs Ekklēsias kathistasthai.*" There is some confirmation of this reading in the sentence found later on: "Et ideo locus hic duo pariter docet, *et haberi, ut diximus, feminas ministras in Ecclesia*, et tales debere assumi in ministerium quae astiterint multis," where the words in italics can hardly be translated back into Greek otherwise than ". . . *kai einai*, hōs *eipamen, gynaikas diakonous en tē Ekklēsia.*"

[44] Gen. 19:1-3.

[45] Gen. 18:1-5.

[46] Origen, *Commentary on Romans* 10, 17 (PG 14, 1278 A-C).

[47] "Altkirchliche Einrichtung," p. 33.

[48] Rom. 12:13; 1 Peter 4:9; etc.

[49] "*Altkirchliche Einrichtung,*" pp. 95-112.

[50] *On the Early History*, pp. 308–309; Zscharnack, *Dienst der Frau*, pp. 108–109.

[51] See above, pp. 86–88.

[52] Origen, *Commentary on Romans* 10, 17, quoted above, p. 31.

[53] Origen, *Commentary on Matthew* 14, 22 (GCS 40, 337, 19–338, 28), tr. ANF, X, p. 510, which is the following of the text quoted above, p. 26. For the meaning of this text, see H. Crouzel, *Virginité et mariage selon Origène* (Museum Lessianum, Section Theologique, 58), Paris, 1963, pp. 157–159.

[54] See Origen, *Contra Celsum* 1, 65 (GCS 2, 118, 24-26); *Following of the Commentaries on Matthew* 141 (GCS 38, 293, 1-33); *Fragments on Matthew* 563 (GCS 41, 231-232).

[55] *The Ministry of Women*, p. 17.

Chapter Five — pages 35–43

[1] The *Didascalia* was written in Syria in the first half of the third century. The original Greek text is lost, except for a short fragment, in poor condition, of Book III, but a Syriac version from the beginning of the fourth century and important fragments of a Latin version from the end of the fourth century are extant. The *Didascalia* was used as a source in the six first books of the *Apostolic Constitutions*. Therefore, in the sections where the *Constitutions* agree with the versions of the *Didascalia*, one may presume that the

original Greek of the *Didascalia* is preserved.

We have used concurrently the editions of F.X. Funk (*Didascalia et constitutiones Apostolorum*, 2 vols., Paderborn, 1905; reprint, Turin, 1964) and of R.H. Connolly (*Didascalia Apostolorum. The Syriac Version Translated and Accompanied by the Verona Latin Fragments. With an Introduction and Notes*, Oxford, 1929). The Greek fragment (*Didasc.*, 3, 5, 6–6, 4) is edited by J.V. Bartlet, "Fragments of the *Didascalia Apostolorum* in Greek," in JTS, XVIII (1917), pp. 301–309.

[2] *Didasc.* 2, 4, 1 (Funk, 34, 16-17; Connolly, 32, 27-28).

[3] *Didasc.* 2, 4, 1-2 (Funk, 36, 1-5; Connolly, 32, 31–34, 6).

[4] *Didasc.* 2, 25, 1-3 (Funk, 92, 14–94, 7; Connolly, 78, 7-27); 2, 25, 8 (Funk, 96, 11-17; Connolly, 81, 7-13). The widows are also mentioned together with the orphans and foreigners in *Didascalia* 4, 3, 1 (Funk, 220, 5-6; Connolly, 154, 1-3). They are associated with the destitute more generally in *Didascalia* 3, 3, 1–4, 4 (Funk, 186, 1–188, 2; Connolly 131, 4–132, 4). They are found in the same association in another document of the same time, the *Epistle to Virgins* of Pseudo-Clement (1, 12, 1; Funk-Diekamp, 22, 18–24).

[5] *Didasc.* 2, 26, 1–3 (Funk, 102, 1-16; Connolly, 85, 1–86, 18; 87, 1-16). A text of the Pseudo-Clementine *Homilies*, the sources of which are at least partly from the same time as the *Didascalia*, mentions among those whom the faithful must "honor" (in the material sense of the term) presbyters, catechists (*katēchētas*), deacons, widows who lived honestly (*chēras eu bebiōkyias*), and orphans, who are the children of the Church (3, 71, 5; GCS 42, 83, 2-4).

[6] *Ep. to Philippians* 4, 3, quoted above, p. 12.

[7] *Didasc.* 2, 26, 8 (Funk, 104, 9-10; Connolly, 88, 5-6; 89, 4-5).

[8] *Didasc.* 2 57, 8 (Funk, 164, 9; Connolly, 120, 21-22). For this reason, when a woman who does not belong to the community comes to the assembly, the deacon asks her whether she is married or a widow (*Didasc.* 2, 58, 1 (Funk, 166, 6-9; Connolly, 120, 28-33; 121, 2-6).

[9] *Didasc.* 2, 28, 1-5 (Funk, 108, 1-15; Connolly, 88, 23–90, 16; 89 19–91, 9).

[10] The Latin *Didascalia*, in 2, 28, 1, uses the word *aniculas* for the recipients of these charities (Funk, 108, 2; Connolly, 89, 19), which means literally "petites vieilles"; the corresponding term in the *Apostolic Constitutions* is *presbyteras* (Funk, 109, 2). A little further on, in *Didascalia* 2, 28, 3, the same people are referred to as *praesbyterorum* (Connolly, 91, 3), which must be corrected, as another hand did in the manuscript itself, to *praesbyterarum* (Funk, 108; 6; see E. Tidner, *Sprachlicher Kommentar zur lateinischen Didascalia Apostolorum*, Stockholm, 1938, p. 166); the parallel to this word in the *Constitutions* is *presbytidōn* (Funk, 109, 6).

Anicula reappears in *Didascalia* 2, 58, 5 (Funk, 168, 14-20; Connolly, 122, 21-29; 123, 17-22): the deacon must see to it that an old man or an old woman (*senior aut anicula*) is not standing up in church while young people are sitting down. In the *Constitutions*, the sentence is reworked, and there is no parallel to these words (cf. *Apost. Const.* 2, 58, 5; Funk, 169, 15-20); the Greek original of the *Didascalia* probably read *presbyteros ē presbytera.* In the Greek fragment which preserves part of the text of *Didascalia* 3, 5, 6, J.V. Bartlet (*art. cit.*, p. 303) restores the word *presbyteras*: "*Myktērisantes chleu]asousin m[allon ē] doxasōs[in tois lo]gois tēs p[resbyte]ras enoch[os de autē] esti amart[ias].*" As one can see, only the first and the three last letters of the word are preserved, so that the restoration is very questionable.

The Syriac version offers a different reading, which can hardly be reconciled with the letters preserved in the Greek fragment: "They will mock and scoff, instead of applauding the word of doctrine; and she shall incur a heavy judgment for sin" (Funk, 190, 5-7; Connolly, 133, 8-10). The *Constitutions* alter this text, but give the term *presbytis* in this section, which to some extent confirms the reconstitution offered by Bartlet: *Myktērisantes chleuasousin mallon hōs pseudē ē doxasousin, kai enochos estai tēs propeteias ē presbytis*" (Funk, 191, 4-5).

Anyway, in all these references the context shows sufficiently that the terms *presbytera* and *presbytis* in the *Didascalia* and the *Constitutions* mean simply an advanced age, and not a dignity or a function. The "old women" (*presbyterai* or *presbytides*) are not exactly the same as the widows (*chērai*), since old women and widows are mentioned conjointly in *Didascalia* 2, 57, 8 (Funk, 164, 9; Connolly, 120, 21-22); the *Constitutions* here read *ai chērai kai ai presbytides* (2, 57 12; Funk, 165, 8). However, in *Didascalia* 2, 28, 1 and 3, instead of "old women," the Syriac version mentions "widows" (Connolly, 88, 23; 90, 5).

11 The Greek term used by the *Didascalia* for this kind of meal was certainly *agapē*, since this term reappears in the *Apostolic Constitutions*, where it is glossed by *dochē*, "a meal with guests" (*Apost. Const.* 2, 28, 1; Funk, 109, 1), and it is transliterated simply as *agapam* in the Latin version (Funk, 108, 1; Connolly, 89, 19). The Syriac version uses a term which refers more particularly to the funeral meals organized for widows in the *Apostolic Tradition* (30; see above, p. 23), but the term "agape" does not appear in this place.

12 The Syriac version mentions only distributions of gifts (Connolly, 88, 25–90, 1). According to Connolly (*op. cit.*, p. 89, footnote), these words would be interpolated and would perhaps witness to a later practice or later ideas. In my opinion, though, they may have existed in the original text and, as suggested by F. Nau (*La Didascalie des douze apôtres*, 2nd ed., Paris, 1912, p. 83, n. 5), they may have disappeared later on because of a *homoioteleuton*. The Latin version, which does not contain the contested words, speaks, though, in the following sentence, of *agapis et erogationibus* (*Didasc.*, 2, 28, 2; Funk, 108, 5; Connolly, 91, 2). Later on the *Didascalia* seems to refer to such distributions (*Didasc.* 3, 10, 8; Funk, 204, 12-21; Connolly, 143, 22–144, 4).

13 The Greek term paralleling it in the *Didascalia* is *kathistēmi*, (*Apost. Const.* 3, 1, 1 and 2; Funk, 183, 3 and 5). It is found also for widows in the *Apostolic Tradition* (10; see above, p. 24).

14 The Greek term used by the *Didascalia* was probably *to chērikon*, which figures four times in the *Apostolic Constitutions*, but three times out of these four in texts taken from the *Didascalia* (*Apost.* 3, 1, 2 Funk, 183, 5 and 7; 3, 2, 1, p. 185, 14; 8, 25, 2, p. 528, 12). Two parallel sections of the Pseudo-Clementine *Homilies* and *Recognitions*, which, because of this parallelism, may come from the Syrian *Grundschrift* of the first half of the third century — thus being from the same time as, and close to, the *Didascalia* — explain that Peter, about to leave Tripoli in Phoenicia, appointed Maron, who had been his host, as bishop, appointed twelve presbyters, selected deacons, and organized an order of widows: *chērika sustēsamenos* (Pseudo-Clement of Rome, *Homilies* 11, 36, 2; GCS 42, 172, 10; cf. *Recognitions* 6, 15, 5; GCS 51, 196, 18). Here we find the same word as in the *Constitutions*, but in the plural form, which is not surprising, since it is a collectivity. The word reappears in the singular in Theodore of Mopsuestia (?), *Commentary on 1 Timothy*, on 1 Tim. 5:9 (Swete, 2, 159, app. ad lin. 22ff.).

15 *Didasc.* 3, 1, 1 (Funk, 182, 1-3; Connolly, 130 1-3).

16 *Didasc.* 3, 1, 2 (Funk, 182, 3–184, 1; Connolly, 130, 3-10).

17 *Didasc.* 3, 1, 3 (Funk, 184, 1-8; Connolly, 130, 10-19).

18 *Didasc.*, 3, 2, 1–3, 1 (Funk, 184, 9–186, 2; Connolly, 130, 20–131, 5).

19 *Didasc.* 3, 5, 1 (Funk, 188, 3–6; Connolly, 132, 5-10).

20 *Didasc.* 3, 5, 2 (Funk, 188, 6-7; Connolly, 132, 10-11).

21 *Didasc.* 3, 5, 3-6 (Funk, 188, 7–190, 7; Connolly, 132, 12–133, 10; Bartlet, p. 303).

22 Such is the way in which the Greek formula *Maria hē tou Iakōbou* is read in the old Syriac version of the Gospel (see Connolly, p. 133, footnote). It is usually interpreted as "Mary, the mother of James."

23 The Greek fragment reads "Salome" instead of "the other Mary." The reading of the Syriac version seems to be better; see Connolly, *ed. cit.*, p. xxi, tr. R.H. Connolly, *Didascalia Apostolorum*, XV (1969), p. 133.

24 *Didasc.* 3, 6, 1-2 (Funk, 190, 8, 17;

Connolly, 133, 11-23; Bartlet, pp. 304, 305). J. Daniélou (The Ministry of Women, p. 19ff.) gives as coming from the *Didascalia* the parallel text of the *Constitutions*, which is notably different.

25 *Didasc.* 3, 6, 3–7, 5 (Funk, 190, 17–194, 17; Connolly, 133 23–136, 24; 135, 1–137, 21; Bartlet, pp. 305, 306; the Greek fragment stops at the end of *Didascalia* 3, 6, 4).

26 *Didasc.* 3, 7, 6-8 (Funk, 194, 6–196, 16; Connolly, 136, 25–138, 20; 137, 21–139, 20). These descriptions of the good and the wicked widow recall many of the traits found in 1 Timothy 5:3-16.

27 *Didasc.* 3, 8, 1-5 (Funk, 196, 17–198, 30; Connolly, 138, 21–140, 34; 139, 21–141, 16).

28 *Didasc.* 3, 9, 1-3 (Funk, 198, 31–200, 5; Connolly, 142, 1-9).

29 *Didasc.* 3, 10, 1–11, 5 (Funk, 202, 1–208, 7; Connolly, 142, 10–145, 30), tr. Connolly.

30 *Didasc.* 4, 5, 1-4 (Funk, 222, 15–224, 11; Connolly, 156, 8–158, 1; 157, 7-11).

31 *Didasc.* 4, 6, 1-5 (Funk, 224, 12–226, 4; Connolly, 158, 1-20).

32 *Didasc.* 4, 6, 6–7, 3 (Funk, 226, 4–228, 4; Connolly, 158, 20–159, 22).

33 *Didasc.* 4, 8, 1–9, 2 (Funk, 228, 5–230, 7; Connolly, 159, 22–160, 18).

34 *Didasc.* 4, 10, 1-2 (Funk, 230, 8-14); Connolly, 160, 19-28).

35 *Didasc.* 3, 1, 1-3 (Funk, 182, 1–184, 8; Connolly, 130, 1-19).

36 *Didasc.* 3, 6, 4 (Funk, 192, 4-5; Connolly, 134, 6-7; 135, 2-3): "Quaeque si tales fuerint, non iudicabuntur dignae eius qui eas vocavit."

37 *Didasc.* 3, 7, 5 (Funk, 194, 16-17; Connolly, 136, 22-24; 137, 20-21): "Nescit qui ei locus creditus est vel quo gradu digna effecta est."

38 In my opinion, it is not proved, contrary to the interpretation of Huls ("Dienst der vrouw," p. 64) and Zscharnack (*Dienst der Frau*, pp. 112–113), by this sentence found in *Didascalia* 3, 11, 5; Funk, 208, 3-7; Connolly, 145, 25-29): "Let not the bishop, nor a presbyter, nor a deacon, nor a widow utter a curse out of their mouth, that they may not inherit a curse but a blessing. And let this also be thy care, O bishop, that not even one of the laity utter from his mouth a curse." The fact that the widow is mentioned in an enumeration after the bishop, priest, and deacon, and apart from the laity, does indeed mean that she enjoys a place apart in the community, but not necessarily that she herself (or her ministry) has a clerical character, as these scholars contend. From another sentence one could derive as well that the widow is included in the same defense as the laity, and is, consequently, part of the laity; see *Didasc.* 3, 5, 4-5 (Funk, 188, 12-13, 17-18; Connolly, 132, 17-20; 133, 1-3): "But concerning punishment and reward, and the kingdom of the name of Christ, and His dispensation, neither a widow nor a layman ought to speak. . . . Wherefore our Lord said in the Gospel, to widows and to all the laity: 'Cast not your pearls before swine' (Matthew 7:6)."

Notice also that the author of the *Didascalia* seems to ignore the term *klēros*; in spite of its occurrences in the *Apostolic Constitutions*, we find no counterpart in the *Didascalia* (see the *Index vocabulorum* in Funk, *ed. cit.*, p. 672, at *klēros*). The author mentions the members of the clergy: "bishop and deacons," "bishops and deacons" (presbyters appear less frequently and seem to have a more humble part); he does not seem to possess a concept needed to refer to the ministers of the Church as a whole.

39 *Didasc.* 3, 1, 1-2 (Funk, 182, 1–184, 1; Connolly, 130, 1-10).

40 *Didasc.* 3, 6, 2; 7, 1, 4-7; 10, 4-7; 4, 5, 2-3; 6, 8-9; 7, 2; 10, 2).

41 *Didasc.* 3, 8, 1-3 (Funk, 196, 17–198, 14; Connolly, 138, 21–140, 15; 139, 21–141, 12).

42 *Didasc.* 3, 11, 4 (Funk, 208, 2-3; Connolly, 145, 23-25).

43 It is not clear where G. Huls finds evidence for "other caritative activities" which he ascribes to the widows, in a general reference to *Didascalia* 3, 5-8 ("Dienst der vrouw," pp. 63–64). Only because he ascribes to widows a text concerning deaconesses (*Didasc.* 3, 12), J. Colson can write: "They [the widows] have no other function than to assist the bishop and deacons in providing help to those assigned to them by the bishop and

deacons, when the bishop and deacons cannot do it by themselves and because it is fitting that this work of assistance should be performed by a woman" (*Fonction diaconale*, pp. 133–134).

[44] *Didasc.* 3, 5, 2 (Funk, 188, 6-7; Connolly, 132, 10-11).

[45] *Didasc.* 3, 5, 3 (Funk, 188, 7-10; Connolly, 132, 12-15).

[46] *Didasc.* 3, 6, 1-2 (Funk, 190, 8-17; Connolly, 133, 11-23).

[47] *Didasc.* 3, 9, 1-3 (Funk, 198, 31–200, 5; Connolly, 142, 1-9).

[48] *Didasc.* 3, 5, 4-6 (Funk, 188, 12–190, 7; Connolly, 132, 17–133, 10).

[49] *Didasc.* 3, 1, 2 (Funk, 182, 7; Connolly, 130, 9).

[50] *Didasc.* 2, 28, 1 (Funk, 108, 1-2; Connolly, 89, 19-20).

[51] *Didasc.* 3, 2, 1 (Funk, 184, 9-11; Connolly, 130, 20–131, 1).

[52] *Didasc.* 2, 4, 1-2; 25, 2-3, 8; 26, 3, 8; 4, 3, 1; 5, 1; 6, 1; 8, 1-3).

[53] *Didasc.* 4, 3, 3, (Funk, 220, 9-17; Connolly, 154, 7-16; 155, 6-14).

[54] *Didasc.* 2, 26, 8; 3, 6, 3; 10, 7; 4, 5, 1; 7, 1, 3.

[55] *Didasc.* 3, 6, 4–7, 5; 8, 3-5; 10, 8-12.

[56] See, for instance, *Ep. to Magnesians* 6, 1 (AV 1, 90, 7-9).

[57] *Didasc.* 2, 26, 6 (Funk, 104, 7-8; Connolly, 88, 3-4; 89, 2-3).

[58] After this word the Latin version is preserved. We give its text, which can be compared with the Syriac version, the translation of which we continue to give in the body of the page; only small discrepancies appear in the comparison: ". . . et Maria Iacobi et Ioseph mater et mater filiorum Zebedei. Tu ergo in aliis rebus disconissam necessariam habebis, ut eas gentilium domes ingredia[n]tur, ubi vos accedere non potestis, propter fideles mulieres, et ut eis quae infirmantur ministret quae necessantur, et in balneis iterum eas quae meliorant ut labe[n]t. Diacones sint in actibus similes episcopis suis, sed exercitatiores, et non malum adpetentes lucrum, ut bene ministrent. Secundum multitudinem Ecclesiae sufficientes erunt, ut et senioribus mulieribus quae iam non possunt, fratribus et sororibus quae in infirmitate ditinentur, possint placere, in celeritate ministeria sua conplentes. Et mulier circa mulieres festinabit, diaconus vero, quoniam vir est, [et] circa viros, et ad peregrinationem et ministerium et servitium ad iussionem episcopi paratissimus et mobilis sit" (Connolly, 149, 1-15).

[59] Cf. Matthew 27:56; Mark 15:40; Luke 8:2-3.

[60] *Didasc.* 3, 12, 1–13, 1 (Funk, 208, 8–214, 3; Connolly, 146, 1–148, 22), tr. Connolly.

[61] In *The Apostolic Constitutions, hē diakonos* (or *gynē diakonos*) appears regularly in the sections paralleling the *Didascalia* (*Apost. Const.* 2, 26, 3; Funk 103, 21; 2, 26, 6, p. 105, 15 and 20; 2, 58, 6, p. 171, 3; 3, 8, 1, p. 197, 19; 3, 16, 1 [=*Didasc.* 3, 12, 1] p. 209, 13 and 16; 3, 16, 2 (=*Didasc.* 3, 12, 2), p. 209, 18, and p. 211, 2; 3, 16, 4 [=*Didasc.* 3, 12, 3], p. 211, 15); and *diakonissa* appears regularly in the sections proper to the *Apostolic Constitutions* (3, 11, 3; Funk, 201, 29; 6, 17, 4, p. 341, 9; 8, 19, 1, p. 524, 11; 8, 19, 2, p. 524, 13; 8, 28, 6, p. 530, 22; 8, 28, 7, p. 530, 25; 8, 28, 8, p. 530, 28; 8, 31, 2, p. 532, 26), with the exception of a text giving the aberrant reading *diakonē*, which is absent from the *Patristic Greek Lexicon* (PGL) but is attested here by all the manuscript except for one, which reads *diakonissa* (*Apost. Const.* 8, 13, 14; Funk, 516, 24). The first text giving *diakonissa* is Canon 19 of Nicaea. Therefore, it is practically certain that the *Didascalia* used the form *hē diakonos* for the deaconess.

[62] *Diasc.* 3, 12, 1 (Funk, 208, 10-11; Connolly, 146, 4-5).

[63] *Didasc.* 3, 13, 1 (Funk, 214, 1-3; Connolly, 148, 21-22).

[64] *Didasc.* 2, 28, 6 (Funk, 108, 15–110, 3; Connolly, 90, 17-23); 2, 44, 2-4 (Funk, 138, 6-13; Connolly, 109, 7-17).

[65] *Didasc.* 2, 57, 6-7 (Funk, 162, 2-7; Connolly, 120, 3-9).

[66] *Didasc.* 2, 26, 6 (Funk, 104, 7-8; Connolly, 88, 3-4); 2, 26, 8 (Funk, 104, 9-10; Connolly, 88, 5-6).

[67] Forget, "Diaconesses," p. 687.

[68] Colson, *Fonction diaconale*, p. 135.

[69] In this sense, P.H. Lafontaine (*Conditions positives*, p. 41), referring to

Didascalia 3, 1, 1, states: "La *Didascalie* avait porté l'âge d'admission des femmes au diaconissat à cinquante ans – The *Didascalia* raised the age of admission for women to the diaconate to fifty years."

70 F.X. Funk affirms it without evidence when he writes: "In *Didascalia* diaconissae nonnisi viduae esse videntur quibus ministerium ad feminas pertinens commissum erat – In the Didascalia the deaconesses seem to be nothing else but widows to whom the ministry of women was committed." (*ed. cit.*, p. 182, footnote on *Apost. Const.* 3, 1, 1).

Chapter Six — pages 44–74

1 ECA 1, 1–2, 1 (Schermann, 13, 1–14, 5): "We being all by command of our Lord Jesus Christ gathered together. He commanded us: 'Before you are about to divide the eparchies by lot, (first) reckon the places of number (*sic*), the authority of bishops, the seals of the priests, the attendance of the deacons, the instructions of the readers, the blamelessness of the widows (*chērōn anegklēsias*), and all things that are required for the foundation and the stability of the Church, in order that when they know the pattern of these heavenly things, they may be warned and keep themselves from all fault, knowing that they have an account to give in that great day of judgment of the things, which, having heard, they did not keep.' And He commanded us to send forth His words into all the world. Therefore it seemed good unto us, for a testimony and admonition of the brotherhood, that we should, as far as our Lord had revealed to each one of us, according to the will of God through the Holy Ghost, enjoin upon you words of admonition" (tr. by J.P. Arendzen, "An Entire Syriac Text of the *Apostolic Church Order*," JTS, III (1902), p. 61.

2 ECA 21, 1-2 (Schermann, 29 9–30, 5; Arendzen, *op. cit.*, p. 71. Let us notice "*Chērai kathistanesthōsan treis . . . eudiakonos . . .*".

3 The same verb *kathistanō* (or its classical form *kathistēmi*) is used for the bishop (ECA 17, 1; Schermann, 25, 5); presbyters (17, 1, p. 25, 6); readers (19, 1, p. 27, 1); and deacons (20, 1, p. 28, 4).

4 At least in the last state of the text (ECA 17, 2; Schermann, 25, 7-8). From the context it appears that a first redaction mentioned only two presbyters, and that the words "not two, but three" were added later on; see A. Harnack, *Die Quellen der sogenannten Apostolischen Kirchenordnung* (TU 2, 5), Leipzig, 1886, p. 11.

5 ECA 20, 1 (Schermann, 28, 4-5). The sentence is not clear. It is difficult to say exactly whether the reference to a text of Scripture prescribing to decide in all things from the word of three witnesses means that the deacons should be three in number, as understood by the Syriac version, or that before they are appointed, they should be given a good testimony from three witnesses at least, as understood by the Coptic version (see J.M. Hanssens, *Liturgie d'Hippolyte*, pp. 56–59, n. 16).

6 Dealing with the election of the bishop, the author considers the case where there would not be in the community twelve faithful with the right to vote (ECA 16, 1: Schermann, 24, 3-5).

7 The formula comes for 1 Timothy 5:5.

8 Cf. 1 Tim. 3:8.

9 Daniélou, *The Ministry of Women*, p. 18: "Care of the sick implies not only material assistance, but religious ministrations as well." The French reads, "*actions cultuelles.*"

10 Hanssens, *Liturgie d'Hippolyte*, p. 61, n. 17.

11 *Ibid.*, pp. 58–59, n. 17.

12 See above, p. 139, n. 2.

13 It is probably correct to change *ouketi* to *ouch oti*, as suggested by Hauler.

14 ECA 24, 1–28, 1 (Schermann, 31, 10–33, 6), tr. Arendzen, *op. cit.*, p. 71, altered.

15 The verbs used are *anapiptō* or *anakeimai*; see Luke 22:14; John 13:12, 23, 25, 28.

16 About this *agraphon*, see A. Resch, *Agrapha* (TU 30, 3-4), Leipzig, 1906, pp. pp. 104, 105. The true meaning seems to be that mankind, weakened by sin, will be saved by the divine power working in

Jesus Christ. This *agraphon* is not attested elsewhere.

[17] All versions, except for the Latin, which is remarkably faithful, alter the text at this place; see Hanssens, *Liturgie d'Hippolyte*, pp. 62–65, n. 20.

[18] Huls, "Dienst der vrouw," p. 67.

[19] C. Robinson, *Ministry of Deaconesses*, pp. 192–193.

[20] Daniélou, *The Ministry of Women*, p. 20.

[21] In ECA 24, 1, Andrew says, according to the Greek text (Schermann, 31, 10-11): "*Euchrēston estin, adelphoi, tais gynaixi diakonian katastēnai*." The Latin version, usually very faithful, here reads: "*Utile est, fratres, mulieribus diaconissam ordinare*," and the Coptic versions speaks also at this place of deaconesses, which suggests that some Greek manuscripts read *diakonissan* instead of *diakonian* — undoubtedly wrongly. The Syriac version confirms the Greek text preserved. Cf. ECA 28, 1 (Schermann, 33, 4-6)), where all versions, in this reference, confirm "*Pōs oun dynametha peri gynaikōn diakonian horisai, ei mē ti diakonian hina epischyōsi tais endeomenais*."

[22] The conjunction *epei* used in this sentence (*epei mēde cheirothesian tina echousin*) has, most often, a causal or temporal connotation, but sometimes also an adversative sense, which seems to fit here very well. Notice, though, that the interpretation of this text proposed by us is still possible if *epei* is interpreted in a causal sense. In addition, I prefer the reading *mēde*, which is retained by most editors (see, for instance, Bruns, 1, 19), to the reading *mēte* adopted by P.P. Joannou, because *mēte* does not seem, according to dictionaries, to be used alone in an adverbial sense, whereas *mēde* does.

[23] First Council of Nicaea (325 A.D.), can. 19 (Joannou, 1-1, 40, 10–41, 7), tr. ANF, XIV, p. 40.

[24] There is no serious study known of this canon understood in this sense. See what P.H. Lafontaine says about it in *Conditions positives*, pp. 47–53 (with some bibliography). But, contrary to what this author says, the registration in the canon does not mean that deaconesses belong to the clergy, since canon 19 of Nicaea affirms that they belong to the laity. Lafontaine supposes that this affirmation concerns only the deaconesses of the Paulianists, because their ordination is void; but he is among those who do not correctly understand canon 10 of Nicaea, as shall be seen later on.

[25] A. Kalsbach "Die Diakonissenweihe im Kan. 19 des Konzils von Nicäa," in *Römische Quartalschrift*, XXXII (1924), pp. 166–169; repeated almost identically in Kalsbach, "Altkirchliche Einrichtung," pp. 46–69. For the opposite, see the objections (not very convincing) of O. Casel in *Jahrbuch für Liturgiewissenchaft*, V (1925), pp. 242–243, and XI (1931), p. 274. One of the solutions offered in order to solve the contradiction is that the deaconesses of the Paulianists did not receive a laying on of hands, whereas Catholic deaconesses received it (Thomassin, Binterim). Another solution is that among the deaconesses of the Paulianists, some were ordained and others were not (Morin, Schaefer, Ludwig, Casel).

[26] Literally, "honor"; in Greek, probably *timē*; it would be better to translate by "dignity."

[27] CH 9.

[28] See above, p. 24.

[29] See the index of articles in Hanssens, *Liturgie d'Hippolyte*, p. 24.

[30] See above, p. 24.

[31] CH 32.

[32] ECA 21, 2; see above, p. 45.

[33] Cf. 1 Tim. 5:3; "*Chēras tima*."

[34] CH 5.

[35] In *Patrologia orientalis* 31, 357, n. 2.

[36] See above, p. 23.

[37] CH 35.

[38] CH 32 (p. 405); 34 (p. 407); 35, first paragraph (p. 409).

[39] Basil of Caesarea, *Ep. to Amphilochius on the Canons* 44 (Joannou, 2, 136, 3-7); tr. R.J. Deferrari, *Saint Basil; The Letters*, III, p. 131 (Loeb).

[40] *Ibid*., 22, p. 113 (Loeb).

[41] *Ibid*., 59, p. 255 (Loeb).

[42] *Ibid*., 22, p. 113 (Loeb).

[43] *Ibid*., 32, p. 123; 51, p. 245 (Loeb).

[44] *Ibid*., 3, p. 23 (Loeb).

[45] *Ibid*., 44, p. 131 (Loeb)

[46] *Ibid*., p. 131 (Loeb).

[47] For instance, 3, 4, 18, 19, 47, etc.

[48] "Altkirchliche Einrichtung," p. 109, n. 1.

[49] *Ep. on the Canons* 18 (p. 119, 27-28).

[50] *Apost. Const.* 6, 17, 4; see later on, p. 60.

[51] *Ep. on the Canons* 41 (pp. 134, 21–135, 4).

[52] *Ibid.*, 4 (p. 101, 20–102, 22).

[53] *Ibid.*, 24 (p. 126, 3-17).

[54] A superior of a religious community of men, on whom a community of women depends canonically; see PGL, at *presbyteros*, sense 11c, where this text is cited among others.

[55] Instead of *presbyteran*, a manuscript reads *presbytin* (PG 31, 1157, n. 7).

[56] Basil of Caesarea, *Shorter Rule* 110 (PG 31, 1157 A).

[57] *Ibid.*, 111.

[58] See PGL, at *presbytera*, sense 3.

[59] Council of Laodicea, can. 11 (Joannou, 1-2, 135, 6-8).

[60] Forget, "Diaconesses," p. 688; Leclercq, "Diaconesse," p. 725.

[61] De Labriolle, "*Mulieres . . . taceant*," pp. 116–117.

[62] Hefele-Leclercq, *Histoire des conciles*, 1-2, 1003; G. Bardy, "Laodicée," in DDC 6, 340-341; Gaudemet, *L'Église*, p. 124, n. 1.

[63] Lafontaine, *Conditions positives*, p. 39, n. 99.

[64] See references later on, p. 146, nn. 197–198.

[65] *Martyrdom of Matthew* 28 (Lipsius-Bonnet, 2-1, 259, 1-6, 9-12, 27-32).

[66] See PGL, at *presbytis*, sense A; to the texts in this section, one can add the three texts of the *Apostolic Constitutions* quoted under B 1, where the subject is old women, but not necessarily old widows (see above, p. 135, n. 10). Theodoret of Cyrus, in his commentary on the Epistle to Titus (on Titus 2:3; PG 82, 864 B), interprets *presbytidas* by *tas gegērakyias*. For Epiphanius (*Panarion* 79, 4, 1; GCS 37, 478, 28-29), the *presbytides* of Titus 2:3 are the eldest among the widows. Nothing can be learned in this regard from the epitaph of a certain Epikto, found on the island of Thera, which belongs to the end of the third century or more probably to the fourth century. It consists only of these three words: "*Angelos Epiktous presbytidos*" (see H. Grégoire, *Recueil des inscriptions grecques chrétiennes d'Asie Mineure*, fasc. 1, Paris, 1922, p. 58, n. 167). There is no reason for the connection made by PGL between this text and that of the *Martyrdom of Matthew* cited in the preceding note.

[67] See Pseudo-Athanasius, *On Virginity* 14(TU 29-2, 48, 16-20); cf. *ibid.*, 11 (44, 20-22). See also Pseudo-Palladius, *Prologue to the Lausiac History* (Butler, 3, 5).

[68] Council of Laodicea, can. 45 (Joannou, 1-2, 148, 16-17).

[69] *Testamentum Domini*, 1, 19, 7; 23, 1; see later on, pp. 65–66.

[70] *Apost. Const.* 4, 3, 1-3 (Funk, 221, 7-21).

[71] *Ibid.*, 2, 4, 1 (Funk, 35, 17).

[72] *Ibid.*, 4, 2, 1 (Funk, 219, 19).

[73] *Ibid.*, 2, 25, 2 (Funk, 93 22-25); 3, 3, 2 (p. 187, 11-15).

[74] *Ibid.*, 7, 29, 2-3 (Funk, 418, 5-10).

[75] *Ibid.*, 2, 26, 3. (Funk, 103, 20-21).

[76] *Ibid.*, 2, 26, 8 (Funk, 105, 26-28).

[77] *Ibid.*, 2, 28, 1-3 (Funk, 109, 1-7).

[78] *Ibid.*, 3, 2, 1 (Funk, 185, 16-18). The *Constitutions*, though, seem to judge second marriage more leniently than the *Didascalia*; compare *Didasc.* 3, 2, 2 (Funk, 183, 11-13) with *Apost. Const.* 3, 2, 2-3 (Funk, 185, 18-187, 6).

[79] *Ibid.*, 3, 1, 1 and 2 (Funk, 183, 3 and 5).

[80] For this term, see above, p. 136, n. 14. Pseudo-Ignatius uses the phrase *to tagma tōn chērōn* (*Ep. to Philippians* 15, 1; Funk-Diekamp, 168, 6).

[81] *Apost. Const.* 8, 25, 2-3 (Funk, 528, 9-15). This text corresponds to chapter 11 of the *Apostolic Tradition* of Hippolytus (see above, pp. 22-23). The differences between the two texts are the following. One does not find in the *Constitutions* the equivalent of the sentences: "She shall be chosen by name" and "Let the widow be instituted by word only"; the *Constitutions* say simply, "*Katatassestho eis to chērikon*," which is equivalent to

"Let her be reckoned among the (enrolled) widows" in the *Tradition*. This detail suggests that the author of the *Constitutions* does not think of a rite including a "nomination" or an "appointment," but only of an actual enrollment in the order of the widows. The *Constitutions* use here the verb *katatattō,* not *kathistēmi,* which was used by Hippolytus; but elsewhere, as is evident, one finds in the *Constitutions* the verb *kathistēmi* used for widows (see references on p. 141, n. 79 above).

The *Constitutions* agree with the *Tradition* on an undelayed "appointment" of a widow who lost her husband long ago. The *Constitutions* explain – but it is only expected – that the widow should subsequently have lived in continence and blamelessly, and particularly that she ought to have taken good care of those who lived under her roof (cf. 1 Tim. 5:8). The same *Constitutions* cite as a model in this regard Judith and Anna, two types of the Christian widow they refer to elsewhere (for Judith, see *Apost. Const.* 3, 7, 6; Funk, 195, 18-19; for Anna, *Apost. Const.* 3, 1, 5, p. 185, 5-11).

However, the *Constitutions* as well as the *Tradition* refuse, without a time of probation, to trust a widow who lost her husband recently; according to the *Tradition,* it should be so even if the widow is an old woman. This hypothesis is not considered by the *Constitutions,* which say: "Let her youth be tested with time" (*Chronō neotēs krinesthō*).

Finally, the *Constitutions* do not retain the explanation of the *Tradition* that the widow is not ordained because she does not perform a liturgical ministry. The *Constitutions* also do not say here that the widow is appointed for prayer, but they have developed on these points abundantly above (*Apost. Const.* 3, 1, 5, Funk, 185, 5-8; 3, 5, 2, p. 189, 18-20; 3, 7, 6, p. 195, 15-17). The parallel text offered by the *Epitome* of Book 8 of the *Constitutions* (ch. 16; Funk, *Didascalia et Constitutiones Apostolorum*, II, p. 82, 1, 20-28) is exactly like that of the *Constitutions.*

[82] Compare *Didasc.* 3, 1, 2 (Funk, 182, 3–184, 1) and *Apost. Const.* 3, 1, 2-3 (Funk, 183, 5-11).

[83] Cf. 1 Tim. 5:9.

[84] Compare *Didasc.* 3, 1, 1 (Funk, 182, 1-2) with *Apost. Const.* 3, 1, 1 (Funk, 183, 1).

[85] Cf. 1 Tim. 5:5.

[86] Compare *Didasc.* 3, 1, 3 (Funk, 184, 6) and *Apost. Const.* 3, 1, 5 (Funk, 185, 6-8). About Anna, the daughter of Phanuel, the *Didascalia* notices only that she proclaimed the coming of Christ; the *Constitutions* notice first of all that she did not quit the Temple, where she spent nights and days in prayer (Luke 2:37).

[87] *Apost. Const.* 3, 3, 1 (Funk, 187, 7-10), unparalleled in *Didascalia*; cf. 1 Tim. 5:10.

[88] *Apost. Const.* 3, 3, 1 (Funk, 187, 10-11).

[89] Compare *Didasc.* 3, 5, 3-6 (Funk, 188, 7–190, 7) with *Apost. Const.* 3, 5, 3-6 (Funk, 189, 20–191, 7).

[90] See above, pp. 88-89.

[91] Compare this sentence with *Didasc.* 3, 6, 1 (Funk, 190, 8-9), which says simply: "It is neither right nor necessary that women should be teachers."

[92] 1 Cor. 11:3.

[93] *Apost. Const.* 3, 6, 1-2 (Funk, 191, 8-18), tr. ANF, VII, p. 427.

[94] Cf. *Didasc.* 3, 6, 2 (Funk, 190, 12-17).

[95] Similarly, the *Constitutions* explain elsewhere that the prophetesses of the Old and New Testament did not speak out against men, but preserved the measure proper to themselves" (*Apost. Const.* 8, 2, 9; Funk, 470, 1-6).

[96] Compare *Didasc.* 3, 6, 3-7, 5 (Funk, 190, 17–194, 17) with *Apost. Const.*, 3, 6, 3-7, 5 (Funk, 191, 19–195, 15); *Didasc.* 3, 7, 6-8 (Funk, 194, 17–196, 16) and *Apost. Const.* 3, 7, 6-8 (Funk, 195, 15–197, 16). An echo of these descriptions is found in Pseudo-Ignatius; see *Ep. to Philadelphians* 4, 8 (Funk-Diekamp, 178, 14-16): "*Estōsan de kai hai chērai mē remboi, mē lichnoi, mē peritrochades, all' hōs Ioudith hē semnotatē, hōs hē Anna hē sōphronestatē.*" For *mē remboi,* cf. *Apost. Const.* 3, 6, 4 (Funk, 191, 24); for *mē lichnoi, Apost. Const.* 3, 7, 7 (p. 197, 5); for *mē peritrochades, Apost. Const.* 3, 6, 4 (191, 23). The example of Judith is referred to in *Apost. Const.* 3, 7, 6 (195, 18-19), that of Anna in *Apost. Const.* 3, 1, 5 (185, 6-11). Elsewhere,

Pseudo-Ignatius uses the terms of First Timothy to say that the widows should not "live in pleasures," lest "their desire turn against Christ": "*Hai chērai mē spatalatōsan, hina mē katastrēniasōsi tou Logou* (*Ep. to Antiochians* 11, 1: (Funk-Diekamp, 220, 12-13; cf. 1 Tim. 5:6 "*Hē de spatalōsa zōsa tethnēken*"; 5:11, "*Hotan gar katastrēniasōsin tou Christou. . .*"

[97] *Apost. Const.* 3, 7, 6 (Funk, 195, 18-21).

[98] *Apost. Const.* 3, 7, 7 (Funk, 197, 7-8). Notice the mention of fasting and watching before prayer, which is absent from the *Didascalia.*

[99] Compare *Didasc.* 3, 8, 1-5 (Funk, 196, 17–198, 30) with *Apost. Const.* 3, 8, 1-3 (Funk, 197, 17–199, 20).

[100] *Apost. Const.* 4, 5-10 (Funk, 223, 16–231, 19).

[101] *Didasc.* 4, 6, 4 (Funk, 224, 23-24).

[102] See, for instance, *Apost. Const.* 4, 10, 4 (Funk, 231, 15-18).

[103] 1 Cor. 11:3.

[104] Gen. 2:21.

[105] Gen. 3:16.

[106] This argument is the only one given in the *Didascalia*; see *Didasc.* 3, 9, 2 (Funk, 200, 1-3).

[107] *Apost. Const.* 3, 9, 1-4 (Funk, 199, 21–201, 17); tr. ANF, VII, p. 429.

[108] *Apost. Const.* 3, 10, 1 (Funk, 201, 18-20).

[109] Compare *Didasc.* 3, 10, 1-6 (Funk, 202, 1-24) with *Apost. Const.* 3, 12, 1–13, 2 (Funk, 203 1-26).

[110] Compare *Didasc.* 3, 10, 6-7 (Funk, 204, 1-12) with *Apost. Const.* 3, 14, 1 (Funk, 205, 1-8).

[111] Compare *Didasc.* 3, 10, 8-11 (Funk, 204, 12–206, 3) with *Apost. Const.* 3, 14, 2-4 (Funk, 205, 8–207, 3).

[112] Compare *Didasc.* 3, 10, 11–11, 4 (Funk, 206, 3–208, 3) with *Apost. Const.* 3, 14, 4–15, 4 (Funk, 207, 3–209, 3).

[113] *Didasc.* 3, 11, 5 (Funk, 208, 3-5).

[114] *Apost. Const.* 3, 15, 5 (Funk, 209, 3-5). Cf. Apost. Const. 8, 47, 8, 17, 18, 51, 63.

[115] *Didasc.* 3, 11, 5 (Funk, 208, 7).

[116] *Apost. Const.* 3, 15, 5 (Funk, 209, 8-9).

[117] *Eccles.* 5:4.

[118] *Apost. Const.* 4, 14, 1-3 (Funk, 235, 4-15); 8, 24, 2 (528, 5-7). For the latter, cf. *Apost. Trad.* 12 (Botte, 32, 33). Pseudo-Ignatius notices also that the vow of virginity should be motivated by the desire for perfection, not by a contempt for marriage (*Ep. to Philadelphians* 4, 3; Funk-Diekamp, 174, 24–176, 2).

[119] Compare *Didasc.* 2, 26, 3 (Funk, 102, 15-16) with *Apost. Const.* 103, 18–105, 1).

[120] Compare *Didasc.* 2, 26, 8 (Funk, 104, 9-10) with *Apost. Const.* 2, 26 8 (Funk, 105, 26-29).

[121] Compare *Didasc.* 2, 57, 8 (Funk, 164, 9) with *Apost. Const.* 2, 57, 12 (Funk, 165, 7-9).

[122] Compare *Didasc.* 3, 6, 4 (Funk, 190, 20-21) with *Apost. Const.* 3, 6, 4 (Funk, 191, 23-24).

[123] *Apost. Const.* 8, 10, 10 (Funk, 490, 7-10).

[124] *Ibid.*, 8, 12, 43 (Funk, 512, 4-9).

[125] *Ibid.*, 8, 12, 44 (Funk, 512, 9-14).

[126] *Ibid.*, 8, 13, 14 (Funk, 516, 21-26).

[127] *Ibid.*, 8, 30, 2 (Funk, 532, 15-21).

[128] *Ibid.*, 8, 24, 1-2 (Funk, 528, 5-7).

[129] *Ibid.*, 8, 25, 1-3 (Funk, 528, 8-15). By so doing, the author of the *Constitutions* deliberately reversed the order of the *Apostolic Tradition*, where the rule concerning the widow came before that concerning the virgin, in all versions, either when the widow comes immediately before the virgin, after the reader and the subdeacon, or when she comes after the confessor and before the reader, the subdeacon, and the virgin (Arabic and Ethiopic versions). The *Testamentum Domini* follows the order of the Arabic and Ethiopic versions. The *Canons of Hippolytus* reject the rule concerning the widow — which is completely reworked; see above, pp. 49–51 — to the end of the series, after that concerning the healer to whom the exorcist corresponds in the *Constitutions*). See Hanssens, *Liturgie d'Hippolyte*, p. 24).

[130] *Apost. Const.* 2, 26, 3 (Funk, 103, 21–105, 1).

[131] *Apost. Const.* 2, 26, 8 (Funk, 105, 26-29). This comparison is already found in Methodius of Olympus (*Symposion* 5,

8; SC 95, 150-162). Pseudo-Ignatius commands, in an even more striking way (*Ep. to Tarsians* 9, 1; Funk-Diekamp, 142, 9-11): "*Tas en parthenia timate hōs hiereias Christou, tas en semnotēti chēras hōs thysiastērion tou Theou,*" i.e., "Honor those (who continue) in virginity, as the priestesses of Christ; and the widows (that persevere) in gravity of behavior, as the altar of God" (ANF, I, p. 109). The use of *hiereia* is surprising, since the *Constitutions*, to which Pseudo-Ignatius is so close that he is supposed to be its author, stigmatizes the ordination of priestesses (*hiereias*) to female deities as a mark of the impious ignorance of pagans and absolutely opposed to the order established by Christ.

Virgins are also mentioned before widows in *Ep. to Philippians* of Pseudo-Ignatius (15, 1; Funk-Diekamp, 168 6): "*Aspazomai to systēma tōn parthenōn, to tagma tōn chērōn, hōn kai ovaimēn*"; and in *Ep. to Antiochians* (12, 3; Funk-Diekamp, 222, 3-5): "*Aspazomai tas christolēptous parthenous, hōn kai onaimēn en Kyriō Iēsou• aspazomai tas semnotatas chēras.*" In the same sense, the genuine text of *Ep. to Smyrneans* of Ignatius of Antioch quoted above (13, 1; see above, p. 13) was altered by the interpolator in a very meaningful way; instead of "*Aspazomai . . . tas parthenous tas legomenas chēras,*" Pseudo-Ignatius writes (*Ep. to Smyrneans,* 13, 1; Funk-Diekamp, 204, 16-17): "*Aspazomai . . . kai aeiparthenous kai tas chēras.*"

[132] *Didasc.* 2, 57, 8 (Funk, 162, 7–164, 9).

[133] *Apost. Const.* 2, 57, 12 (Funk, 165, 7-9).

[134] *Didasc.* 2, 26, 6; see above, p. 41.

[135] *Didasc.* 3, 12, 1–13, 1; see above, pp. 41–42.

[136] See above, p. 138, n. 61.

[137] Compare *Didasc.* 3, 12, 1 (Funk, 208, 8-11) with *Apost. Const.* 3, 16, 1 (Funk, 209, 10-14).

[138] *Apost. Const.* 6, 17, 4 (Funk, 341, 9-11).

[139] *Apost. Const.* 3, 16, 1 (Funk, 209, 14-17).

[140] *Didasc.* 3, 12, 4 (Funk, 201, 18-22), without a parallel in the *Constitutions.*

[141] *Didasc.* 3, 13, 1 cited above, pp. 41-43.

[142] *Apost. Const.* 3, 19, 1 (Funk, 215, 1-3).

[43] John 14:26; 16:13-14.

[144] *Apost. Const.* 2, 26, 6 (Funk, 105, 15-21).

[145] See, for instance, Jerome, *Ep. 52* (to Nepotian) 5, 6 (CSEL 54, 424, 3-7).

[146] *Didasc.* 3, 12, 2-3 (Funk, 208, 14–210, 14).

[147] Compare *Didasc.* 3, 12, 2 (Funk, 208, 14–210, 5) with *Apost. Const.* 3, 16, 2 (Funk, 209, 18–211, 3).

[148] *Didasc.* 3, 12, 4 (Funk, 208, 14-18), without a parallel in the *Constitutions.*

[149] Compare *Didasc.* 3, 12, 3 (Funk, 210, 12-14) with *Apost. Const.* 3, 16, 4 (Funk, 211, 14-16).

[150] *Apost. Const.* 2, 58, 4-6 (Funk, 169, 8–171, 4). Here the *Didascalia* deals only with the deacon and does not mention the deaconess.

[151] *Apost. Const.* 8, 20, 1, cited later on, p. 62. The author probably refers to the women ministering at the door of the Tabernacle in Exodus 38:8; see above, p. 126, n. 2. Repeating the very terms of the prayer for ordination given in *Constitutions,* Pseudo-Ignatius expressly refers to the deaconesses as the "keepers of the holy gates": "*Aspazomai tas phrourous tōn hagiōn sou pulōnōn, tas en Christō diakonous*" (*Ep. to Antiochians* 12, 2; Funk-Diekamp, 222, 2-3); cf. *Apost. Const.* 8, 20, 1 (Funk, 524, 18-19): "*Tas phrourous tōn hagiōn sou pulōn.*"

[152] *Apost. Const.* 8, 28, 6 (Funk, 530, 22-25).

[153] *Apost. Const.* 8, 13, 14 (Funk, 516, 21-26).

[154] For instance, *Apost. Const.* 2, 26, 3 (Funk, 103, 18–105, 1). Also in Pseudo-Ignatius of Antioch, *Ep. to Antiochians* 12, 2-3 (Funk-Diekamp, 222, 2-5).

[155] Compare *Didasc.* 3, 8, 1 (Funk, 196, 17-20) with *Apost. Const.* 3, 8, 1 (Funk, 197, 17-21).

[156] *Apost. Const.* 8, 31, 2 (Funk, 532, 22–534, 1).

[157] *Apost. Const.* 8, 19, 2 (Funk, 524,

11-13). This ordination, like all other ordinations, is a rite strictly reserved to the bishop, and the presbyters cannot confer it: *Apost. Const.* 3, 11, 3 (Funk, 201, 28-31).

[158] Cf. *Apost. Const.* 8, 24, 2 (Funk, 528, 5-6); 8, 25, 2 (528, 9).

[159] There is also a mention of the presence of the presbyterium and of the deacons for the ordination of a presbyter (*Apost. Const.* 8, 16, 2; Funk, 522, 3) and of a deacon (8, 17, 2, p. 522, 28-29), not for the ordination of a subdeacon (8, 21, 2; p. 524, 26–526, 1), and not for the ordination of a reader (8, 22, 2, p. 526, 10-11).

[160] 2 Cor. 1:3.

[161] Cf. Exod. 38:8; 1 Sam. 2:22; see above, p. 126, n. 2.

[162] Cf. 2 Cor. 7:1.

[163] *Apost. Const.* 8, 20, 1-2 (Funk, 524, 13-24), tr. ANF, VII, p. 492.

[164] Ordination of a deacon (*Apost. Const.* 8, 17-18); ordination of a deaconess (8, 19-20); ordination of a subdeacon (8, 21); ordination of a reader (8, 22).

[165] *Apost. Const.* 3, 11, 3 (Funk, 201, 28-31).

[166] *Apost. Const.* 8, 10, 9 (Funk, 490, 5-7): "*Hyper pasēs tēs en Christō diakonias kai hypēresias deēthōmen, hopōs ho Kyrios amempton autois tēn diakonian paraschētai.*" The term *hypēresia* refers to the subdeacons, who are sometimes called *hypēretai* in the *Constitutions*. The readers and singers are mentioned in the following demand (*Apost. Const.* 8, 10, 10; p. 490, 7-8).

[167] *Apost. Const.* 8, 12, 41 (Funk, 510, 23-26); 8, 12, 43 (512, 4-9).

[168] *Apost. Const.* 2, 26, 3 (Funk, 103, 18–104, 1); 6, 17, 1-4 (339, 29–341, 11); 8, 28, 2-6 (530, 9-25); 8, 28, 7 (530, 25-27); 8, 28, 8 (530, 27-29); 8, 31, 2 (532, 22–534, 1). Also in Pseudo-Ignatius of Antioch, *Ep. to Antiochians* 12, 2 (Funk-Diekamp, 22, 1-3).

[169] *Apost. Const.* 8, 13, 14 (Funk, 516, 21-26).

[170] *Arabic Canons of Nicaea*, can. 74 in the version of Turrianus (Mansi, 2, 978 C) = can. 79 in the version of Ecchellensis (Mansi, 2, 1008 BC).

[171] Council of Chalcedon (451), can. 15 (Joannou, 1-1, 81, 18–82, 4), tr. ANF, XIV, p. 279.

[172] Gaudemet, Église, p. 123.

[173] CT 16, 2, 27, June 21, 390 (Mommsen, 1-2, 843). Cf. 1 Tim. 5:9.

[174] See above, pp. 87–89.

[175] Majorian, *Novellae* 6, 3 (Mommsen, 2, 164).

[176] *Ibid.*, 5 (pp. 164–165).

[177] Council of Chalcedon, can. 16 (Joannou, 1-1, 82, 8-15).

[178] Only the Syriac version has been published: *Testamentum Domini nostri Iesu Christi*, ed. I.E. Rahmani, Mainz, 1899 (with a Latin translation). There is a French translation in F. Nau, *La version syriaque de l'Octateuque de Clément*, re-edited by P. Ciprotti, Paris, 1967. For the versions in Arabic and Ethiopic, see Hanssens, *Liturgie d'Hippolyte*, p. 3, n. 1.

The edition of Rahmani gives only a division into "books" and chapters; but, since they are sometimes very long, it is difficult to locate a reference. Therefore, I have regularly added to the number of the "book" and chapter that of the paragraphs introduced by Nau in his translation. Thanks must go to my colleague A. de Halleux, professor of Syriac language and literature at the University of Louvain, for his help in the solution of some philological problems found in the Syriac version of the *Testamentum Domini*.

[179] See above, pp. 22–24.

[180] *Test.* 1, 40-43.

[181] Cf. for the bishop, *Test.* 1, 20-28; for the presbyter, 1, 29-32; for the deacon, 1, 33-38.

[182] *Test.* 1, 33, 1 (Rahmani, pp. 78–79; Nau, p. 48).

[183] *Test.* 1, 40, 1 (Rahmani, pp. 94–95; Nau, p. 52).

[184] Cf. respectively *Test.* 1, 44, 45 and 46.

[185] See the conspectus in Hanssens, *Liturgie d'Hippolyte*, p. 24.

[186] Rahmani suggests reading, instead of subdeacons, "readers" (*ed. cit.*, p. 83), but he gives no evidence to support this position. He might have noted that when the clergy gather around the altar for the offering of the Eucharistic sacrifice, subdeacons come after readers (*Test.* 1,

23, 1) and receive Communion after them (1, 23, 14). But they are mentioned before them in the diaconal litany (1, 35, 5); and in the general outline followed by the *Testamentum*, the subdeacon (1, 44) comes before the reader (1, 45), whereas he comes after the reader in the Coptic version of the *Apostolic Tradition* and in the *Canons of Hippolytus*, after the reader and the virgin in the Arabic and Ethiopic versions of the *Apostolic Tradition.* The author of the *Testamentum*, therefore, has deliberately altered the order followed by the *Apostolic Tradition.*

In addition, the term "to ordain" reappears for the subdeacon (*Test.* 1, 44, 1), but is absent for the reader; the text says positively that the reader is not given a laying on of hand (1, 45, 1). Consequently, readers are clerics of a lower rank than subdeacons, and there is no reason to alter the text to read that the number of the readers is limited, whereas that of the subdeacons is not.

Furthermore, Rahmani suggests reading "four" instead of "fourteen" (*ed. cit.*, p. 82, n. 5). Such a mistake by a copyist is made rather easily in a manuscript if the figure is not written in full letters; but it is unlikely that the number of subdeacons would be inferior to that of deacons, and arithmetically unrelated to it; but it is quite likely that in this symbolic arithmetic (twelve presbyters parallel twelve apostles; seven deacons parallel seven deacons in Jerusalem, according to the Acts of Apostles), the number of the subdeacons was fixed as twice that of the deacons.

187 *Test.* 1, 34, 4 (Rahmani, pp. 82-83; Nau, p. 49).

188 *Ed. cit.*, p. 82, n. 5.

189 ECA 21, 1-2, cited above, p. 45.

190 See references above, p. 139, nn. 3-4.

191 The text quoted above (*Test.* 1, 34, 4) is unparalleled in the *Apostolic Tradition.*

192 *Test.* 1, 44.

193 *Test.* 1, 45.

194 *Test.* 1, 19, 7 (Rahmani, pp. 26–27; Nau, p. 32). About the "front-stage," cf. 1, 19, 2. The Syriac text is not free from ambiguity, since the term which I interpreted as "place," following Nau, means literally "house," and could therefore be interpreted, at first, as "abode, place of indwelling" (Rahmani translated *aedes*). However, the context points to the sense of "place," which the Syriac term may certainly possess in the constructed form. Anyway, the text quoted in the following footnote is exempt from ambiguity and sufficient to support my hypothesis.

195 *Test.* 1, 23, 1 (Rahmani, pp. 36–37; Nau, p. 36).

196 *Ibid.*

197 *Test.* 1, 19, 7; 34, 4; 41, 1; 43, 2; 2, 4, 4; 8, 12.

198 *Test.* 1, 35, 5 (Rahmani, pp. 86–87; Nau, p. 50). The reference here is certainly to the widows "sitting in front," and not to old women generally, as interpreted by Nau in his translation. The reason is that these "senior women" are mentioned among the clergy, between the deacons, on the one hand, and the subdeacons and readers, on the other hand; laymen are mentioned only later on (1, 36, 6).

The term "senior women" (in the Greek original, probably *presbyterai* or maybe *presbytides*) reappears in Book 2 in a text on the Paschal Vigil, and the context concerns widows: "Let the widows stay till dawn in the temple, having food there. Let the virgins abide together in the temple, and let the bishop help and provide for them, and let the deacons minister to them. Let the presbyteresses stay with the bishop till dawn, praying and resting" (*Test.* 2, 19, 6-7; Rahmani pp. 140–141; Nau, p. 66; English tr. J. Cooper and A.J. Maclean, *The Testament of the Lord*, Edinburgh, 1902, p. 134). In my opinion, in this text the "widows" are taken in the general sense of the term, whereas the "presbyteresses" or "senior women" are the widows who sit in front: they stay with the bishop (cf. 1, 19, 7), and whereas the former take food, the latter pray and continue in fasting, two exercises which are typical of the spirituality of the widows who sit in front (cf. 1, 40, 3).

199 *Test.* 1, 23, 14 (Rahmani, pp. 46–47; Nau, p. 39).

200 *Test.* 1, 40, 1 (Rahmani, p. 94–95; Nau p. 52). The author insists on this idea again at the end of the chapter: "Therefore let her be *chosen* who can go

to meet the holy phials," i.e., the congregation (1, 40, 4; Rahmani, pp. 96–97; Nau, p. 53).

[201] Compare respectively with *Test.* 20, 1; 29, 1; 33, 1.

[202] See *Test.* 1, 44, 1; 45, 1.

[203] *Test.* 1, 40, 1 (Rahmani, pp. 94–95; Nau. p. 52).

[204] *Ibid.*

[205] *Ibid.*

[206] Cf. 1 Tim. 5:9.

[207] Cf. *Test.* 1, 20, 2; 33, 1.

[208] *Test.* 1, 23, 13 (Rahmani, pp. 46–47; Nau, p. 38); 1, 42, 2 (Rahmani, pp. 100–101; Nau, p. 54). Because of this detail, I incline to consider as less important an addition in the Arabic version introducing the condition of age and of "monogamy" which was traditional since First Timothy (see Rahmani, *ed. cit.*, p. 95, n. 2).

[209] *Test.* 1, 40, 1 (Rahmani, pp. 94–95; Nau, p. 52).

[210] *Ibid.*

[211] *Test.* 1, 23, 11 (Rahmani, pp. 44–45; Nau, p. 38).

[212] *Test.* 1, 29, 1 (Rahmani, pp. 68–69; Nau, p. 45).

[213] *Test.* 1, 40, 2 (Rahmani, pp. 94–95; Nau, p. 52).

[214] ECA 21, 1, cited above, p. 45.

[215] *Test.* 1, 40, 2 (Rahmani, pp. 96–97; Nau, pp. 52–53).

[216] *Ibid.*

[217] *Test.* 2, 8, 12 (Rahmani, pp. 128–131; Nau, p. 63).

[218] *Test.* 2, 4, 4 (Rahmani, pp. 118–119; Nau, p. 59).

[219] *Test.* 1, 42, 1 (Rahmani, pp. 100–101; Nau, p. 54).

[220] *Test.* 1, 40, 3 (Rahmani, pp. 96–97; Nau, p. 53).

[221] *Test.* 1, 40, 2 (*ibid.*). Cf. *Test.* 1, 20, 1 (Rahmani, pp. 26–27; Nau, p. 33); the bishop must love the widows, the orphans, and the poor; *Test.* 2, 6, 1 (Rahmani, pp. 118–121; Nau, p. 60): in the examination of the candidates for baptism, it shall be inquired whether they have honored the widows, visited the sick, lived with humility and charity, and been zealous in good deeds (a text parallel to *Apost. Trad.* 20 — cf. above, p. 22; *Test.* 2, 11, 1 (Rahmani, pp. 132–133; Nau, p. 64): if a man receives a gift for a widow or someone who is always busy with the service of the Church he must give it on the same day; if he does not, he must on the next day add of his own and give it, since the bread of the poor has remained too long in his possession (a text parallel to *Apost. Trad.* 24 — cf. above, p. 23).

[222] *Test.* 1, 40, 3 (Rahmani, pp. 96–97; Nau, p. 53).

[223] *Test.* 1, 42, 2–43, 3 (Rahmani, pp. 100–105; Nau, pp. 54–55).

[224] *Test.* 1, 41, 1 (Rahmani, pp. 98–99; Nau, p. 53). There is no mention of a laying on of hands; one recalls that the *Apostolic Tradition* excluded it positively in the case of a widow (*Apost. Trad.* 10, cited above, p. 24).

[225] Cf. above, p. 62.

[226] *Test.* 1, 41, 2-3 (Rahmani, pp. 98–99; Nau, pp. 53–54).

[227] *Test.* 1, 23, 1 (Rahmani, pp. 36–37; Nau, p. 36). The Syriac term which I interpreted by "submitted to a rule" is a transliteration of the Greek *kanonikos.*

[228] *Test.* 1, 19, 7 (Rahmani, pp. 26–27; Nau, p. 33).

[229] *Test.* 1, 23, 1 (Rahmani, p. 36–37; Nau, p. 36).

[230] *Test.* 1, 35, 5 (Rahmani, pp. 86–87; Nau, p. 50).

[231] *Test.* 1, 23, 14 (Rahmani, pp. 46–67; Nau, p. 39).

[232] *Apost. Const.* 3, 8, 1 (Funk, 197, 17-19).

[233] *Test.* 1, 40, 2 (Rahmani, pp. 96–97; Nau, p. 52). Nau translates wrongly: "Qu'elle (la veuve) suive les traces des diaconessess"; the Syriac verb used here means properly "to trace," and figuratively "to scrutinize, to watch, to inspect."

[234] *Test.* 1, 36, 1-4 (Rahmani, pp. 88–91; Nau, pp. 50–51).

[235] *Test.* 2, 19, 1 (Rahmani, pp. 138–139; Nau, p. 66).

[236] *Test.* 1, 36, 4 (Rahmani, pp. 90–91; Nau, p. 51).

[237] *Test.* 2, 20, 7 (Rahmani, p. 142–143; Nau, p. 66).

[238] CT 9, 25, 1 (Mommsen, 1-2, 478).

[239] CT 9, 25, 2 (pp. 478–479).

[240] See above, pp. 58–61.

[241] Cf. CJ 1, 3, 5 (Krueger, 19); *The Roman Law of the Burgundians*, 9, 4 (MGHL 1-2, 132, 14–133, 2).

[242] CT 9, 25, 3 (Mommsen, 1-2, 479). The sentence here is no longer the death sentence, but exile and seizure of property.

[243] Majorian, *Novellae* 6, 4 (Mommsen, 2, 164). To encourage the denunciation of such crimes, the emperor gives to the denouncer the property of the criminal.

[244] CT 16, 2, 20 (Mommsen, 1-2, 841). St. Ambrose refers to this law in a letter to Valentinian II in 384. (*Ep.* 18, 13-14; PL 16, 1017 A–1018 A); see Gryson, *Le Prêtre selon saint Ambroise*, Louvain, 1968, p. 303.

[245] Cf. 1 Tim. 5:9-10.

[246] Sozomen reports, in his *Ecclesiastical History* (7, 16, 1-10; GCS 50, 322, 17–324, 9) that Bishop Nectarius (381–397) put an end to the function of the priest in charge of penitence at Constantinople after a scandal which occurred there. A high-class woman complained that she had been treated violently by a deacon while she was in church praying and fasting according to the command of the priest in charge of penitence. Nectarius left to the moral conscience of everyone to decide whether he was worthy of receiving Communion, and Sozomen laments the relaxation of mores which gave occasion to such a decision. Then, he continues (*ibid.*, 7, 16, 11; p. 324, 9-13): "I believe it was from similar considerations that the Emperor Theodosius, who was always zealous in promoting the glory of the Church, issued a law enacting that women should not be admitted into the ministry (*diakonian Theou mē epitrepesthai*) unless they had had children, and were upwards of sixty years of age, according to the precept of the Apostle Paul" (tr. E. Walford, *Ecclesiastical History of Sozomen*, London, 1855, p. 336).

[247] CT 16, 2, 27 (Mommsen, 1-2, 843–844).

[248] CT 16, 2, 28 (p. 844). This law is dated August 23, 370. Note that in this text deaconesses are positively identified with widows, as if the two terms referred to the same persons: "Legem quae *de diaconissis vel viduis* nuper est promulgata. . . ." The part rescinded from the law of June 21, of course, does not figure in the Justinian Code; cf. CJ 1, 3, 9 (Krueger, 19).

[249] Marcian, *Novellae* 5 (Mommsen, 2, 193-196). The chief sentence of this constitution is repeated in the Code of Justinian without alteration (CJ 1, 2, 13; Krueger, 13).

[250] CT 5, 3, 1 (Mommsen, 1-2, 220). The text is repeated in CJ 1, 3, 20 (Krueger, 20).

[251] Majorian, *Novellae* 6, 5 (Mommsen, 2, 164-165).

[252] For the Code, I have used the text of P. Krueger (10th ed., Berlin, 1929); for the *Novellae*, that of R. Schoell and G. Kroll (5th ed. Berlin, 1928).

[253] For the circumstances of this law, see J. Pargoire, *L'Église byzantine de 527 à 847*, 2nd ed., Paris, 1905, pp. 60–61.

[254] *Novellae* of Justinian (NJ) 3, 1, 1 (Schoell-Kroll, 21, 3-12).

[255] NJ 3, prol. (Schoell-Kroll, 19, 16-17); 3, 1, 1 (21, 5-6); 3, 2, 1 (22, 10); 6, tit. (35, 19-21). Cf. CT 5, 3, 1, cited above, same page.

[256] CJ 1, 3, 45, 9 (Krueger, 32); NJ 3, prol. (Schoell-Kroll, 18, 18 and 26); 3, 1, (20, 12); 123, 21 (609, 17-18); 123, 28 (615, 1); 123, 37 (620, 29); 131, 13 (662, 24).

[257] These terms reappear at least eleven times in NJ 6, 6 (Schoell-Kroll, 43, 24–45, 13). See also NJ 3, prol. (18, 26); 6, tit. (35, 17-18); 123, 13 (604, 20); 131, 13 (662, 27).

[258] CJ 1, 3, 53, 3-4 (Krueger, 37); NJ 6, 6 (Schoell-Kroll, 44, 4-10); 123, 30 (616, 31-32); 123, 37 (620, 24-29); 131, 13 (662, 26-27).

[259] CT 16, 2, 27, partly repeated in CJ 1, 3, 9; see above, p. 70.

[260] *Novella* 6 states that women still young and in full vigor should not be ordained to the diaconate because their virtue is too fragile, but deaconesses should be chosen among "those who have outpassed the first half of their life and are about fifty years old, according to the holy canons" (NJ 6, 6; Schoell-Kroll, 43, 27-32). I do not see what canons are referred to here; the Council of Chalcedon fixed

the minimum age at forty years (can. 15, cited above, p. 63). *Novella* 6 permits, though, that when necessary, a younger deaconess be ordained, under the condition that she reside in a convent, where she cannot have relations with men, and is submitted to severe discipline (*ibid.*, p. 44, 4-10).

261 NJ 123, 13 (Schoell-Kroll, 604, 19-21). The same text fixes the minimum age for a presbyter at thirty, for a deacon at twenty-five, for a reader at eighteen (604, 16-19). The law is therefore more demanding for a deaconess than for the male members of the hierarchy.

262 NJ 6, 6 (Schoell-Kroll, 43, 33-34); 123, 13 (604, 21-22). Once more, the law is more severe than for male clerics, who can be married people (see Gryson, *Origines du célibat*, pp. 110–116).

263 NJ 6, 6 (Schoell-Kroll, 43, 35-36; 44, 20-25); cf. Council of Chalcedon, can. 15 (Joannou, 1-1, 81, 19-20): "*Meta akribous dokimasias.*"

264 Cf. above, pp. 51 and 63–64.

265 NJ 6, 6 (Schoell-Kroll, 44, 30–45, 13).

266 NJ 123, 43 (Schoell-Kroll, 623, 25–624, 18). Anyway, these sanctions are much more severe than those for male clergy who are guilty of the same crime; the latter are reduced to lay condition but are not deprived of their property or of their freedom, and, even less, of their life (see Gryson, *Origines du célibat*, pp. 110–116).

267 CJ 1, 3, 53 (Krueger, 37); NJ 6, 6 (Schoell-Kroll, 45, 3-5); 123, 43 (623, 25–624, 18). According to the first of these laws, the possessions of the criminal are ascribed to the monastery or to the church of the victim, who is supposed to be innocent, and she will enjoy the use of them all the rest of her life; among the accomplices, only those who have directly helped the aggressor in the very act of the rape are deprived of their property, not the others; but both are sentenced to death. According to *Novella* 6, the property of the guilty man goes to the treasury of the State. According to *Novella* 123, it ought to be claimed by the bishops or their intendants, and by the governors of the province or their representatives, and delivered to the holy place to which the deaconess was attached; if after one year there is no claim, the property must go to the treasury of the State.

268 All these terms are often used in reference to the male partner of a "spiritual marriage"; see the bibliography mentioned above, p. 132, n. 28.

269 NJ 6, 6 (Schoell-Kroll, 44, 10-20 and 25-29).

270 NJ 123, 30 (Schoell-Kroll, 616, 17-32).

271 NJ 123, 29 (Schoell-Kroll, 615, 26–616, 10).

272 NJ 123, 21 (Schoell-Kroll, 609, 17–611, 9).

273 NJ 123, 28 (Schoell-Kroll, 614, 27–615, 25).

274 NJ 3, 1, 1; see above, p. 72.

275 NJ 123, 30 (Schoell-Kroll, 616, 23).

276 CJ 1, 3, 45, 9 (Krueger, 32). The law prescribes that the right to this rent cannot be negotiated by the beneficiary and that the rent, in spite of any other agreement, is perpetually claimable.

277 NJ 123, 37 (Schoell-Kroll, 620, 18–621, 14).

278 NJ 131, 13, 3 (Schoell-Kroll, 662, 23-27).

279 NJ 6, 6 (Schoell-Kroll, 44, 1-4).

280 See *Didasc.* 3, 12, 2-3, (Funk, 208, 14–210, 14); *Apost. Const.* 3, 16, 2-4 (Funk, 209, 18–211, 17); Epiphanius of Salamis, *Panarion* 79, 3, 6 (GCS 37, 478, 18); *Idem, Anchoratus* 21, 10 (GCS 37, 522, 18-20); *Arabic Canons of Nicaea*, can. 74 [79] (Mansi, 2, 978 C and 1000 BC). See also Cassiodorus, *Commentary on the Epistle to Romans*, on Rom. 16:1, cited in Peter Abelard, *Sermons* 31 (for the festivity of St. Stephen; PL 178, 572 B): "Quem quidem locum Cassiodorus in huius epistolae commentariis suis exponens: Significat, inquit, diaconissam fuisse matris Ecclesiae, quod in partibus Graecorum hodie usque peragitur, quibus et baptizandi usus in Ecclesia non negatur"; about this text, see "On the Early History and Modern Revival of Deaconesses," in *Church Quarterly Review*, XLVIII (1898–1899), p. 321, n. 1.

It is noted that these functions (anointing) were not entrusted to the deaconesses everywhere, in spite of the ministry's existence in that locality. The following story is a witness to this fact. It happened in Palestine in the sixth century.

"At the monastery of Penthucla was a certain Conon of Cilicia, a priest destined to the ministry of baptism. Since Conon was a monk of high repute, the Fathers appointed him to baptize. Thus he was anointing and baptizing those who were presented to him for this. When he was anointing the women, he was ashamed, and because of this, he wanted to leave the monastery. When he was on the verge of leaving, St. John appeared to him and said: 'Have patience, and I will deliver you from this struggle.'

"One day a young woman from Persia came to be baptized. She was so beautiful and so fair that the priest did not have the courage to anoint her with holy oil. Since she stayed there for two days, Archbishop Peter heard about this. He was startled and *wanted a deaconess to accomplish this function; but he did not do it, since it was not the custom.* Father Conon took his bag, left, and said: 'I will not stay here any longer.'

"As he was walking through the hills, St. John the Baptist appeared to him and said in a soft voice: 'Come back to your monastery and I will deliver you from your struggle.' Father Conon answered angrily: 'Believe me, I will not go back, because you often made a promise and you never kept it.' Then St. John calmed him and requested that he sit upon a hill, and having taken off his clothes, he marked him three times with the sign of the cross below his navel and said: 'Have confidence in me, Father Conon; I wanted you to prove yourself worthy of a reward in regard to this struggle; but since you do not want it, I have nevertheless delivered you from it, but you will not have the reward that would have been coming to you.'

"Father Conon returned to the monastery where he used to baptize. The next morning he anointed and baptized the young woman from Persia without even knowing that she was a woman. He kept this office for twelve years, anointing and baptizing, without any movement of the flesh and without noticing any woman. Thus he finished his days" (Jean Moschus, *Pratum Spirituale* 3; PG 87, 2853 C).

281 For the Armenian Churches, see C. Dvin (527), can. 17 (Hefele-Leclercq, 2-2, 1079). Earlier the Catholicoi Narses and Isaac the Great had absolutely forbidden women to assist the priest in the celebration of baptism; see H. Denzinger, *Ritus Orientalium*, I Würzburg, 1863, p. 22. For the Nestorian Churches, see G. Diettrich, *Die nestorianische Taufliturgie*, Giessen, 1903, pp. 97–98. The Nestorians apply to deaconesses the text of 1 Timothy 5-9 imposing a minimum age of sixty years.

282 See the texts cited in Barhebraeus, *Nomocanon* 7, 7, 9 (Bedjan, 98-99).

Chapter Seven — pages 75–91

1 See G. Ficker, "Widerlegung eines Montanisten," in *Zeitschrift für Kirchengeschichte*, XXVI (1905), pp. 447–463.

2 See above, pp. 28–29.

3 Cf. Acts 21:9.

4 Cf. Judg. 4:4.

5 1 Cor. 11:5.

6 Luke 1:48.

7 Cf. Exod. 15:20.

8 Cf. 1 Cor. 14:34-35; 1 Tim. 2:12.

9 The following eight words cannot be easily translated and connected to the context: "*Kai ou katēschynen tēn kephalēn toutesti(n) ton andra.*" Ficker (*art. cit.*, p. 457, n. 3) corrects *katēschynen* to *katēischyne*, which does improve the clearness of the text. A good supposition would be either that the verb ought to be read in the infinitive form (*kataischynein* or *kataischynai*) or that there is a short lacuna.

10 Cf. 1 Cor. 11:5.

11 *Anakekalymmenōs*: the Montanist is playing on the word, which reminds one of *akatalyptō*, used in the phrase "with the head *uncovered*."

12 Cf. Gal. 4:22, 24.

13 Under the pretext that their head is not uncovered at this time, since those who are being baptized must be completely naked.

14 Here occurs the word *kakōsin*, followed by a small lacuna of three to five

letters; the context shows undoubtedly that this word must be interpreted in a medical sense.

15 1 Thess. 5:17.

16 *Confutation of a Montanist* (Ficker, 456, 24–458, 12).

17 Cf. Acts 21:9.

18 Cf. Judg. 4:4.

19 Cf. Exod. 15:20.

20 Luke 1:48.

2 Cf. 1 Tim. 2:12.

22 1 Cor. 11:5.

23 1 Cor. 11:3.

24 Cf. 1 Tim. 2:14. – Didymus the Blind, *On the Trinity* 3, 41, 3 (PG 39, 988 C–989A).

25 This name does not figure either in the contemporary sources of the same period as the origins of Montanism or in Eusebius of Cesarea, where only the names of Maximilla and Priscilla are mentioned.

26 Cf. Gen. 3:6.

27 Gal. 3:28.

28 Augustine, *On Heresies* 27 (PL 42, 31 C); John Damascene, *On Heresies* 49 (PG 94, 767 A).

29 See Lafontaine, *Conditions positives*, pp. 16–18.

30 Gen. 3:16.

31 1 Tim. 2:12.

32 1 Cor. 11:8.

33 1 Tim. 2:14. – Epiphanius, *Panarion*, 49, 1, 1–3, 4 (GCS 31, 241, 18–244 11).

34 It is the sixty-ninth heresy of Epiphanius. It is already mentioned briefly at the end of the letter against the Antidicomarianites, which is cited in the preceding section of the book; see *Panarion* 78, 23, 4 (GCS 37, 473, 8-16).

35 *Panarion* 78, 23, 4 (GCS 37, 473, 8-12); 79, 1, 7 (476, 16-20).

36 See Lafontaine, *Conditions positives*, pp. 13–15.

37 It is already one of two criticisms formulated against them in *Panarion* 78, 23, 4 (GCS 37, 473, 13-14): "*Hierourgein dia gynaikōn.*"

38 Panarion 79, 1, 6-7 (GCS 37, 476, 11-15).

39 *Ibid.*, 79, 2, 1-6 (476, 25–477, 26).

40 *Ibid.*, 79, 3, 1-2 (477, 27–478, 2). The same remark is found in the *Didascalia* (3, 9, 2; above, p. 38), and in the *Apostolic Constitutions* (3, 9, 4; above, pp. 56–57).

41 Cf. Mark 15:40; 16:1.

42 Cf. Rom. 16:13.

43 Cf. Matthew 27:55-56; Mark 15:40-41.

44 Cf. John 11:1.

45 Cf. Luke 8:2-3.

46 Cf. Matthew 15:22-28 and parallels.

47 Cf. Matthew 9:20-22 and paralles. – *Panarion* 79, 7, 3-4 (GCS 37, 482, 4-14).

48 Cf. Acts 21:9.

49 Cf. Luke 2:36-38. – *Panarion* 79, 3, 3-5 (GCS 37, 478, 2-16).

50 Cf. 1 Cor. 14:34-35; 1 Tim. 2:12 – *Panarion* 79, 3, 6–4, 1 (GCS 37, 478, 16-31); cf. *Anchoratus* 21, 10 (GCS 37, 522, 18-20).

51 *Anchoratus* 21, 7-8 (GCS 37, 522, 7-13).

52 *Ibid.*, 21, 9 (522, 13-18).

53 *Ibid.*, 21, 10 (522, 18-22).

54 *Ibid.*, 21, 11 (522, 22-25).

55 *Ibid.*, 21, 10 (522, 18-19).

56 Epistle of Epiphanius of Salamis to John of Jerusalem, in Jerome, *Ep.* 51, 2, 2 (GSEL 54, 398, 12-13).

57 See above, p. 24.

58 See *Saint Jerôme. Letters*, tr. J. Labourt (Coll. des Universités de France), II, Paris, 1951, p. 203.

59 Cf. Titus 2:3.

60 *Panarion* 79, 4, 1 (GCS 37, 478, 27-29).

61 Cf. Rom. 16:1-2.

62 *Homilies on Romans* 30, 2 (PG 60, 663, C–664 A).

63 See later on, pp. 88–89.

64 1 Tim. 3:11.

65 1 Tim. 3:12.

66 *Homilies on 1 Timothy* 11, 1 (PG 62, 553 CD).

67 Cf. Rom. 16:3-5.

68 *Homilies on Romans* 30, 2 (PG 60, 664 AB). Cf. Acts 18:26.

[69] *Homilies on Romans* 30, 3 (PG 60, 664 C–665 C). Actually, Paul does not call Priscilla *sulleitourgon* exactly, as Chrysostom says, but he calls both Priscilla and Aquila *tous synergous mou* (Rom. 16:3).

[70] *Homilies on the Acts* 40, 1 (PG 60, 281 D).

[71] See above, p. 4.

[72] 2 Tim. 4:19.

[73] *Homilies on 2 Timothy* 10, 2 (PG 62, 658 A).

[74] There are two homilies on the salutation addressed to Priscilla and Aquila in the Epistle to the Romans, besides the series containing the complete commentary on this Epistle; they follow one another, and were given after an interval of a few days; they are found in PG 51, 187-208.

[75] Rom. 16:3.

[76] Cf. Acts 18:24-26.

[77] Cf. Rom. 16:12.

[78] Cf. Rom. 16:6-12.

[79] 1 Tim. 2:12.

[80] 1 Cor. 7:13, 16.

[81] *First Homily on "Salute Priscilla et Aquila,"* 3 (PG 51, 191 D–192 C).

[82] Cf. Rom. 16:6.

[83] 1 Tim. 2:12.

[84] 1 Cor. 7:16.

[85] 1 Tim. 2:15.

[86] Luke 8:2-3. — *Homilies on Romans* 31, 1-2 (PG 61, 668 D—669 C), tr. LNPF, 1st ser., XI, p. 554.

[87] Titus 2:3-4.

[88] 1 Tim. 2:12.

[89] *Ibid.*

[90] *Homilies on Titus* 4, 1 (PG 62, 683 B); tr. LNPF, 1st ser., XIII, p. 532.

[91] 1 Cor. 14:34.

[92] Gen. 3:16.

[93] *Homilies on 1 Corinthians* 37, 1 (PG 61, 315 C–317 C).

[94] 1 Tim. 2:11.

[95] 1 Tim. 2:12.

[96] 1 Tim. 2:13.

[97] 1 Cor. 11:9.

[98] 1 Tim. 2:14.

[99] Gen. 3:16.

[100] *Homilies on 1 Timothy* 9, 1 (PG 62, 543 C–545 B).

[101] *On the Priesthood* 2, 2 (PG 48, 633 AB), tr. LNPF, 1st ser., IX, p. 40.

[102] Cf. 1 Cor. 14:34-35.

[103] *On the Priesthood* 3, 9 (PG 48, 646 CD), tr. LNPF, 1st ser., IX, p. 49.

[104] See *Homilies on 1 Timothy* 13, 2–15, 1 (PG 62, 566 C–581 A).

[105] *Homily on Widows* (PG 51, 321 B–338 B).

[106] *Ibid.*, 3 (PG 51, 323 D).

[107] See *On the Priesthood* 3, 16 (PG 48, 654 D–656 D).

[108] *Homilies on Matthew* 66, 3 (PG 58, 630 B).

[109] *Homilies on 1 Corinthians* 30, 4 (PG 61, 254 B–255 C).

[110] 1 Cor. 7:16 (Jerusalem Bible).

[111] 1 Tim. 2:13.

[112] 1 Tim. 2:14. — *Commentary on 1 Timothy*, on 1 Tim. 2:11-14 (Swete, 2, 93, 10–95, 8).

[113] *Commentary on 1 Timothy*, on 1 Tim. 3:11 (Swete, 2, 128, 9–129, 12).

[114] Cf. 1 Tim. 5:9; compare with CT 16, 2, 27 (see above, pp. 72–74).

[115] *Commentary on 1 Timothy*, on 1 Tim. 5:3-16 (Swete, 2, 153, 14–167, 22).

[116] *Commentary on 1 Corinthians*, on 1 Cor. 14:34-35 (PG 82, 348 A).

[117] 1 Cor. 7:16 (Jerusalem Bible).

[118] An opinion already found in Theodore of Mopsuestia; see above, p. 85.

[119] 1 Cor. 11:3.

[120] *Commentary on 1 Corinthians*, on 1 Cor. 11:3 (PG 82, 309 C.

[121] Cf. 1 Tim. 2:13.

[122] Cf. 1 Tim. 2:14. — *Commentary on 1 Timothy*, on 1 Tim. 2:11-14 (PG 82, 801 BC).

[123] 1 Tim. 3:8, and the same for the following.

[124] *Commentary on 1 Timothy*, on 1 Tim. 3:11 (PG 82, 809 A).

[125] *Commentary on Romans*, on Rom. 16:1-2 (PG 82, 217 D–220 A).

[126] Cf. Acts 16:15; Rom. 16:1-2.

[127] *Commentary on 1 Timothy*, on 1 Tim. 5:3-16 (PG 82, 817 A–820 C).

[128] Translated by A.M. Malingrey in

Sources chrétiennes, XIII, 2nd ed., Paris, 1968, to which one can add *Lettre d'exil à Olympias et à tous les fidèles*, usually known as *Quod nemo laeditur*, ed. and tr. by the same author in the same collection, CIII, Paris, 1964.

129 Palladius of Helenopolis, *Dialogue on the Life of John Chrysostom* 11 (PG 47, 35 BC); 16 (cols. 56 A–58 A); 17 (cols. 60 A–61 D).

130 *Lausiac History* 56 (Butler, 149, 21–150, 12).

131 Text and translation by A.M. Malingrey, in SC 13 *bis*, Paris, 1968.

132 *Eccl. Hist.* 8, 9, 1-3 (GCS 50, 361, 21–362, 6): 8, 24, 4-7 (382, 1-21).

133 For the letters to Olympias, see above, p. 153, n. 128. Chrysostom's correspondence includes three letters to Pentadia (*Ep.* 94, 104, 185), and three letters to Procla (or Amproucla) (*Ep.* 96, 103, 191). They are found in PG 52.

134 See Chrysostom, *Ep.* 6 (13), 1 d (SC 13 *bis*, 130, 53-63); Palladius *Lausiac History* 41 (Butler, 129, 4-6).

135 Sozomen, *Eccl. Hist.* 4, 24, 16 (GCS 50, 181, 16-18): "Elpidius was deposed . . . because he had, contrary to the decrees of the Council of Melitina, restored to his former rank in the presbytery a man named Eusebius, who had been deposed for having created Nectaria a deaconess after she had been excommunicated on account of perjury; and to confer this honor upon her was clearly contrary to the laws of the Church" (tr. E. Walford, *op. cit.*).

136 Theodoret of Cyrus, *Eccl. Hist.* 3, 14, 1-11 (GCS 44, 190, 9–192, 14).

137 *Ep.* 105.

138 Cyril of Scythopolis, *Life of St. Euthymius* 3 (TU 49-2, 10, 19–11, 2): ". . . *diakonon echeirotonēsen tēs hagiōtatēs Ekklēsias.*"

139 Sozomen, *Eccl. Hist.* 9, 2, 1-2 (GCS 50, 392, 8-15).

140 *Epistles*, Patmos 48 (44), (SC 40, 118): "*Axia diakonō*"; *Sirm.* 17 (SC 98, 62-64): "*Kasianē diakonō*"; *Sirm.* 101 (SC 111, 18-20): "Kelerinē diakonō."

141 Elisanthia is mentioned in the *Life of Olympias the Deaconess* (6, 7, and 12).

142 Gregory of Nyssa, *Life of Macrina* (PG 46, 988 D and 992 C). Macrina was the sister of Basil and of Gregory of Nyssa; there is no evidence that she was a deaconess, as supposed by Forget "(*Diaconesses*," 694) without any reference.

143 In the *Life* of St. Euphrasia, the superior (Theodula) of the monastery where she spent the greater part of her life is called indifferently, and many times, *diaconissa* (*hē diakonos*) or *abbatissa*; see this text in *Acta sanctorum Martii* 2, 261-270.

144 Etheria, *Pilgrimage* 23, 3 (SC 21, 184).

145 Marcus the Deacon, *Life of Porphyri, Bishop of Gaza* 102 (Grégoire-Kugener, 78).

146 *Lausiac History* 70 (Butler, 165, 15-166, 30).

147 See G. Jacopi, *Esplorazioni e studi in Paflagonia e Cappadocia*, Rome, 1937, pp. 33–36.

148 See P. Thomsen, *Die lateinische und griechische Inschriften der Stadt Jerusalem und ihrer nächsten Umgebung*, Leipzig, 1922, n. 130.

149 See J. Germer-Durand, "Epigraphie chrétienne de Jérusalem," in *Revue Biblique*, I (1892), pp. 560–588, n. 10.

150 See J. Laurent, "Delphes chrétien," in *Bulletin de correspondance hellénique*, XXIII (1899), pp. 273–278.

151 See *Monumenta Asiae Minoris antiqua*, I, ed. W.M. Calder, London, 1928, n. 323 b, 324, 326 and 383.

152 *Ibid.*, n. 178, 194, 226.

153 *Ibid.*, p. xxv.

154 *Monumenta Asiae Minoris antiqua*, III, ed. J. Keil and A. Wilhelm, London, 1931, n. 744.

155 H. Grégoire, *Recueil des inscriptions grecques chrétiennes d'Asie Mineure*, fasc. 1, Paris, 1922, n. 258.

156 See C. Bayet, "De titulis Atticae christianis antiquissimis commentatio historica et epigraphica" (doctoral thesis, University of Paris), Paris, 1878, n. 105.

157 See Grégoire, *op. cit.*, n. 209.

158 CIL 3, 13845: a deaconess by name Ausonia, at Doclea, on the Dalmation coast; CIL 5, 6467: epitaph of deaconess Theodora, buried in Pafia on July 22, 539. I gave up providing an exhaustive account of the inscriptions. It would be easy,

through the indices of the specialized collections (especially, the eight volumes of *Monumenta Asiae Minoris antiqua*), to find a more important list than the present one. However, as I said before, most of these inscriptions, except for the few instances reported on the preceding page, do not tell more than the presence of deaconesses in a particular time and place, more particularly in the Syro-Byzantine milieu from the fourth century, but they tell us nothing about their status and functions.

The present conclusion relies on a wide inquiry entrusted to a group of students as an seminar exercise during the first semester of the academic year 1970–1971 at the University of Louvain. The same group also studied many epitaphs mentioning widows, but it was impossible to derive conclusions from this inquiry, since there is almost never any indication from which one can affirm positively whether, in these often very short texts, this term means the simple fact of being a widow or is truly the title of an ecclesiastical function.

Chapter Eight — pages 92–99

[1] 1 Cor. 14:34.

[2] Cf. 1 Cor. 11:5.

[3] Cf. 1 Cor. 11:3.

[4] 1 Cor. 14:34.

[5] Gen. 3: 16.

[6] Gen. 18:12; cf. 1 Peter 3:6.

[7] Cf. 1 Tim. 2:13-14.

[8] Cf. Gen. 2:21-22.

[9] Cf. Gen. 3:6.

[10] 1 Cor. 14:35.

[11] *Commentary on 1 Corinthians*, on 1 Cor. 14:34-35 (CSEL 81-2, 163, 3–164, 7).

[12] 1 Tim. 2:11-12.

[13] Cf. 1 Tim. 2:9-10.

[14] 1 Tim. 2:13-14.

[15] *Commentary on 1 Timothy*, on 1 Tim. 2:11-14 (CSEL 81-3, 263, 18–264, 8).

[16] 1 Cor. 11:10.

[17] Cf. Apoc. 2:1ff. – *Commentary on 1 Corinthians*, on 1 Cor. 11:8-10 (CSEL 81-2, 122, 11–123, 4).

[18] *Commentary on 1 Corinthians*, on 1 Cor. 11:7 (CSEL 81-2, 121 24–122, 7).

[19] Gen. 2:21-22.

[20] Gen. 1:27.

[21] 1 Cor. 11:7.

[22] 1 Cor. 11:6.

[23] 1 Tim. 2:12. – *Quaestiones veteris et novi testamenti* 21 (SCEL 50, 47, 27–48, 16).

[24] Gen. 1:28.

[25] Gen. 1:26.

[26] Cf. *Eph.* 1:21; Col. 1:16.

[27] *Quaestiones veteris et novi testamenti* 45, 2-3 (CSEL 50, 82, 14–83, 7).

[28] Lev. 19:2.

[29] Cf. Acts 6:1-6.

[30] Cf. Acts 1:14.

[31] Cf. 1 Cor. 14:34-35.

[32] *Commentary on 1 Timothy*, on 1 Tim. 3:11 (CSEL 81-3, 267, 28–268, 16).

[33] *Ibid.*, on 1 Tim. 2:11-12, cited above, p. 93.

[34] Rom. 16:1-2.

[35] *Commentary on Romans*, on Rom. 16:1-2 (CSEL 81-1, 476, 10-23; 477, 10-22).

[36] Rom. 16:6-12.

[37] *Commentary on Romans*, on Rom. 16:12 (CSEL 81-1, 484, 1-10; 485, 1-9); cf. *ibid.* on Rom. 16:6 (480, 3-6; 481, 4-6).

[38] This formula appears in *Commentary on 1 Timothy*, on 1 Tim. 5:4 (CSEL 81-3, 279, 8).

[39] *Ibid.*, on 1 Tim. 5:9-10 (281, 6-7).

[40] *Ibid.*, on 1 Tim. 5:5 (279, 21); on 1 Tim. 5:9-10 (281, 9-10).

[41] These terms occur frequently in this section; see *ibid.*, on 1 Tim. 5:6 (280, 6 and 7); on 1 Tim. 5:11 (281, 12 and 14); on 1 Tim. 5:12 (281, 25); on 1 Tim. 5:13 (282, 8 and 14); on 1 Tim. 5:14-15 (283, 4, 8 and 9).

[42] *Ibid.*, on 1 Tim. 5:3 (278, 24–279, 2); on 1 Tim. 5:6-7 (279, 26–280, 16).

[43] *Ibid.*, on 1 Tim. 5:3 (278, 25); on 1 Tim. 5:4 (279, 10); on 1 Tim. 5:6 (280, 6); see also *ibid.*, on 1 Tim. 5:13 (282,

8-9): "Gloriosum est huius rei vocabulum."

[44] *Ibid.*, on 1 Tim. 5:4-5 (279, 3-25).

[45] *Ibid.*, on 1 Tim. 5:8-10 (280, 17–281, 9).

[46] *Ibid.*, on 1 Tim. 5:11-12 (281, 10–282, 4).

[47] *Ibid.*, on 1 Tim. 5:13 (282, 5–19).

[48] *Ibid.*, on 1 Tim. 5:14-15 (282, 20–283, 12).

[49] *Ibid.*, on 1 Tim. 5:16 (283, 13–284, 3).

[50] *Ibid.*, (284, 3-6).

[51] 1 Cor. 14:34.

[52] Cf. Titus 2:4-5.

[53] 1 Cor. 14:34.

[54] Cf. Gen. 2:21-22.

[55] Gen. 18:12.

[56] 1 Cor. 14:35.

[57] *Commentary on 1 Corinthians*, on 1 Cor. 14:34-35 (PLS 1, 1227).

[58] Titus 2:4.

[59] *Commentary on Titus*, on Titus 2:4 (PLS 1, 1370).

[60] 1 Tim. 2:12.

[61] *Commentary on 1 Timothy*, on 1 Tim. 2:12 (PLS 1, 1349).

[62] *Commentary on 1 Corinthians*, on 1 Cor. 11:5 (PLS 1, 1214).

[63] *Commentary on 1 Timothy*, on 1 Tim. 3:11 (PLS 1, 1351).

[64] Rom. 16:1.

[65] *Commentary on Romans*, on Rom. 16:1 (PLS 1, 1178).

[66] Rom. 16:3.

[67] Cf. Acts 18:24-26.

[68] *Commentary on Romans*, on Rom. 16:3 (PLS 1, 1179).

[69] 1 Tim. 5:9.

[70] 1 Tim. 5:11.

[71] *Commentary on 1 Timothy*, on 1 Tim. 5:9, 11 (PLS 1, 1354–1355).

Chapter Nine — pages 100–108

[1] Sulpicius Severus, *Chronicle*, 2, 46, 6 (CSEL 1, 99, 31–100, 2).

[2] *Ibid.*, 2, 50, 8 (103, 27-28).

[3] Council of Saragossa I (380), can. 1 (Bruns, 2, 13).

[4] Augustine, *Ep.* 237, 4 (CSEL 57, 528, 4-28).

[5] See above, pp. 95–96 and 98.

[6] Council of Nîmes (394/396), can. 2 (CCL 148, 50, 14-19).

[7] For instance, Wahl, *Exclusion of Women*, p. 10.

[8] Cf. 1 Cor. 11:6; 14:35.

[9] Cf. 1 Cor. 11:14-15.

[10] First Council of Orange (441), can. 25 (26); (CCL 148, 84, 102-103).

[11] Above, pp. 97–98.

[12] See especially *Ep.* 38 (to Marcella); 79 (to Salvina); 107 (to Laeta); 108 ("Epitaphium sanctae Paulae"); 123 (to Geruchia); 127 (to Principia).

[13] *De viduis* (PL 16, 247-276).

[14] First Council of Toledo (400), can. 9 (Bruns, 1, 205).

[15] Jerome, *Ep.* 22, 13, 1 (CSEL 54, 160, 6-9); 38, 4, 1-4 (291, 16–292, 18); 127, 3, 2-4 (CSEL 56, 147, 15–148, 6).

[16] First Council of Orange (441), can. 26 (27), (CCL 148, 85, 104-107).

[17] Pseudo-Council of Arles II, can. 46 (CCL 148, 123, 178-179).

[18] See C. Munier, *Les Statuta Ecclesiae antiqua, Études critiques* (Bibliothèque de l'Institut de droit canonique de l'Université de Strasbourg, 5), Paris, 1960, pp. 125–146.

[19] SEA can. 68 (102), (CCL 148, 177, 169); can. 100 (12), (CCL 148, 184, 268).

[20] SEA, can. 36 (101), (CCL 148, 172, 97-98).

[21] *Didasc.* 3, 2, 1 (Funk, 184, 9-11); *Apost. Const.* 3, 2, 1 (Funk, 185, 14-18).

[22] SEA, can. 68 (102), (CCL 148, 177, 167-170).

[23] SEA, can. 7 (17), (CCL 148, 167, 16-18).

[24] SEA, can. 102 (103), (CCL 148, 185, 278-280).

[25] *Apost. Const.* 3, 5, 2 (Funk, 189, 18-20).

[26] SEA can. 37 (99), (CCL 148, 172, 99-100).

[27] *Apost. Const.*, 3, 6, 1-2 (Funk, 191, 8-18).

[28] Cf. 1 Cor. 14:34-35; 1 Tim. 2:12; *Didasc.* 3, 6, 1-2 (Funk, 190, 8-17).

[29] SEA, can. 41 (100), (CCL 148, 173, 107).

[30] *Didasc.* 3, 9, 1-3 (Funk, 198, 31–200, 5); *Apost. Const.* 3, 9, 1-4 (Funk, 199, 21–201, 17).

[31] *Didasc.*, 3, 12, 3 (Funk, 210, 12-14).

[32] SEA, can. 100 (12), (CCL 148, 184, 268-273).

[33] Gelasius of Rome, *Ep.* 14, 13 and 21 (Thiel, 369–370 and 374).

[34] *Ibid.*, 26 (pp. 376–378).

[35] Text and French translation in P. de Labriolle, *Les sources de l'histoire du montanisme*, Paris, 1913, pp. 226–230.

[36] For instance, CJ 1, 5, 5 (Krueger, 51).

[37] See Lafontaine, *Conditions positives*, pp. 22–24.

[38] Council of Epaon (517), can. 21 (CCL 148 A, 29, 163-165).

[39] See É. Griffe, *La Gaule chrétienne à l'époque romaine*, III, 1965, pp. 128–148, 151-163.

[40] Second Council of Orleans (533), can. 17 (CCL 148 A, 101, 64-69).

[41] *Idem*, can. 18 (101, 70-71).

[42] Remi of Reims, *Testament* (CCL 117, 477, 95-98): "Delegoque benedictae filiae meae Helariae diaconae ancillam nomine Nocam et vitium pedaturam que suae iungitur vineae quam Cattusio facit."

[43] Venantius Fortunatus, *Life of St. Radegund*, 12, 26-28 (MGHAA 4-2, 41, 20-31).

[44] Second Council of Tours (567), can. 21 (20), (CCL 148 A, 187, 341–188, 349).

[45] Third Council of Orléans (538), can. 19 (16), (CCL 148 A, 121, 184-194).

[46] Fifth Council of Orléans (549), can. 19 (CCL 148 A, 155, 191-194); Second Council of Tours (567), can. 21 (20), (CCL 148 A. 184, 260–188, 356); Second Council of Paris (556/573), can. 5 (CCL 148 A, 207, 88–208, 97).

Appendix — pages 115–120

[1] A-G Martimort, "A propos des ministeres feminins dans l'Église," *Bulletin de Litterature Ecclesiastique*, LXXIV, pp. 103–108. This work contains all the bibliographical notes and references necessary to follow the discussion.

[2] It may be useful here to prevent an objection. If you derive from the *Apostolic Constitutions* an argument favoring the sacramentality of ordination of deaconesses, why not do the same for subdeacons and readers and conclude that their ordination is also sacramental, since it is considered such in the *Apostolic Constitutions*? The answer is that the testimony of the *Constitutions* concerning subdeacons is isolated and contradicted by later Eastern tradition, whereas it is confirmed by this tradition for deaconeses. Already the *Epitome of the Apostolic Constitutions* refused to follow the *Constitutions* concerning readers, and the Byzantine medieval tradition made a clear distinction between the sacramental orders, extended to and including the female diaconate, and the non-sacramental orders, from the subdiaconate on down. The assimilation of the female diaconate into the sacramental orders in the *Apostolic Constitutions* is representative of a tradition, whereas the promotion of the subdiaconate and readers to this same rank is nothing more than a personal opinion of the author and is rejected by tradition. A theological argument, therefore, can be derived in the first case, but not in the second.

Moreover, if we look in the *Constitutions* themselves for traces of a difference of status among the various orders which, because of his own conceptions, would have escaped the systemization which the author achieved, we find that a difference appears, not between the male and female diaconate, contrary to M. Martimort's wishes, but between the female diaconate and the subdiaconate. Actually, from the subdiaconate down, ordination did not present the same degree of solemnity: the text no longer states that it should take place before the presbyters and deacons. This detail is significant. Involuntarily, no doubt, and in spite of his desire to present all ordinations in the same manner, the author reveals the fact that actually the first four ordinations (including the female diaconate) were most solemn celebrations, whereas the following ones (from the subdiaconate down) were far more simple rites.